Living by the Light of the Moon

2020 Moon Book

Beatrex Quntanna

Disclaimer

Before following any Yoga advice or practice suggested by this book, it is recommended that you consult your doctor as to its suitability, especially if you suffer from any health problems or special conditions. The publishers, the author, and associates cannot accept responsibility for any injuries or damage incurred as a result of following the exercises in this book, or using any of the therapeutic methods described or mentioned.

Copyright ©2019 by Beatrex Quntanna

All Rights Reserved. No part of this book may be reproduced or transmitted in any form or by any means without the written permission of the publisher, except for the inclusion of brief quotations in a review.

ISBN 978-0-578-57299-4

Printed in the United States of America

ART ALA CARTE PUBLISHING
760-944-6020
beatrex@cox.net
www.beatrex.com

I would like to dedicate this book
TO MY SON, CHRISTOPHER,
and my grandsons,
SPENCER, ASHER, AND CURRAN,
who inspire me to know that
life is a celebration.

ACKNOWLEDGMENTS

Thank you Jennifer Masters for the cover art and your ability to capture the Inspirational theme with your magical graphic art. Additionally, for your dedication to refinement on all levels in the book and beyond.

Michelenne Crab for the daily Tibetan Numerology intentions that inspire and direct us to make the most of each day. Inspiring us to live in harmony with the universal timing of all things.

Jill Estensen for the astrological calculations for the entire year. Also, for sharing aspects from *Dimensional Astrology* that add an innovative approach to the Sabian Symbols, experiencing the degrees and the polarity that they create for each moon phase.

Jennifer "Tashi" Vause, R.Y.T., for *Sky Power Yoga*, taking the time to determine yoga poses for each moon. This adds special support to our physiology to be in alignment with our intention for each moon cycle.

Thanks to Meg Colloton for editing with such ease and grace. Kaliani Devinne for contributing the goddess profiles that correspond to each moon cycle and the moon charts. Candice Covington for her approach to the elements. Ann Meyer for the freedom affirmations from *Teaching of the Inner Christ*. Melinda Pajak and Jennifer "Tashi" Vause for being the overlighting divas and adding the finishing touches.

Thanks to Felicia Bond for bringing the goddesses to life in Moon Class!

Special thanks to the countless students who come to Moon Class—without you this teaching would not exist!

Production Credits

Art Direction, Book Design, Cover Art, and Video Editing (*How to Use the Moon Book* video class series)

Jennifer Masters
www.JenniferMastersCreative.com

Daily Tibetan Numerology

Michelenne Crab
www.mydailytarotcard.com

Astrological Calculations, Sabian Symbols and *Dimensional Astrology*

Jill Estensen
intuvision@roadrunner.com

Goddess Profiles

Kaliani Devinne
StepsOnTheSacredSpiral.blogspot.com

Sky Power Yoga

Jennifer "Tashi" Vause, R.Y.T.
yogatashi@yahoo.com

Book and Calendar Editor

Meg Colloton
megcolloton@sbcglobal.net

Video Production (online classes with Beatrex)

Melinda Pajak
www.BlueMoonAcademy.com

TABLE OF CONTENTS

About the Art	6
The Importance of Cycles	7
How To Use This Book	9

January — 12
- Full Moon 20° Cancer 00' 11:22 AM Lunar Eclipse — 14
- New Moon 4° Aquarius 22' 1:42 PM — 22

February — 30
- Full Moon 20° Leo 00' 11:33 PM — 32
- New Moon 4° Pisces 29' 7:32 AM — 40

March — 48
- Full Moon 19° Virgo 37' 10:48 AM — 50
- New Moon 4° Aries 12' 2:29 AM — 58

April — 66
- Full Moon 18° Libra 44' 7:36 PM — 68
- New Moon 3° Taurus 24' 7:26 PM — 76

May — 84
- Full Moon 17° Scorpio 20' 3:45 AM — 86
- New Moon 2° Gemini 05' 10:39 AM — 94

June — 102
- Full Moon 15° Sagittarius 34' 12:13 PM Lunar Eclipse — 104
- New Moon 0° Cancer 21' 11:42 PM Solar Eclipse — 112

July — 120
- Full Moon 13° Capricorn 38' 9:44 PM Lunar Eclipse — 122
- New Moon 28° Cancer 27' 10:33 AM — 130

August — 138
- Full Moon 11° Aquarius 46' 8:59 AM — 140
- New Moon 26° Leo 35' 7:41 PM — 148

September — 156
- Full Moon 10° Pisces 12' 10:22 PM — 158
- New Moon 25° Virgo 01' 4:00 AM — 166

October — 174
- Full Moon 9° Aries 08' 2:06 PM — 176
- New Moon 23° Libra 53' 12:31 PM — 184
- Full Moon 8° Taurus 38' 7:50 AM — 192

November — 200
- New Moon 23° Scorpio 18' 9:07 PM — 202
- Full Moon 8° Gemini 38' 1:30 AM Lunar Eclipse — 210

December — 218
- New Moon 23° Sagittarius 08' 8:17 AM Solar Eclipse — 220
- Full Moon 8° Cancer 53' 7:29 PM — 228

Appendices — 237
- Tarot Glossary — 241
- Sky Power Yoga — 247

About the Author — 257
- Other Publications By Beatrex — 258
- Online Classes With Beatrex — 259

ABOUT THE ART

Beatrex and I talked about the theme of the year, Unity, and what a "4" year encompasses; form, foundation, organization, unification, trust, and truth. We ended up on an odyssey that took us from looking at ancient Buddhist and Hindu symbolism to Renaissance architecture to modern art to contemporary art, which was quite fun! Victor Vasarely, Wassily Kandinsky, and other modern artists of the twentieth century were all about modernity, universality, spirituality, unification, and emotional expression through line, shape, form, function, and design. Collectively, their work led me to looking at contemporary artists Alex Grey and Android Jones, whose art is more overtly steeped in spirituality and spoke to me about form and unification on different levels.

With all of this floating around in my mind and in my world, I set out to create the art for this edition of *Living By the Light of the Moon*. I wanted to capture the ideas of 'unification of form,' of structures, and of sacred geometry. Lines becoming shapes, and shapes becoming something more; two dimensions becomes three dimensions, three dimensions becomes four....

For the cover art I started with the three large circles—a circle being a symbol of the unity of all things—to represent Sun, Moon, and Earth. I then surrounded them with various geometric forms taking shape. One of these is the cube, a shape that is scattered throughout the artwork and is at the center of each moon cycle Astro chart. The cube is the sacred geometry that corresponds with the number 4 in Numerology. The square becomes a cube, the cube becomes a Merkabah, then the Metatron Cube.

Along my journey of creating both the overall look and design, and the twelve Zodiac symbols, I started to gravitate toward the Art Deco movement as a source of inspiration. It just felt like it fit in perfectly with what I was seeing in my mind. In my research I stumbled across a few zodiac designs the artist Erté created—I've explored his work plenty of times and had never seen them! I was enamoured. If you know Erté's work, I'm sure you already see his influence here. A "decorative art" and a cross-section of modern art, Art Deco came about after the Industrial Revolution, at a time when people were embracing social change, modernity, and globalism, as well as new technologies, craftsmanship, and beauty.

As I explored modern art from its early days through the middle of the twentieth century, I noticed many parallels to our time now—as we organize and build new structures for the future we want, write the social contracts we want to live by, look for better ways to learn and teach emotional intelligence, and seek out ways to inject more art and beauty into our everyday lives.

—Jennifer Masters
Artist, Illustrator, Creative

THE IMPORTANCE OF CYCLES

The Moon is the keeper of the secrets of life and its cycles set the stage for successful living. Beatrex has developed a valuable collection of knowledge about how to use the cycles of the Moon to enhance the quality of your life. This workbook reveals those secrets and supports you in implementing them. Each cycle offers a different combination of light energy to give you the chance to grow harmoniously into wholeness. Following the luminaries, the Sun and the Moon, through the zodiac and noting the cycles of illumination and reflection can bring you to a deeper creative experience of life. The Moon is the great cosmic architect—the builder and the dissolver of form. Full Moons are about dissolving and New Moons are about building. This workbook will assist you in knowing what and when to build and what and when to dissolve with activities for each cycle of the Moon throughout 2020.

Life, at the highest spiritual level, moves beyond time and uses cycles to increase your ability to actualize your full potential. Cycles are in charge of your personal development; while time is in charge of the change in direction that happens when you evolve by trusting in divine timing. This workbook synthesizes techniques that allow for the power of development and direction to occur in the entire spectrum of wholeness. Each Zodiac sign holds the knowledge necessary to integrate an aspect of yourself to become whole. As the Moon and the Sun travel around our planet each month, a different aspect of self-development is presented to you via the zodiac sign constellation that it visits.

The year 2020 is a "4" year in Tibetan Numerology. The number 4 is all about building form and creating a system for fulfillment. The celestial body that rules the number 4 is the Moon. This year will bring many power plays between pride, perfection, production, and transformation. It will be up to us to materialize the structure of our personal power in this ever-changing reality, and living by the light of the Moon will show us the way.

I like what my cousin Claudia Oliveri Quintana says, "the number 4 is a powerful number that aims to struggle for order in this chaotic world ... we have the four cardinal points; North, East, South, and West ... four seasons ... four elements; Fire, Water, Air, and Earth ... it all has to come together: unity."

When the Moon is Full

It is time to release and set yourself free when the Moon is full and in direct opposition to the Sun. This polarity dissolves anything that stands in the way of your personal recalibration. Sixty hours before a full moon you may experience tension as the Sun and the Moon oppose each other. Learn to understand the opposite natures without feeling the need to separate them. Find the middle ground so that you are not manipulated by polarity as the integration of opposites creates the unity that creates harmony.

The polarity themes are on each full moon's page. Use the astrological theme to inspire you to renew your life by writing a releasing list. Light a candle and read your list out loud. Place your releasing list under a circle-shaped mirror and put your candle on top of the mirror. Make sure to use a candle in glass—a votive or seven-day candle—to protect from fire. Place outside in the moonlight or in a special place in your home. Let the candle burn out. When your candle is finished burning, your list is in operation. Empty space allows manifestation to occur. Before writing your list you might want to look over the full moon cycle's trigger points to see if there is anything you need to let go of first. Remember recalibration allows you to live without resistance.

When the Moon is New

When the Moon is new, it is in the same sign as the Sun. This unites the power of the magnetic and the dynamic fields that are in perfect resonance for manifesting. This is a potent time to make your desires known by writing your manifesting list. Use the astrological theme to write your list like a child who is writing to Santa Claus. Be comfortable with extending your list's boundaries beyond what you believe is possible by thinking: *This, or something better than this, comes to me in an easy and pleasurable way for the good of all concerned.* Then light a candle and read your list out loud. Place it under an eight-sided mirror and put your candle on top of the mirror. Make sure to use a candle in glass—a votive or seven-day candle—to protect from fire. Place outside in the moonlight or in a special place in your home. Let the candle burn out. By the time the candle burns out, your list is in operation.

HOW TO USE THIS BOOK

Your Time Zone

All times listed in the book are local to the Pacific time zone. Add or subtract hours accordingly to adjust times for your time zone. It is best to do your manifestation and freedom ceremonies at the specific times noted.

These Sections Will Help You To Live By the Light of the Moon

Planetary Highlights

This section explains the planets and how they will affect your life each month. It does not contain all of the aspects; it simply highlights points of interest that promote personal growth during each month. If you are interested in more study, take an astrology class. If you are an astrologer and want more information, we have provided a chart for each moon phase for your convenience.

The Monthly Calendar

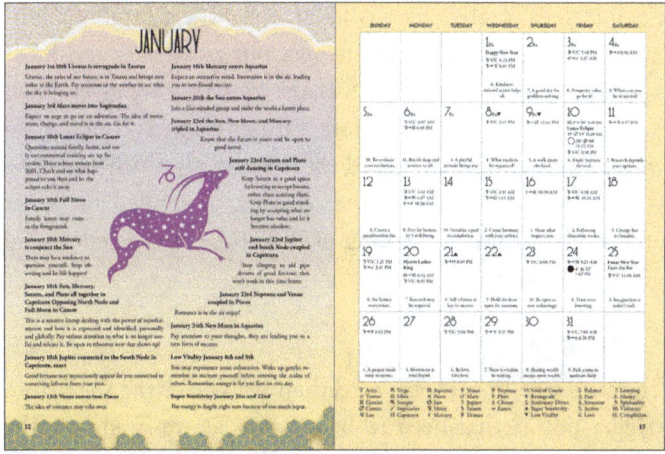

This section provides you with a monthly overview and keeps you connected to the lunar, solar, and planetary cycles. It lets you know when the Moon is void-of-course, when it moves into a new sign, when the Sun and planets change signs, and when a planet goes retrograde or stationary direct (shown by the ℞ and ⚚ symbols). The calendar also has the Tibetan Numerology of the Day, along with an affirmation, to help you align with the energy and set your intentions for the day.

Void Moon

When the Moon is void-of-course, it has made its last major aspect in a sign and stays void until it enters the next sign. When the Moon is void-of-course, you will see the icon V/C on the calendar. This is not a good time to start new projects, relationships, or to take trips, unless you intend to never follow through. When the Moon ☽ enters a new sign, you will see this arrow → It will be followed by the symbol for the new sign and the time that the Moon enters it.

Low-Vitality ▼

This happens when the Moon is directly opposite the center of the galaxy. When this fixed-star opposition occurs, the Earth becomes very fragile and gets depleted. This leads to exhaustion in our physical bodies and is a sign for us to nurture ourselves by resting. The depletion can create Earth changes. Endings can also happen and resistance to these completions will bring on exhaustion. Best to detach and let go.

Super-Sensitivity ▲

This happens when the Moon travels across the sky, hits the center of the galaxy, and connects with a fixed star. When this happens the atmosphere becomes chaotic. An extra amount of energy pours down in a spiral at a very fast speed making it difficult to focus. This fragility can make you depressed, anxious, dizzy, and accident-prone. It is a good idea to keep your thought process away from this energy. This is global, not personal.

The Sun

Each month you will see the icon for the Sun ☉ with an arrow → indicating when the Sun enters a new sign. When the Sun changes signs, the climate of energy takes on a new theme for your personal development. Look for the Sun icon, with an arrow followed by an astrological sign, to indicate sign change and time.

Planets

Planets also change signs and move in retrograde and direct motions. Retrograde planets are next to the date in each day's box followed by retrograde icon ℞. In the middle of each box is information about planetary changes of time and direction.

Goddesses

When the Moon enters a new zodiac sign, a changing of guardians occurs. Deep within each sign lives a goddess who is the keeper of this cyclical domain. This archetype's assignment is to hold the space for an aspect of wholeness to actualize.

Build Your Altar

An altar is an outer focus for inner work. Esoteric coordinates such as Tarot cards, flowers, colors, gemstones, fragrances, and numerology are provided as an enhancement to better assist you in working with each moon phase. Perhaps you are working on a love theme; you might want to add six hearts, six flowers, and six gemstones on your altar with your manifesting or freedom list, mirror, and candle. The coordinating Tarot card can be used as a visual activation. Flowers, colors, and gemstones accent your intentions. The fragrance provides a special connection to Spirit. You may want to burn candles of this scent, spritz your aura or your altar with the fragrance, or simply sniff the fragrance to awaken your olfactory system. Go to www.beatrex.com for moon mists, mirrors, and candle wraps.

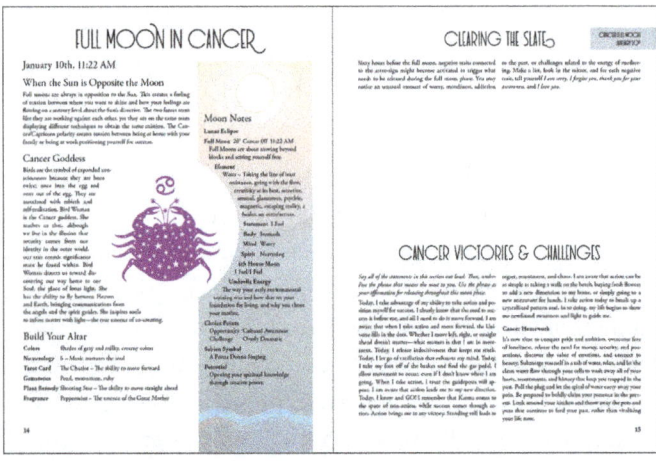

"I" Statements

These statements align the Self with the characteristics of the astrological sign and the house the sign lives in.

Dropping Moon

This happens when a new or full moon peaks at the same time as it goes void. During a "dropping moon" it becomes very important for you to write your manifesting or your freedom list about half an hour before the designated time.

The Elements

Each moon cycle has a primary element (earth, air, fire or water), attached to the astrological sign to which it is assigned, that brings you more awareness of what to work on during the cycle.

Body – Mind – Spirit

Each astrological sign rules a body part, a mental trait or attitude, and a spiritual condition. This section is provided to increase understanding of the tendencies and patterns that are activated during the moon transit.

House Themes

Each house the Moon moves through brings a focus for that moon as a baseline for self-development during the moon phase.

Karmic Awakenings

Every once in a while the chart for the Moon will show an intercepted astrological sign in a house on the chart. This indicates that a karmic pattern is in operation on that day.

Choice Points: Opportunity – Challenge – Potential

Dimensional Astrology presents us with a prescribed action for each of the 360-degrees on the astrology wheel. The object of Dimensional Astrology is to depolarize and neutralize. The degree of the Moon is described to better enhance your understanding of the phase and its effects on you and your world. The wisdom comes with the actualization of potential; when we experience and combine the opportunity and the challenge without judgment.

Sabian Symbols

Each degree in the chart is identified with a symbolic language that speaks to your unconscious awareness and leads you to a new potential. The Sabian Symbols were given birth in California in 1925 by Mark Edmond Jones, a noted astrologer, working with gifted clairvoyant Elsie Wheeler. The symbol for the degree of the Moon is described to better enhance your understanding of the phase and its effects on you and your world.

Clearing the Slate

The first step to accepting freedom is to clear the slate from trigger points that need to be released as we head into the full moon cycle. Each section is filled with trigger points that are specific to the astrological sign where the Moon resides. See if any of them feel familiar. Acknowledge what's familiar and then follow the instructions by writing down what happened and perform Ho'oponopono, the Hawaiian forgiveness ritual. For example, a negative trigger point for Leo is impatience. When you find yourself being impatient, write down the circumstances or journal about it. Then, looking in the mirror, apologize to yourself, ask for forgiveness, have gratitude for yourself with thanks that you could see your impatience as a trigger, and then return to love.

Victories and Challenges

These are sets of affirmations designed to say out loud during a specific moon cycle to determine a motivational tone for your self-discovery. After saying all of them out loud, you will know which statement applies to you. Circle the one that is yours and use it as a personal mantra daily during the moon phase.

Victory List

Acknowledge what you have overcome. Keep this list active throughout this cycle. Honoring victories allows you to accept success.

Manifesting List

Write down what you want to create and manifest in your life.

Gratitude List

Keep this list active throughout this cycle. This will bring you to a level of completion so that a new cycle of opportunity can occur in your life.

Releasing List

What do you need to let go of in order to set yourself free?

List Ideas

Use these ideas to jump start your own lists. Let your imagination take off from here.

Tarot

Sometimes it is good support to get another opinion on how you are doing with each cycle. Included for each moon is a new section where you can pull a Tarot card, using just the Major Arcana cards, and get more information on your process from a Universal perspective. There is a glossary of meanings beginning on page 240, and cards that you can cut and paste (pp.243-5). You will likely want to make a copy of the cards in case you pull the same card more than once. For a more in-depth look at the Tarot, go to *www.beatrex.com/the-book-store* and look for Tarot: A Universal Language by Beatrex Quntanna.

The Astro Wheel

Western astrological charts are placed within a circle or wheel. The wheel is a picture of the sky from a particular place and time on Earth. It is divided into 12 parts called "houses." Each house deals with a particular area of life. Key concepts for each house are written outside the wheel. Compare the wheel in the book to your very own chart and dis-

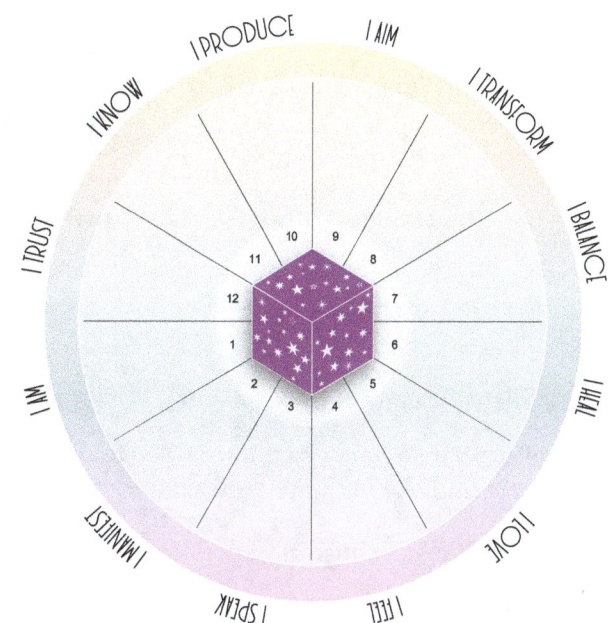

cover the theme that you will be living personally during the moon phase. (See glossary for the houses in the appendix.)

You will want to use a natal chart for yourself that clearly shows the degrees and the houses. For the preferred chart to use with this book, visit www.beatrex.com and look for the link to download a free chart. You will need to know the date, time, and place of your birth.

Cosmic Check-In

"I" statements are designed specifically to keep you in touch with all of the signs and their houses each time the Moon is new or full. Fill in the blanks to complete each statement during each full and new moon phase to activate all parts of your birth chart and keep you in touch with Oneness. Have fun noticing how different you are during each cycle.

Blank Pages

Between each moon phase blank pages are provided for journaling.

Appendices

This section in the back of the book contains expanded information to support you as you work through the book; lists of the eclipses and retrogrades this year, and Tibetan Numerology, houses, heavenly bodies, Astro signs, colors, and Tarot glossaries. See pages 237-245.

Sky Power Yoga

Now with its own section in the back of the book, these yoga poses are designed to support transformations in the physical dimension, for each moon cycle. See pages 247-255.

JANUARY

January 1st-10th Uranus is retrograde in Taurus

Uranus, the ruler of our future, is in Taurus and brings new order to the Earth. Pay attention to the weather to see what the sky is bringing us.

January 3rd Mars moves into Sagittarius

Expect an urge to go on an adventure. The idea of movement, change, and travel is in the air. Go for it.

January 10th Lunar Eclipse in Cancer

Questions around family, home, and early environmental training are up for review. These echoes remain from 2001. Check and see what happened to you then and let the eclipse take it away.

January 10th Full Moon in Cancer

Family issues may come to the foreground.

January 10th Mercury is conjunct the Sun

There may be a tendency to question yourself. Stop obsessing and let life happen!

January 10th Sun, Mercury, Saturn, and Pluto all together in Capricorn Opposing North Node and Full Moon in Cancer

This is a massive lineup dealing with the power of transformation and how it is expressed and identified, personally and globally. Pay serious attention to what is no longer useful and release it. Be open to whatever new that shows up!

January 10th Jupiter connected to the South Node in Capricorn, exact

Good fortune may mysteriously appear for you connected to something leftover from your past.

January 13th Venus moves into Pisces

The idea of romance may take over.

January 16th Mercury enters Aquarius

Expect an overactive mind. Innovation is in the air, leading you to new-found success.

January 20th the Sun enters Aquarius

Join a like-minded group and make the world a better place.

January 23rd the Sun, New Moon, and Mercury tripled in Aquarius

Know that the future is yours and be open to good news!

January 23rd Saturn and Pluto still dancing in Capricorn

Keep Saturn in a good space by learning to accept lessons, rather than resisting them. Keep Pluto in good standing by accepting what no longer has value and let it become obsolete.

January 23rd Jupiter and South Node coupled in Capricorn

Stop clinging to old pipe dreams of good fortune; they won't work in this time frame.

January 23rd Neptune and Venus coupled in Pisces

Romance is in the air enjoy!

January 24th New Moon in Aquarius

Pay attention to your thoughts, they are leading you to a new form of success.

Low Vitality January 8th and 9th

You may experience some exhaustion.

Super Sensitivity January 21st and 22nd

There is too much input from the galactic center. Avoid overthinking. There is a download coming from the Universe that is more chaotic than restful.

SUNDAY	MONDAY	TUESDAY	WEDNESDAY	THURSDAY	FRIDAY	SATURDAY
			1 ♅ ♂ ℞ **Happy New Year** ☽ V/C 6:13 PM ☽→♈ 8:01 PM 6. Kindness-infused action helps all.	2 ♅ ♂ ℞ 7. A good day for problem-solving.	3 ♅ ♂ ℞ ☽ V/C 5:18 PM ♂→♐ 1:37 AM 8. Prosperity rules, go for it!	4 ♅ ♂ ℞ ☽→♉ 8:16 AM 9. Where can you be in service?
5 ♅ ♂ ℞ 10. Re-evaluate your resolutions.	6 ♅ ♂ ℞ ☽ V/C 4:07 AM ☽→♊ 6:10 PM 11. Breath deep and connect to all.	7 ♅ ♂ ℞ 3. A playful attitude brings joy.	8 ♅ ♂ ℞ ▼ ☽ V/C 2:15 PM 4. What needs to be organized?	9 ♅ ♂ ℞ ▼ ☽→♋ 12:44 PM 5. A walk clears the head.	10 ♅ ᴅ 2° ♉ 39' 5:48 PM **Lunar Eclipse** 19° ♋ 54' 11:10 AM ○ 20° ♋ 00' 11:22 AM ☽ V/C 3:58 PM 6. Music nurtures the soul.	11 ☽→♌ 4:17 AM 7. Research expands your options.
12 8. Create a manifesting list.	13 ☽ V/C 5:41 AM ☽→♍ 6:07 AM ♀→♓ 10:38 AM 9. Pray for humanity's well-being.	14 10. Visualize a goal to completion.	15 ☽ V/C 4:11 AM ☽→♎ 7:43 AM 2. Create harmony with your actions.	16 ☿→♒ 10:30 AM 3. Share what inspires you.	17 ☽ V/C 4:58 AM ☽→♏ 10:21 AM 4. Following directions works.	18 5. Change has its benefits.
19 ☽ V/C 1:21 PM ☽→♐ 2:41 PM 6. See beauty everywhere.	20 **Martin Luther King** ☉→♒ 6:54 AM ☽ V/C 8:45 PM 7. Research may be required.	21 ▲ ☽→♑ 8:59 PM 8. Self-reliance is key to success.	22 ▲ 9. Hold the door open for someone.	23 ☽ V/C 6:08 PM 10. Be open to new technology.	24 ☽→♒ 5:21 AM ● 4° ♒ 22' 1:42 PM 8. Trust your knowing.	25 **Lunar New Year** Enter the Rat ☽ V/C 11:06 AM 3. Imagination is today's tool.
26 ☽→♓ 3:43 PM 4. A project needs some structure.	27 5. Movement is your friend.	28 ☽ V/C 5:08 PM 6. Be love. Live love.	29 ☽→♈ 3:51 PM 7. There is wisdom in waiting.	30 8. Sharing wealth creates more wealth.	31 ☽ V/C 7:09 AM ☽→♉ 4:28 PM 9. Pick a time to meditate daily.	

♈ Aries	♍ Virgo	♒ Aquarius	♀ Venus	♆ Neptune	V/C Void-of-Course	2. Balance	7. Learning
♉ Taurus	♎ Libra	♓ Pisces	♇ Pluto	℞ Retrograde	3. Fun	8. Money
♊ Gemini	♏ Scorpio	☉ Sun	♂ Mars	⚷ Chiron	ᴅ Stationary Direct	4. Structure	9. Spirituality
♋ Cancer	♐ Sagittarius	☽ Moon	♃ Jupiter	→ Enters	▲ Super Sensitivity	5. Action	10. Visionary
♌ Leo	♑ Capricorn	☿ Mercury	♄ Saturn	♅ Uranus	▼ Low Vitality	6. Love	11. Completion

Full Moon in Cancer

January 10th, 11:22 AM

When the Sun is Opposite the Moon

Full moons are always in opposition to the Sun. This creates a feeling of tension between where you want to shine and how your feelings are flowing on a sensory level about the Sun's directive. The two forces seem like they are working against each other, yet they are on the same team displaying different techniques to obtain the same mission. The Cancer/Capricorn polarity creates tension between being at home with your family or being at work positioning yourself for success.

Cancer Goddess

Selene was the daughter of Titans, sister to Helios, the Sun, and Eos, the dawn. She rides the night sky in a "biga," a chariot drawn by one black horse and one white horse yoked together. As the Moon passes through its phases, she integrates the light and shadow as she leads the Moon on its twin course with the Sun. While the moontides of moods and emotion try to pull us off balance, she is the one who tames the opposing energies to keep us on track and on purpose.

Never static, always phasing, Selene teaches you to allow and accept the constant changes that move through your life. With her guidance, you will not be pulled off center. She invites you to welcome and integrate all phases of the Moon, and of your life, grounded in the fulcrum of a balanced and centered heart.

Build Your Altar

Colors	Shades of gray and milky, creamy colors
Numerology	6 – Music nurtures the soul
Tarot Card	The Chariot – The ability to move forward
Gemstones	Pearl, moonstone, ruby
Plant Remedy	Shooting Star – The ability to move straight ahead
Fragrance	Peppermint – The essence of the Great Mother

Moon Notes

Lunar Eclipse

Full Moon 20° Cancer 00' 11:22 AM
Full Moons are about moving beyond blocks and setting yourself free.

Element
Water – Taking the line of least resistance, going with the flow, creativity at its best, secretive, sensual, glamorous, psychic, magnetic, escaping reality, a healer, an actor/actress.

Statement I Feel
Body Stomach
Mind Worry
Spirit Nurturing

4th House Moon
I Feel/I Feel

Umbrella Energy
The way your early environmental training was and how that set your foundation for living, and why you chose your mother.

Choice Points
Opportunity Cultural Awareness
Challenge   Overly Dramatic

Sabian Symbol
A Prima Donna Singing

Potential
Opening your spiritual knowledge through creative power.

CLEARING THE SLATE

**CANCER FULL MOON
JANUARY 10ᵀᴴ**

Sixty hours before the full moon, negative traits connected to the astro-sign might become activated to trigger what needs to be released during the full moon phase. You may notice an unusual amount of worry, moodiness, addiction to the past, or challenges related to the energy of mothering. Make a list, look in the mirror, and for each negative trait, tell yourself *I am sorry, I forgive you, thank you for your awareness,* and *I love you.*

CANCER VICTORIES & CHALLENGES

Say all of the statements in this section out loud. Then, underline the phrase that means the most to you. Use the phrase as your affirmation for releasing throughout this moon phase.

Today, I take advantage of my ability to take action and position myself for success. I clearly know that the road to success is before me, and all I need to do is move forward. I am aware that when I take action and move forward, the Universe fills in the dots. Whether I move left, right, or straight ahead doesn't matter—what matters is that I am in movement. Today, I release indecisiveness that keeps me stuck. Today, I let go of vacillation that exhausts my mind. Today, I take my foot off of the brakes and find the gas pedal. I allow movement to occur, even if I don't know where I am going. When I take action, I trust the guideposts will appear. I am aware that action leads me to my new direction. Today, I know and GO! I remember that karma comes to the space of non-action, while success comes through action. Action brings me to my victory. Standing still leads to regret, resentment, and chaos. I am aware that action can be as simple as taking a walk on the beach, buying fresh flowers to add a new dimension to my home, or simply going to a new restaurant for lunch. I take action today to break up a crystallized pattern and, in so doing, my life begins to show me newfound awareness and light to guide me.

Cancer Homework

It's now time to conquer pride and ambition, overcome fear of loneliness, release the need for money, security, and possessions, discover the value of emotions, and connect to beauty. Submerge yourself in a tub of water, relax, and let the clean water flow through your cells to wash away all of your hurts, resentments, and history that keep you trapped in the past. Pull the plug and let the spiral of water carry away your pain. Be prepared to boldly claim your presence in the present. Look around your kitchen and throw away the pots and pans that continue to feed your past, rather than vitalizing your life now.

GRATITUDE LIST

Keep this list active throughout the moon cycle. This will bring you to a level of completion so that a new cycle of opportunity can occur in your life. Be prepared for miracles!

TAROT

Ask the question out loud, then draw a card. You may wish to draw it or paste a copy of it here. Then write down what you feel it might be telling you, in response to the question. Use the glossary in the appendix and record here anything about the card that captures your attention. You may wish to come back throughout the moon cycle to meditate or journal more on the card.

How is my heart supporting my releasing?

RELEASING LIST

**CANCER FULL MOON
JANUARY 10th**

Say this statement out loud three times before writing your list:

I am a free spiritual being and it is my desire to be free to think and to express myself fully — to move about my life toward Truth and Wisdom — to accept and enjoy all good which is mine in living my truth.

I am now free and ready to make choices beyond survival!

Cancer Freedom Ideas

Now is the time to set myself free from self-pity, defensive behavior, nurturing everyone else but me, living in the past, being a mother, and having a mother.

Full Moon in Cancer

Your Personal Moon Experience

Fill in the Cosmic Check-In page. Then look up the degree of the Moon on the chart below. Take note of the "I" statement on the outside of the wheel where the Moon is located. Now, locate the same degree on your own chart and make a note of the house and corresponding "I" statement. Go back to the Cosmic Check-In page and circle the two statements from the charts and read what you wrote. This will give you an idea about what to expect from this moon phase on a personal level. For more information on personalizing your *Moon Book*, go to www.BlueMoonAcademy.com and look for *How to Use the Moon Book*.

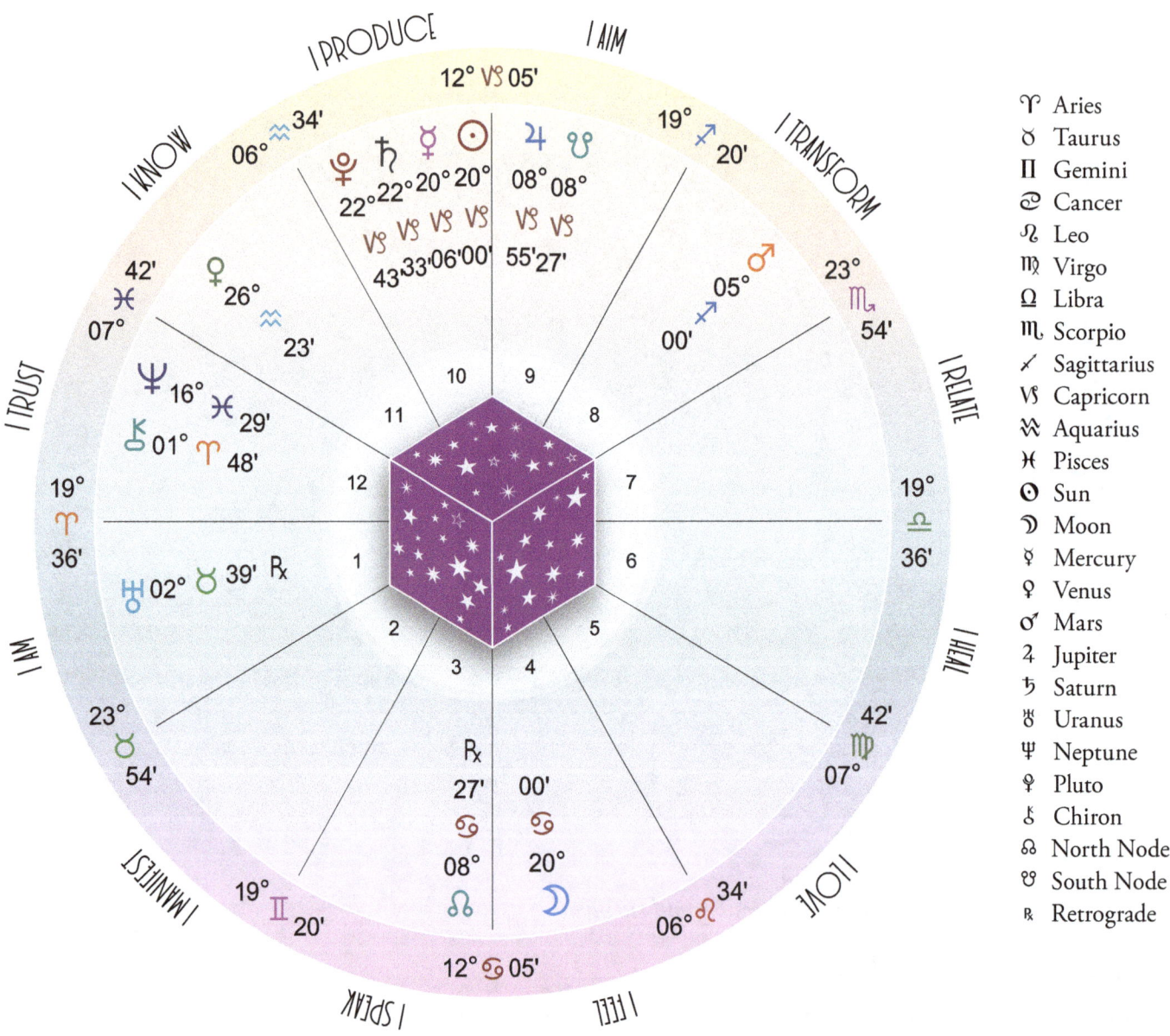

COSMIC CHECK-IN

**CANCER FULL MOON
JANUARY 10ᵀᴴ**

Take a moment to write a brief phrase for each "I" statement. This activates all areas of your life for this creative cycle.

♋ I Feel

♌ I Love

♍ I Heal

♎ I Relate

♏ I Transform

♐ I Aim

♑ I Produce

♒ I Know

♓ I Trust

♈ I Am

♉ I Manifest

♊ I Speak

New Moon in Aquarius

January 24th, 1:42 PM

When the Sun is in Aquarius

This is a time when the higher octave of the mind comes into play and one is given the power of vision. The Aquarian energies promote knowing by being a wellspring of knowledge. They expand the radius of contact by going beyond the known in areas of communication and cooperation. Now is the time to be initiated into greater awareness to serve the fields of human endeavors. Connect and combine magic with science and become a creative influence. When the sun is in Aquarius we must unify with our team players and collect innovative ideas to advance the world to a better place.

Aquarius Goddess

White Tara steps in to assist you with compassionate acceptance and healing of old, deep wounds that are now illuminated by both the Sun and the Moon. With seven eyes (one on her forehead, one on each hand and each foot), White Tara's ability to see encompasses her ability to feel and connect with others and with the Earth. Her name is derived from the root "tri," which means to cross. She has accepted the task of remaining in feminine form until all beings are enlightened, and is here to help all cross the ocean of existence and suffering.

Call upon White Tara's guidance to navigate towards self-acceptance and self-forgiveness on your path to healing.

Build Your Altar

Colors	Violet, neon, crystalline rainbow tints
Numerology	8 – Trust your knowing
Tarot Card	The Star – Golden opportunities for the future
Gemstones	Aquamarine, blue topaz, peacock pearls
Plant Remedy	Queen of the Night Cactus – Ability to see light in the dark
Fragrance	Myrrh – Healing the nervous system

Moon Notes

Lunar New Year Enter the Rat

New Moon 4° Aquarius 22' 1:42 PM
New Moons are about opening new pathways for prosperity.

Element
Air – The breath of life that allows the mind to achieve new insights and fresh perspectives, abstract dreaming, freedom from attachments, codes of intelligence, and academic applications.

Statement I Know
Body Ankles
Mind Genius
Spirit Innovation

9th House Moon
I Aim/I Know

Umbrella Energy
The way you approach spirituality, philosophy, journeys, higher knowledge, and aspiration.

Choice Points
Opportunity   Integrity
Challenge   Conservatism

Sabian Symbol
A Council Of Ancestors Has Been Called To Guide A Man

Potential
Time to manifest a teacher.

AQUARIUS VICTORIES & CHALLENGES

**AQUARIUS NEW MOON
JANUARY 24TH**

Say all of the statements in this section out loud. Then, underline the phrase that means the most to you. Use the phrase as your affirmation for manifesting throughout this moon phase.

Today, I chart my course for my new direction. My future is set on a new, fresh evolutionary course. I am guided by a higher source and trust in that guidance. I know my life has value and I am willing to contribute to the pool of consciousness by experiencing my life and living my life to the fullest view of possibility. Today, I know my possibilities are endless. My Spirit and my Soul are connected to Heaven and to Earth and this knowing brings me to the awareness that I can add to the higher qualities of life because I am connected to the whole. My being is far-reaching and immeasurable. I contribute to existence simply by knowing. All of the guideposts are connected for me today to see my way to a profound new future. My vision is clear and I can clearly set my sights on this new course. Golden opportunities come with this new vision and I trust in my guidance to bring me to this new level of manifesting power. I check in with my inner lights, each day, by meditating and asking for all seven of the energy centers in my body to come into alignment with the outer symbols of guidance. I do this by becoming still and breathing until I feel the stillness. Then, I place my hand on each center in my body, one center at a time, to be activated by light. Next, I ask out loud for each center in my body to let me know what its energetic contribution to the new direction is and how best to use the energy to move forward on my new course of action. I write down each statement and connect each statement to the guiding star in the sky. I am now linked up physically and spiritually and ready to navigate my total self towards my new evolutionary direction.

Aquarius Homework

Aquarians manifest a storehouse of information through innovative telecommunications, technology, social networking and media, and global communication. They are typically found in the fields of psychology, science fiction authoring or film-making, speech writing, and aerospace engineering.

Consider these three Aquarian gifts:

- Opportunity – Become a creative influence
- Enlightenment – When you become aware that you are light
- Brotherhood – Separation doesn't exist anymore

Where do you see these occurring in your life?

VICTORY LIST

Acknowledge what you have overcome. Keep this list active during this moon cycle. Honoring victory allows you to accept success.

TAROT

Ask the question out loud, then draw a card. You may wish to draw it or paste a copy of it here. Then write down what you feel it might be telling you, in response to the question. Use the glossary in the appendix and record here anything about the card that captures your attention. You may wish to come back throughout the moon cycle to meditate or journal more on the card.

How is my mind supporting my manifesting?

MANIFESTING LIST

AQUARIUS NEW MOON
JANUARY 24TH

This or something better than this comes to me in an easy and pleasurable way, for the good of all concerned. Thank you, Universe!

Aquarius Manifesting Ideas
Now is the time to focus on manifesting vision, invention, technology, freedom, friends, community, personal genius, higher awareness, teamwork, science, and magic.

New Moon in Aquarius

Your Personal Moon Experience

Fill in the Cosmic Check-In page. Then look up the degree of the Moon on the chart below. Take note of the "I" statement on the outside of the wheel where the Moon is located. Now, locate the same degree on your own chart and make a note of the house and corresponding "I" statement. Go back to the Cosmic Check-In page and circle the two statements from the charts and read what you wrote. This will give you an idea about what to expect from this moon phase on a personal level. For more information on personalizing your *Moon Book*, go to www.BlueMoonAcademy.com and look for *How to Use the Moon Book*.

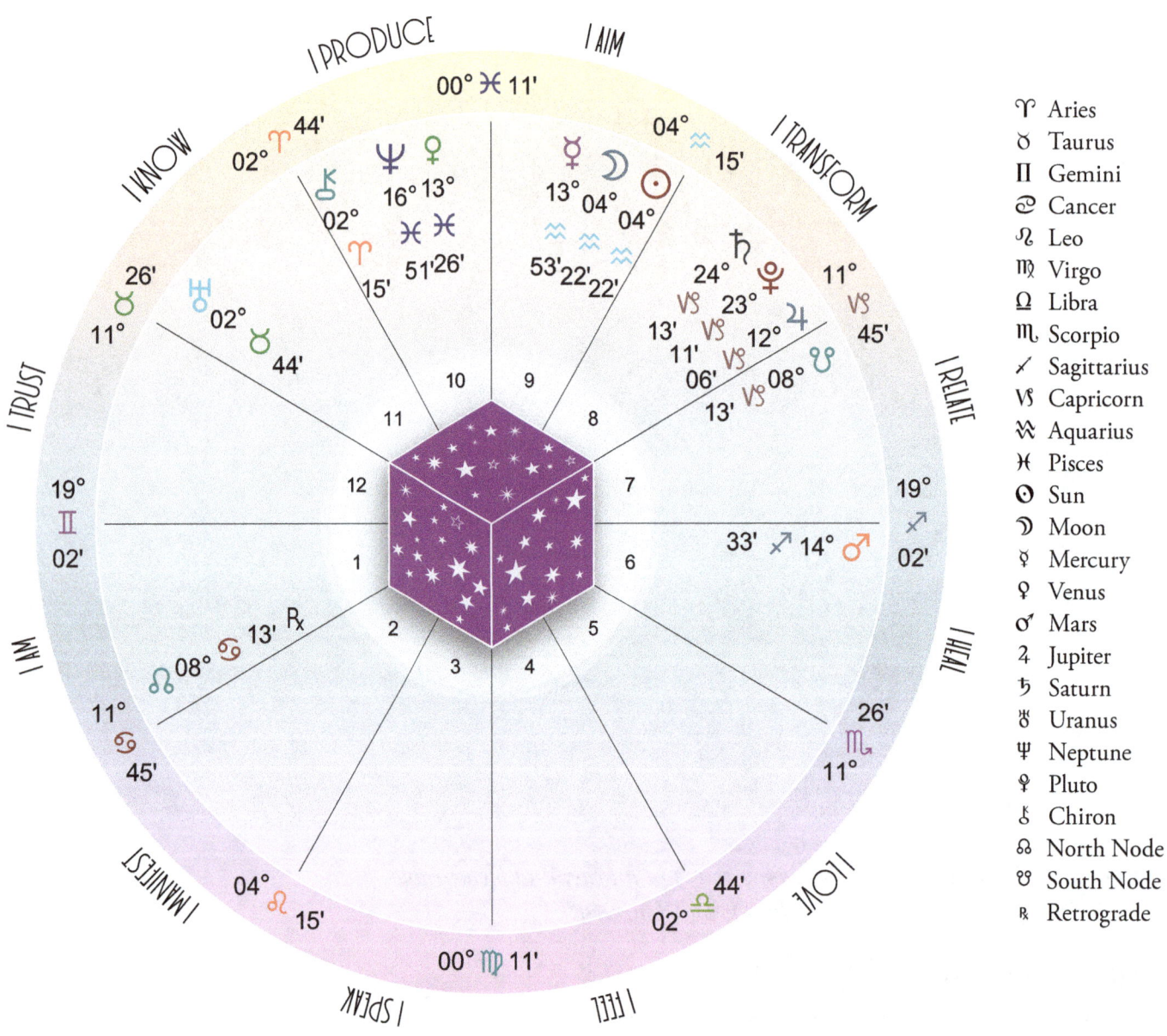

COSMIC CHECK-IN

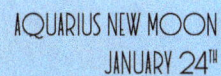
AQUARIUS NEW MOON
JANUARY 24TH

Take a moment to write a brief phrase for each "I" statement. This activates all areas of your life for this creative cycle.

♒ I Know

♓ I Trust

♈ I Am

♉ I Manifest

♊ I Speak

♋ I Feel

♌ I Love

♍ I Heal

♎ I Relate

♏ I Transform

♐ I Aim

♑ I Produce

27

FEBRUARY

The entire month Pluto and Saturn continue their dance in the sky

This transit continues throughout the entire year, working on the redistribution of power. Who will be the most powerful and qualified caretaker of resources? It will be a continued test of integrity and morality for those in power. It's power versus perfection.

February 3rd Mercury moves into Pisces

Expect a steam cleaning of emotional issues. The test here will be to not talk yourself out of dealing with issues showing up to be reconciled.

February 7th Venus moves into Aries

Watch out if you don't get an immediate reaction in the area of romance, tempers could fly!

February 8th Full Moon in Leo

Time to expel unwanted love-related issues.

February 8th Venus and Chiron are coupled in Aries

Time to heal the ego! If you have an extreme need to be right, a healing is necessary!

February 16th Mercury goes retrograde in Pisces until next month, goes direct in Aquarius March 9th

Backlash or whiplash will appear on the horizon of your mind or emotion. Take time to deal with it so it becomes a moment of freedom for you! This is a great time for unleashing any hang-ups in communication needing to be set free.

February 16th Mars moves into Capricorn

High ambition works in your favor during this time. Set your sights on the vision or goal and get going. This is a very good time to manifest your dreams into reality!

February 18th The Sun moves into Pisces

Set your sights on a meet-up with a spiritual group. It is time to be inspired by the power of group energy. Meditate to determine the direction of your awareness.

February 23rd New Moon in Pisces

If used correctly, this new moon will advance your creativity toward a sense of personal value.

February 23rd South Node and Mars are conjunct in Capricorn

The South Node is telling you what you need to move out of the way in order to achieve your goal.

Low Vitality February 5th and 6th

Expect to feel exhausted; so, rest. If you try to push the envelope, you will be sorry.

Super Sensitivity February 14th-16th, 18th and 19th

The fragility of space can lead to anger or depression. Keep your boundaries to yourself and stay in your body. This is not a good time to meditate.

SUNDAY	MONDAY	TUESDAY	WEDNESDAY	THURSDAY	FRIDAY	SATURDAY
						1 10. Back up your electronic devices.
2 11. Breathe, connect to the Universe.	3 ☽ V/C 3:27 AM ☽→♊ 3:29 AM ☿→♓ 3:37 AM 3. Let your "Kid" out. Have some fun!	4 4. Organization is required today.	5▼ ☽ V/C 6:19 AM ☽→♋ 11:02 AM 5. Be up for an adventure today!	6▼ 6. Set the mood for love and romance.	7 ☽ V/C 7:42 AM ☽→♌ 2:45 PM ♀→♈ 12:02 PM 7. You know the solution already.	8 ○ 20° ♌ 00' 11:33 PM 8. Be a success and accept Victory!
9 ☽ V/C 8:08 AM ☽→♍ 3:38 PM 9. Be of service and all will be well.	10 10. Opportunities come with vision.	11 ☽ V/C 10:25 AM ☽→♎ 3:38 PM 11. The vastness is available today.	12 3. Relax, get out the crayons and color.	13 ☽ V/C 1:40 PM ☽→♏ 4:37 PM 4. Know your boundaries.	14▲ **Valentine's Day** 5. Action is required today, just do it.	15▲ ☽ V/C 2:19 PM ☽→♐ 8:07 PM 6. Listen to your body talk today.
16☿℞▲ ☿℞ 12°♓53' 4:54PM ♂→♑ 3:32 AM 7. Ask, the answer will find you.	17☿℞ **President's Day** 8. Ambition leads the way. Follow it.	18☿℞▲ ☽ V/C 1:03 AM ☽→♑ 2:37 AM ☉→♓ 8:56 PM 9. Give without being asked.	19☿℞▲ 10. Future focus is required today.	20☿℞ ☽ V/C 6:18 AM ☽→♒ 11:42 AM 11. Trust your connection to knowing.	21☿℞ ☽ V/C 8:08 PM 3. Turn up the music and dance.	22☿℞ ☽→♓ 10:37 PM 4. Today, it's best to use your logic.
23☿℞ ● 4° ♓ 29' 7:32 AM 5. Expect a change today.	24☿℞ 6. Live Love today and every day.	25☿℞ ☽ V/C 6:11 AM ☽→♈ 10:48 AM 7. What is the big picture?	26☿℞ 8. Take the lead and create victory.	27☿℞ ☽ V/C 7:24 PM ☽→♉ 11:30 PM 9. Bless the Earth in your meditation.	28☿℞ 10. Meet a goal and set a new goal.	29☿℞ 11. Feel the power of the Universe.

♈ Aries
♉ Taurus
♊ Gemini
♋ Cancer
♌ Leo
♍ Virgo
♎ Libra
♏ Scorpio
♐ Sagittarius
♑ Capricorn
♒ Aquarius
♓ Pisces
☉ Sun
☽ Moon
☿ Mercury
♀ Venus
♂ Mars
♃ Jupiter
♄ Saturn
♅ Uranus
♆ Neptune
♇ Pluto
⚷ Chiron
→ Enters
V/C Void-of-Course
℞ Retrograde
§ Stationary Direct
▲ Super Sensitivity
▼ Low Vitality
2. Balance
3. Fun
4. Structure
5. Action
6. Love
7. Learning
8. Money
9. Spirituality
10. Visionary
11. Completion

Full Moon in Leo

February 8th, 11:33 PM

When the Sun is Opposite the Moon

Full moons are always in opposition to the Sun. This creates a feeling of tension between where you want to shine and how your feelings are flowing on a sensory level about the Sun's directive. The two forces seem like they are working against each other, yet they are on the same team displaying different techniques to obtain the same mission. The Leo/Aquarius polarity creates tension about the need to be adored and the need to be free.

Leo Goddess

The depth of Winter is the dreaming time, when your seed has been planted. The colder temperatures and lack of light naturally draw us inside – within. Rhiannon, the Celtic Goddess, rides her horse through your dreams by night and guides your visions as you stare into the hearth fire. She transverses the liminal space, the doorway between the worlds.

Take a ride with Rhiannon, allowing her to transport you as you do your inner work. Revel in the silence of a quiet night before the fireplace. Find comfort in a hot cup of relaxing herbal tea. Rest and allow yourself a few extra hours of well-deserved sleep!

Build Your Altar

Colors Royal purple, gold, orange
Numerology 8 – Be a success and accept Victory!
Tarot Card The Sun – Follow the light, it knows where to go
Gemstones Amber, emerald, pyrite, citrine, yellow topaz
Plant Remedy Sunflower – Standing tall in the center of life
Fragrance Jasmine – Remembering your Soul's original intention

Moon Notes

Lunar Eclipse
Full Moon 20° Leo 00' 11:33 PM
Full Moons are about moving beyond blocks and setting yourself free.

Element
Fire – Igniting, dissolving, accelerating, cleansing, advancing awareness, impatience, leadership, passion, and vitality.

Statement I Love
Body Heart, Spinal Cord
Mind Self-confidence
Spirit Generosity

10th House Moon
I Produce/I Love

Umbrella Energy
Your approach to status, career, honor, and prestige, and why you chose your father.

Choice Points
Opportunity   Self-starter
Challenge   Unusual Behavior

Sabian Symbol
Intoxicated Chickens Dizzily Flap Their Wings Trying To Fly

Potential
Trying to do something that doesn't exist.... Stay in reality!

CLEARING THE SLATE

**LEO FULL MOON
FEBRUARY 8TH**

Sixty hours before the full moon negative traits connected to the astro-sign might become activated to trigger what needs to be released during the full moon phase. You may notice wanting an unusual amount of attention, resistance to authority, or strong impatience that expresses itself as a brat attack. Make a list, look in the mirror, and for each negative trait, tell yourself *I am sorry, I forgive you, thank you for your awareness,* and *I love you.*

LEO VICTORIES & CHALLENGES

Say all of the statements in this section out loud. Then, underline the phrase that means the most to you. Use the phrase as your affirmation for releasing throughout this moon phase.

I no longer feel the need to be in control and dominated by my mind telling me that it is appropriate to repress my feelings. I am going to claim my dominion today and feel the power of life running through me. I accept the privilege of being fully human and fully alive. I look to see where I lack courage to connect to what is natural for me. I see where I have been stubborn and turn to face my resistance. I become aware of when my higher self says "Go" and my lower self says "No." I am aware that my lower self (my body) is a creature of habit and will sabotage me with the idea that change takes too much energy. I take responsibility for the part of me that is a creature of habit and talk to my body about coming into alignment with my new intention to become fully passionate and fully alive. I remember today that in order to get the body to move forward with me, I need two-thirds of my cells to align with my request. First, I become aware of the part of myself that is trying to control all of my outcomes and keep me a slave to those outcomes, rather than trusting in the evolution of nature and the concept of Divine Order. I give up the fight today knowing that this struggle is dissipating all my energy and making me exhausted. In order for my body to respond, I need to awaken my cells through sound and touch. So, today I rub my body and speak out loud by sharing my request for connection, revitalization, rejuvenation, passion, and support. Today, I celebrate the idea that I can connect to my wholeness by activating my cells to support my commitment to my aliveness. I can now stand tall in the center of life and grow in self-confidence.

Leo Homework

Review your memorabilia and see what no longer matches your current love nature, your creative nature, and your loving self. Set your heart free while chanting, "Love is all you need." Become a part of the new consciousness on the Earth that brings a more abundant life when we expand the radius of our love. Live Love Every Day!

GRATITUDE LIST

Keep this list active throughout the moon cycle. This will bring you to a level of completion so that a new cycle of opportunity can occur in your life. Be prepared for miracles!

TAROT

Ask the question out loud, then draw a card. You may wish to draw it or paste a copy of it here. Then write down what you feel it might be telling you, in response to the question. Use the glossary in the appendix and record here anything about the card that captures your attention. You may wish to come back throughout the moon cycle to meditate or journal more on the card.

How is my spirit supporting my releasing?

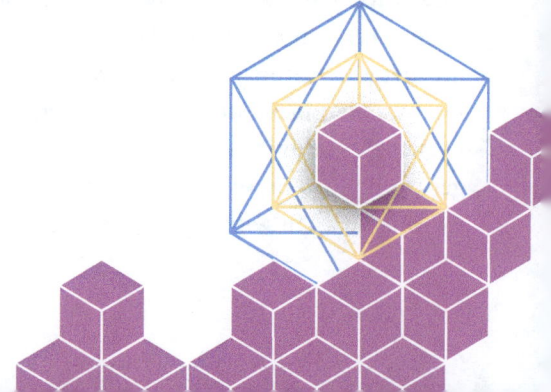

RELEASING LIST

**LEO FULL MOON
FEBRUARY 8TH**

Say this statement out loud three times before writing your list:

I am a free spiritual being and it is my desire to be free to think and to express myself fully.

From this day forward I resolve to be true – first to myself and my highest self, and then to the highest self in me which is the Source of Love That I Am.

Leo Freedom Ideas

Now is the time to activate a game change in my life, and give up the need to be the center of attention, obstacles to generosity, false pride, false identity, blocks to confidence or creativity, excuses that keep me from quality time with my children, blocks to knowing that I am loved and lovable, and the idea that everyone needs to be devoted to me in all situations.

FULL MOON IN LEO

Your Personal Moon Experience

Fill in the Cosmic Check-In page. Then look up the degree of the Moon on the chart below. Take note of the "I" statement on the outside of the wheel where the Moon is located. Now, locate the same degree on your own chart and make a note of the house and corresponding "I" statement. Go back to the Cosmic Check-In page and circle the two statements from the charts and read what you wrote. This will give you an idea about what to expect from this moon phase on a personal level. For more information on personalizing your *Moon Book*, go to www.BlueMoonAcademy.com and look for *How to Use the Moon Book*.

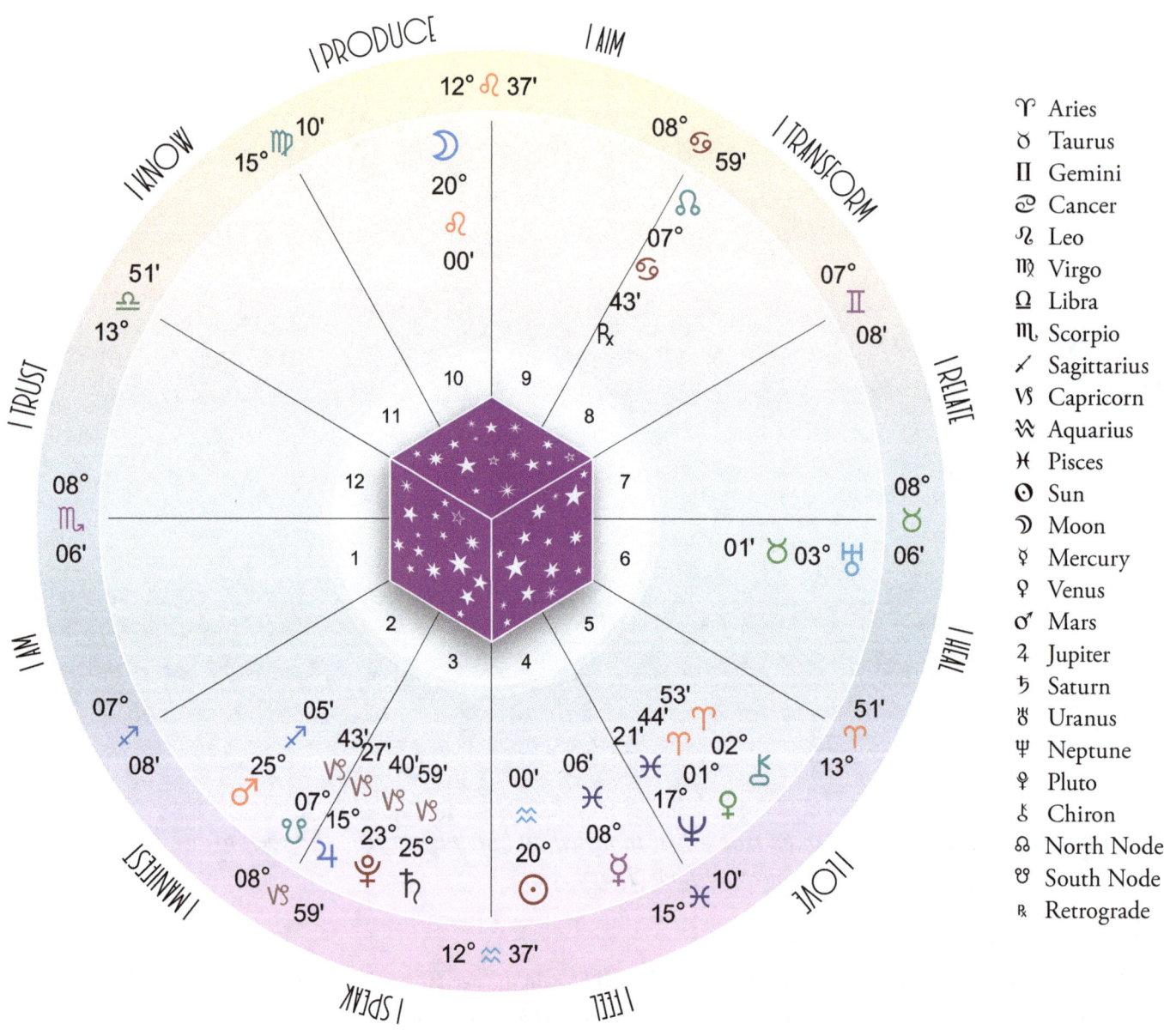

36

COSMIC CHECK-IN

LEO FULL MOON
FEBRUARY 8TH

Take a moment to write a brief phrase for each "I" statement. This activates all areas of your life for this creative cycle.

♌ I Love

♍ I Heal

♎ I Relate

♏ I Transform

♐ I Aim

♑ I Produce

♒ I Know

♓ I Trust

♈ I Am

♉ I Manifest

♊ I Speak

♋ I Feel

New Moon in Pisces

February 23rd, 7:32 AM

When the Sun is in Pisces

This is a time when you come in contact with your most Divine essence. It is a time to meditate and connect to your higher purpose. Let your intuition guide you to a program of service. Let your Soul take control and connect to a space beyond your ego. In order to do this, you must become free of your habits, hang ups, and fantasies. Compassion frees you from the slavery of self-interest and the lure of your personality's blind urges, emotional traps, and mental crystallizations. When the Soul takes control, you unite your personality with Divine essence and radiate the light needed to find your true pathway.

Pisces Goddess

This new moon, Canola, the Irish mistress of the harp, tugs at your heartstrings. In myth, Canola took a walk after quarrelling with her lover one night, and fell asleep outdoors to hypnotic music. The next morning she awoke to find that it was the sound of the wind passing through the sinews of a whale carcass; from this she invented the harp.

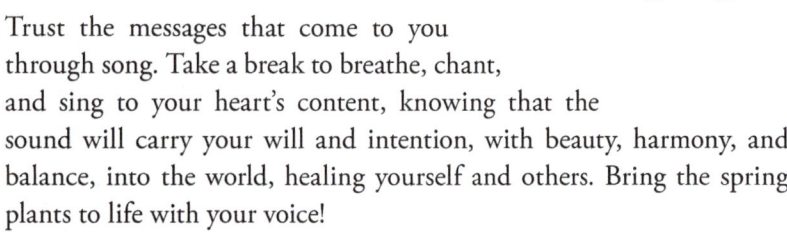

Trust the messages that come to you through song. Take a break to breathe, chant, and sing to your heart's content, knowing that the sound will carry your will and intention, with beauty, harmony, and balance, into the world, healing yourself and others. Bring the spring plants to life with your voice!

Build Your Altar

Colors	Turquoise, blue, green, aqua
Numerology	5 – Expect change today
Tarot Card	The Moon – The inner journey, reflection, illumination
Gemstones	Amethyst, opal, jade, turquoise
Plant Remedy	Passion flower – The ability to live in the here and now
Fragrance	Lotus – Connecting to the Divine without arrogance

Moon Notes

New Moon 4° Pisces 29' 7:32 AM
New Moons are about opening new pathways for prosperity.

Element
Water – Taking the line of least resistance, going with the flow, creativity at its best, secretive, sensual, glamorous, psychic, magnetic, escaping reality, a healer, an actor/actress.

Statement I Trust
Body Feet
Mind Super-sensitive
Spirit Mystical

12th House Moon
I Trust/I Trust

Umbrella Energy
Determines how you deal with your karma, "unconscious software," and what you will experience in order to attain mastery to complete your karma. It is also about the way you connect to the Divine.

Choice Points
Opportunity Philanthropy
Challenge Alienation

Sabian Symbol
A Church Bazaar

Potential
People in a community coming together to have fun.

PISCES VICTORIES & CHALLENGES

**PISCES NEW MOON
FEBRUARY 23RD**

Say all of the statements in this section out loud. Then, underline the phrase that means the most to you. Use the phrase as your affirmation for manifesting throughout this moon phase.

I see my path clearly now. I know I must walk by myself on this journey into the deepest part of my Soul. It is time to clear the way and look beneath the surface to discover the parts of myself that I have placed in the unconscious world to be worked on at a later date. That later date is now. I am aware that the postponement of my inner reality can no longer be delayed.

Evolution is pulling me and it has become greater than my distractions, my fear, my denial, and my refusal to face what I have hidden from myself and others. I am aware of outside influences that pull me away from facing my inner realms. I know, without a doubt, that I am only as sick as the secrets I keep from myself and others. I see clearly how these distractions, illusions, and secrets need to be recognized so I can find the separated parts of myself that have been left in the dark, obscured from the light. I know that it is time to bring myself into wholeness and bring my shadow side to the light of my awareness.

I begin by closing my eyes and experiencing darkness. I imagine walking on a lonely road, in the dark, by myself. I pay particular attention to the sensations in my body and allow for the body to guide me to the places of dullness, numbness, fear, and anxiety. I simply allow for the intelligence of the body to coordinate the feeling with an image, person, or an event. I stay still and know, from the depth of my being, that recognition is all that is required of me right now. When recognition occurs, the light of awareness is ignited and the conscious world will take care of the rest. I know that the road to enlightenment requires me to first take the road into the dark side of my Soul.

Pisces Homework

Pisces manifest by using their psychic powers for counseling, therapy, hypnosis, the ministry, and creating spiritual schools or healing centers. They are also successful in visionary arts, acting, music, medical and pharmaceutical fields, and oceanography.

Take time to go within to discover where new pathways are open for advancement. Blessings pour forth to those who move toward these pathways in the spirit of service. Be open to these pathways and consider the ones that benefit our planet with new ideas, creative expression, and expanded views that lead people to higher levels of service.

VICTORY LIST

Acknowledge what you have overcome. Keep this list active during this moon cycle. Honoring victory allows you to accept success.

TAROT

Ask the question out loud, then draw a card. You may wish to draw it or paste a copy of it here. Then write down what you feel it might be telling you, in response to the question. Use the glossary in the appendix and record here anything about the card that captures your attention. You may wish to come back throughout the moon cycle to meditate or journal more on the card.

How is my heart supporting my manifesting?

MANIFESTING LIST

*PISCES NEW MOON
FEBRUARY 23RD*

This or something better than this comes to me in an easy and pleasurable way, for the good of all concerned. Thank you, Universe!

Pisces Manifesting Ideas

Now is the time to focus on manifesting connection with the Divine, creativity, healing powers, psychic abilities, sensitivity, compassion, and service.

New Moon in Pisces

Your Personal Moon Experience

Fill in the Cosmic Check-In page. Then look up the degree of the Moon on the chart below. Take note of the "I" statement on the outside of the wheel where the Moon is located. Now, locate the same degree on your own chart and make a note of the house and corresponding "I" statement. Go back to the Cosmic Check-In page and circle the two statements from the charts and read what you wrote. This will give you an idea about what to expect from this moon phase on a personal level. For more information on personalizing your *Moon Book*, go to www.BlueMoonAcademy.com and look for *How to Use the Moon Book*.

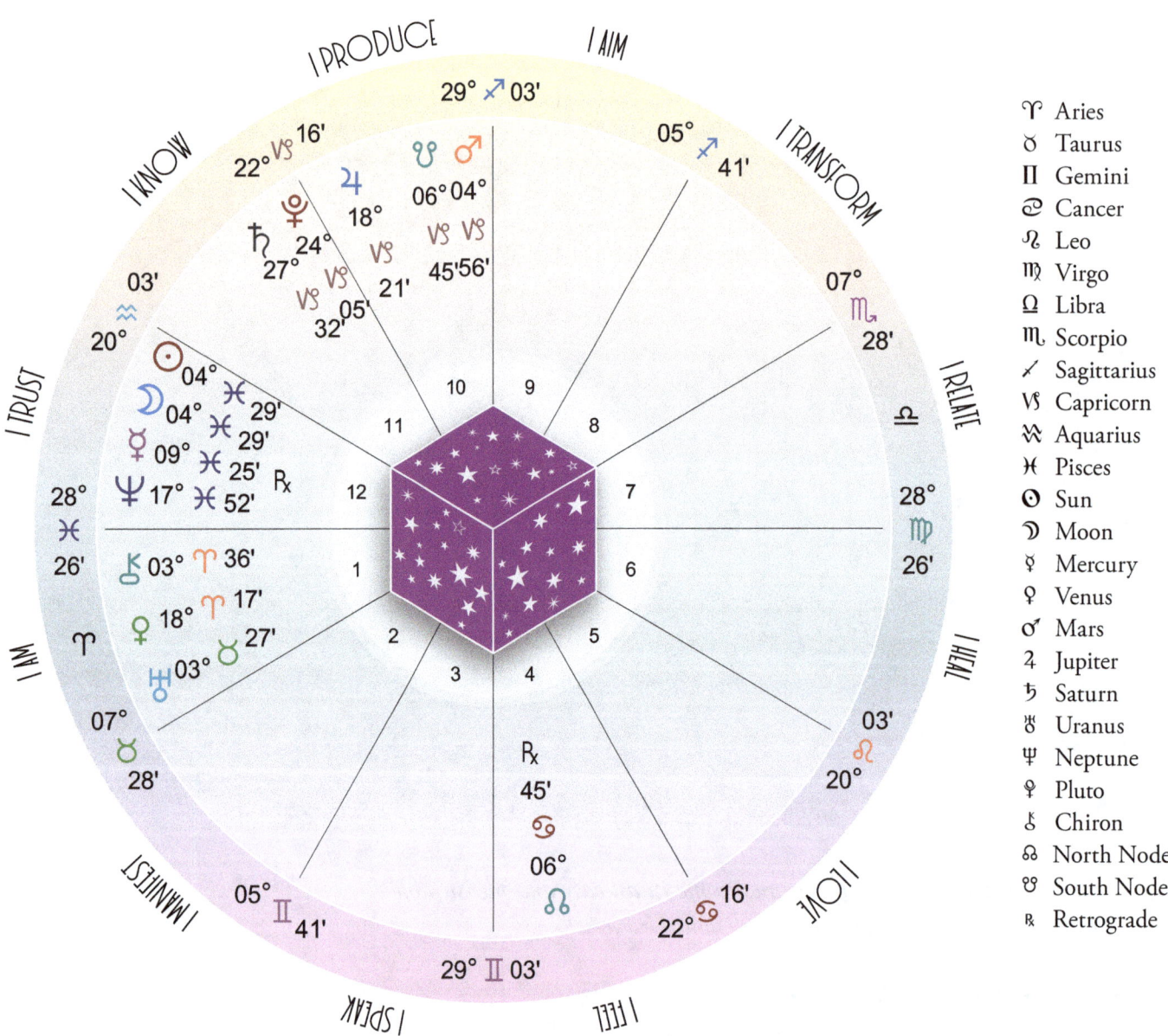

44

COSMIC CHECK-IN

PISCES NEW MOON
FEBRUARY 23RD

Take a moment to write a brief phrase for each "I" statement. This activates all areas of your life for this creative cycle.

♓ I Trust

♈ I Am

♉ I Manifest

♊ I Speak

♋ I Feel

♌ I Love

♍ I Heal

♎ I Relate

♏ I Transform

♐ I Aim

♑ I Produce

♒ I Know

MARCH

March 1st through the middle of the month Pluto and Saturn continue their dance

This works on the struggle between power and perfection.

March 4th Mercury retrograde enters Aquarius

This is a time to open your mind to see what your inventiveness may have missed. Time to redesign and get yourself into the marketplace.

March 9th Mercury direct in Aquarius

Pay attention to your mind. Your innovation is speaking to you now!

March 9th through the 11th Sun and Neptune conjunct

Time to identify with your most spiritual focus. Pay attention, it is calling you!

March 9th Full Moon in Virgo

Let go of small-minded thinking and focus on finding divinity in the details. Time to be very clear about boundaries. Release yourself from lingering health issues. Let go of romancing sickness. Time to fall into the arms of wellness.

March 9th Uranus and Venus dancing in Taurus

Expect the unexpected where love is concerned.

March 16th Mercury enters Pisces

Expressing love may take a front seat in your experience. Write love letters and play straight from the heart. Your romantic dreams may come true, if you come from truth.

March 19th The Sun moves into Aries – Spring Equinox

Happy Spring! The time for dreaming is over. All of life is being sparked with new life. Set your course for this new year by opening to yourself right now!

March 21st Saturn enters Aquarius

This is a great time to advance your ideas. Expect your career to advance as well. Be willing to use the power of your mind by being open, rather than resistant. Options always work to keep the mind open, especially if you have three. Go for it.

March 24th Jupiter, Pluto, Mars tripled in Capricorn

Ambition can skyrocket right now, if you accept the power available to you now. Keep your ego out of it and all will manifest in your favor. At once, blessings; good fortune; action; and great wealth are all available. Hold on to your hat and accept this power. Accept the amazement!

March 24th New Moon in Aries

Identify the top of the mountain, it is yours. Set your intentions with purity of thought and be the champion you are!

March 24th the Sun, Moon, and Chiron tripled in Aries

Balance polarities and know you can heal!

March 30th Mars enters Aquarius

Expect ideas to be extremely active. Remember, action follows thought. If used correctly, success is yours. If you resist, regret will be your reality. Start an idea book to keep up with a rapid-fire mind. You will be amazed at your mental brilliance right now!

Low Vitality March 3rd, 4th, and 31st

The highly charged action potential this month could create exhaustion this month. Please don't push the envelope. The ideas will stick around, if you write them down. Then you can rest and return to your ideas ready to go.

Super Sensitivity March 16th and 17th

The atmosphere is chaotic; stay close to your self (or in your body) and all will be well.

SUNDAY	MONDAY	TUESDAY	WEDNESDAY	THURSDAY	FRIDAY	SATURDAY
1 ☿℞ ☽ V/C 7:52 AM ☽→♊ 11:21 AM 11. Everything is there for you.	2 ☿℞ 3. Who can you inspire today?	3 ☿℞▼ ☽ V/C 6:19 PM ☽→♋ 8:25 PM 4. Today's virtue is patience.	4 ☿℞▼ ♀→♉ 7:07 PM ☿℞→♒ 3:07 AM 5. Let go, it's okay to be different.	5 ☿℞ ☽ V/C 11:11 PM 6. What supports your healing?	6 ☿℞ ☽→♌ 1:28 AM 7. Take time for deep thought.	7 ☿℞ 8. Know manifestation happens now.
8 ☿℞ PDT begins 2:00 AM ☽ V/C 12:12 AM ☽→♍ 3:47 AM 9. Service brings on happiness.	9 ☿SD 28° ♒ 13' 8:48 PM ○ 19° ♍ 37' 10:48 AM 10. You are worthy of high aspirations.	10 ☽ V/C 1:32 AM ☽→♎ 3:02 AM 11. Divine intention opens creativity.	11 3. Bring out the board games.	12 ☽ V/C 1:11 AM ☽→♏ 2:29 AM 4. Follow the directions today.	13 5. Be open, be versatile.	14 ☽ V/C 3:05 AM ☽→♐ 4:10 AM 6. Do what it takes to feel better.
15 8. Generosity increases wealth.	16▲ ☽ V/C 2:34 AM ☽→♑ 9:25 AM ☿→♓ 12:42 AM 9. Notice where you can join a cause.	17▲ **St. Patrick's Day** 10. Pay attention to your dreams.	18 ☽ V/C 5:47 PM ☽→♒ 6:16 PM 11. Will a door open or close?	19 **Spring Equinox** ☉→♈ 8:49 PM 3. Artistic talents are magnified.	20 ☽ V/C 1:59 AM 4. Structure is the foundation for life.	21 ☽→♓ 5:34 AM ♄→♒ 8:58 PM 5. Follow your curiosity and be amazed!
22 6. Nourish with love in your heart.	23 ☽ V/C 7:51 AM ☽→♈ 5:59 PM 7. Collecting awareness is great wealth.	24 ● 4° ♈ 12' 2:29 AM 8. Trust the timing of events.	25 9. Focus on generating harmony.	26 ☽ V/C 12:16 AM ☽→♉ 6:36 AM 10. Have courage to trust the plan.	27 11. Be willing to feel vastness in the sky.	28 ☽ V/C 4:04 PM ☽→♊ 6:38 PM 3. Music supports our vitality today.
29 4. Today's virtue is trustworthiness.	30 ☽ V/C 8:10 AM ♂→♒ 12:43 PM 5. The urge to keep going is strong.	31▼ ☽→♋ 4:44 AM 6. Let's let love go viral.				

♈ Aries	♍ Virgo	♒ Aquarius	♀ Venus	♆ Neptune	V/C Void-of-Course	2. Balance	7. Learning
♉ Taurus	♎ Libra	♓ Pisces	♂ Mars	♇ Pluto	℞ Retrograde	3. Fun	8. Money
♊ Gemini	♏ Scorpio	☉ Sun	♃ Jupiter	⚷ Chiron	SD Stationary Direct	4. Structure	9. Spirituality
♋ Cancer	♐ Sagittarius	☽ Moon	♄ Saturn	→ Enters	▲ Super Sensitivity	5. Action	10. Visionary
♌ Leo	♑ Capricorn	☿ Mercury	♅ Uranus		▼ Low Vitality	6. Love	11. Completion

FULL MOON IN VIRGO

March 9th, 10:48 AM

When the Sun is Opposite the Moon

Full moons are always in opposition to the Sun. This creates a feeling of tension between where you want to shine and how your feelings are flowing on a sensory level about the Sun's directive. The two forces seem like they are working against each other, yet they are on the same team displaying different techniques to obtain the same mission. The Virgo/Pisces polarity creates tension between doing your work and finding your path.

Virgo Goddess

Astraea is the virgin Goddess of Purity, who fled the Earth upon seeing weaponry, warfare, and the rise of patriarchy that destroyed the earth goddess culture during the Iron Age. She ascended to the heavens to become the constellation Virgo, to watch over the Earth until she will one day return issuing in a new Utopian age. Often depicted as a star maiden, she has wings and a shining halo or crown of stars, and carries a flaming torch or thunderbolt.

Ask Astraea to help you as you sort through the details to bring love and light into a fresh new perspective, free from the restrictions of the past. "Because it's always been done that way," is no longer a viable excuse. Sharing what you love, with the intention for the highest and best for all, enlists Astraea's blessings.

Build Your Altar

Colors	Green, blue, earth tones
Numerology	10 – You are worthy of high aspirations
Tarot Card	The Hermit – Knowing your purpose and sharing it with the world
Gemstones	Emerald, sapphire
Plant remedy	Sage – The ability to hold and store light
Fragrance	Lavender – Management and storage of energy

Moon Notes

Full Moon 19° Virgo 37' 10:48 AM
Full Moons are about moving beyond blocks and setting yourself free.

Element
Earth – Practical, determined, structured, enduring, stubborn, traditional, stable, and stuck inside the box.

Statement I Heal
Body Intestines
Mind Critical, Analytical
Spirit Divinity In Details

5th House Moon
I Love/I Heal

Umbrella Energy
The way you love and how you want to be loved.

Choice Points
Opportunity   New Path/New Reality
Challenge   Wastefulness

Sabian Symbol
A Caravan Of Cars Headed For Promised Lands

Potential
Follow your own path.

CLEARING THE SLATE

**VIRGO FULL MOON
MARCH 9TH**

Sixty hours before the full moon, negative traits connected to the astro-sign might become activated to trigger what needs to be released during the full moon phase. You may notice an extreme sense of judgement, an obsession for detail, or letting perfectionism stop your action. Make a list, look in the mirror, and for each negative trait, tell yourself *I am sorry, I forgive you, thank you for your awareness,* and *I love you.*

VIRGO VICTORIES & CHALLENGES

Say all of the statements in this section out loud. Then, underline the phrase that means the most to you. Use the phrase as your affirmation for releasing throughout this moon phase.

Today I take time to go within to be silent. I imagine myself on a country road moving towards a beautiful mountain. I bask in the glory of the power of the mountain and know that it is calling me to the top. I find a pathway to the top and begin to climb. As I climb I become aware of a presence guiding me and empowering me to keep going, creating a sense of peacefulness within me.

I become aware of my own power in this silent journey to the top and revel in the serenity that nature and silence bring me. At last I am about to reach the summit and, just before I do, I feel the power drawing me to go within on a deeper level. I stop for a moment and look back at the path I have just climbed and know that my life's path is a remarkable gift. I connect to the center of the Earth and feel an inner glow.

The top of the mountain calls to me and, as I reach the top, a voice says to me, "Take in the view and look in all directions." As I turn 360-degrees, I sense a light igniting me in every direction. Then the voice says, "Look up!" Now, my awareness shifts and I see that I have become an illuminating light glowing in all six directions. Next I hear, "Sit in your silence and take in the vastness of who you are. Who you are is immeasurable." I sit, feeling the glow of light within me, and become aware of a greater plan for my life. I allow myself to receive this plan. I accept this assignment and slowly walk down the mountain, knowing that I can be a shining light for myself and others. I know I must take my light out to the world and share what I know to be my truth. Today, I become a messenger for the light.

Virgo Homework

Become integrated so that the light of your personality becomes soul-infused. When you are soul-infused and are in service to your Higher Self, you radiate love and light through the power of the inner self through all activities, thoughts, and emotions and become more magnificent. Learn the art of detachment and let your Soul take control.

GRATITUDE LIST

Keep this list active throughout the moon cycle. This will bring you to a level of completion so that a new cycle of opportunity can occur in your life. Be prepared for miracles!

TAROT

Ask the question out loud, then draw a card. You may wish to draw it or paste a copy of it here. Then write down what you feel it might be telling you, in response to the question. Use the glossary in the appendix and record here anything about the card that captures your attention. You may wish to come back throughout the moon cycle to meditate or journal more on the card.

How is my body supporting my releasing?

RELEASING LIST

**VIRGO FULL MOON
MARCH 9TH**

Say this statement out loud three times before writing your list:

I am a free spiritual being and it is my desire to be free to think and to express myself fully.

I hereby fully and completely free my mind from all adhesions to outdated philosophies, habits, relationships, groups of people, man-made laws, moral codes, all rules, set ideas and set ways of thinking, traditions, organizations, duty-motivated activities, guilt, judgment, and being misunderstood!

Virgo Freedom Ideas

Now is the time to activate a game change in my life, and give up finding fault with myself, my addiction to perfection, my addiction to detail, over-indulging in image management, pain-producing thinking patterns, judgment of others, resistance to being healthy, and destructive behaviors.

FULL MOON IN VIRGO

Your Personal Moon Experience

Fill in the Cosmic Check-In page. Then look up the degree of the Moon on the chart below. Take note of the "I" statement on the outside of the wheel where the Moon is located. Now, locate the same degree on your own chart and make a note of the house and corresponding "I" statement. Go back to the Cosmic Check-In page and circle the two statements from the charts and read what you wrote. This will give you an idea about what to expect from this moon phase on a personal level. For more information on personalizing your *Moon Book*, go to www.BlueMoonAcademy.com and look for *How to Use the Moon Book*.

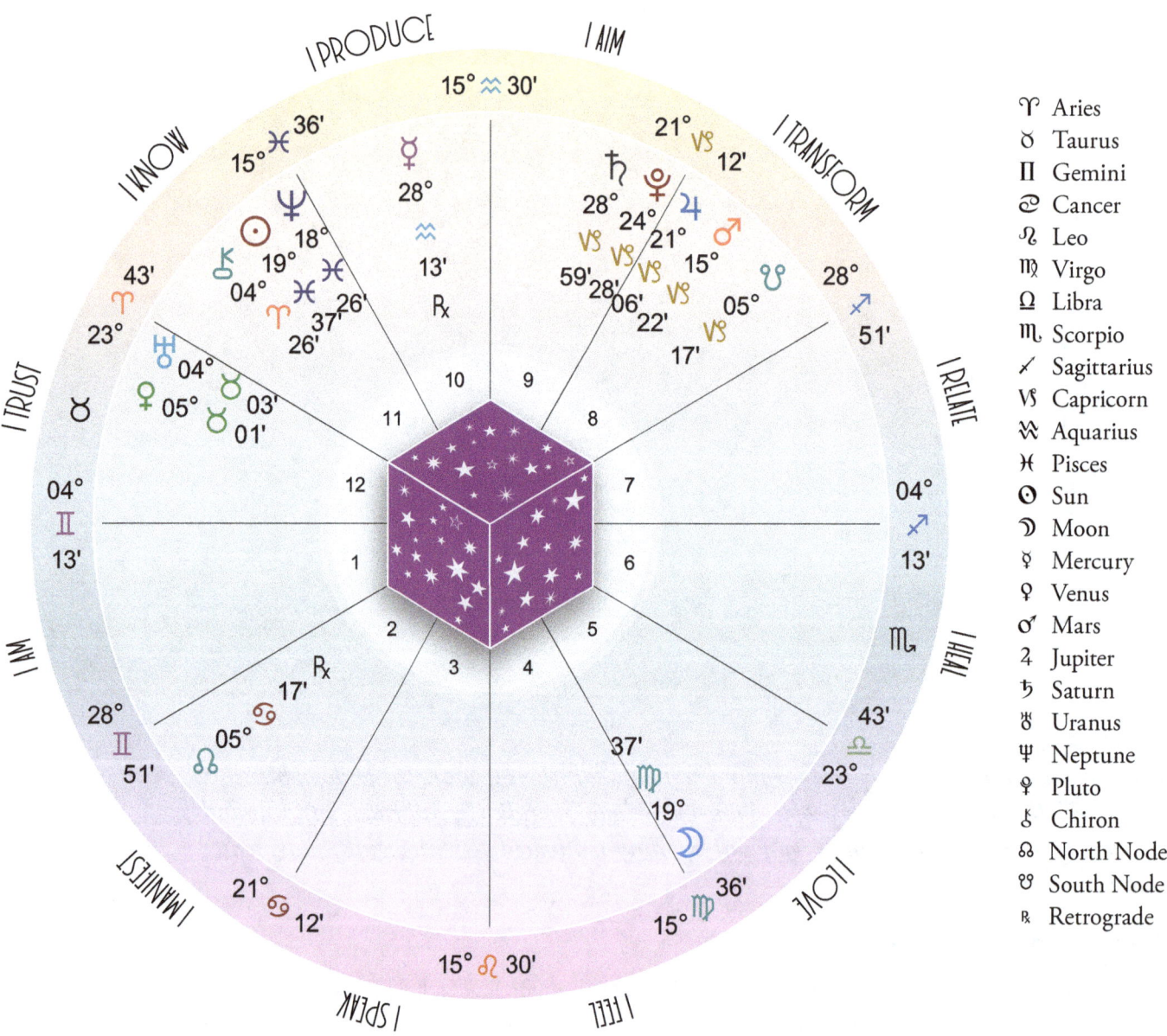

COSMIC CHECK-IN

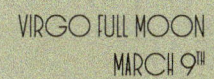
VIRGO FULL MOON
MARCH 9TH

Take a moment to write a brief phrase for each "I" statement. This activates all areas of your life for this creative cycle.

♍ I Heal

♎ I Relate

♏ I Transform

♐ I Aim

♑ I Produce

♒ I Know

♓ I Trust

♈ I Am

♉ I Manifest

♊ I Speak

♋ I Feel

♌ I Love

55

New Moon in Aries

March 24th, 2:29 AM

When the Sun is in Aries

Aries awakens the dreamer from Winter sleep and represents the raw energy of Spring, when the new shoots of life burst forth. Aries is the fundamental, straightforward approach to life. There is no challenge that is too great, no obstacle too daunting, and no rival too powerful for the Aries. Aries symbolizes initiation, leadership, strength, and potency. Competition and achievement are very important to Aries. Now is the time to be a pioneer and break all barriers to become the winner you are.

Aries Goddess

Pandora was created by Zeus, who was angry about Prometheus stealing the secret of fire. She was the first human woman, whose name means "the all-giving." The gods all conspired to each invest her with seductive gifts. Hesiod's story tells us that Pandora's curiosity led her to open a jar (not a box) that unleashed evils upon humanity. However, Pandora, also known as Anesidora, "she who sends up gifts" from the Earth, could instead be interpreted as opening the pithos (the vessel), an ancient symbol of the Divine Feminine, and generously gifting the world with fertility and creativity.

As you reinterpret your identity this moon, ask Pandora to help you get curious and creative about the "I" you present to the world and how that contributes to the "we."

Build Your Altar

Colors	Red, black, white
Numerology	8 – Trust the timing of events
Tarot Card	Emperor – Success on all levels
Gemstones	Diamond, red jasper, coral, obsidian
Plant Remedy	Pomegranates, oak – Planting new life, rooting new life
Fragrance	Ginger – The ability to ingest and digest life

Moon Notes

New Moon 4° Aries 12' 2:29 AM
New Moons are about opening new pathways for prosperity.

Element
Fire – Igniting, dissolving, accelerating, cleansing, advancing awareness, impatience, leadership, passion and vitality.

Statement I Am
Body Head
Mind Ego-centric
Spirit Initiation, Leadership

3rd House Moon
I Speak/I Am

Umbrella Energy
How you get the word out and the message behind the words.

Choice Points
Opportunity Self-transcendence
Challenge   Oblivious

Sabian Symbol
A White Triangle Is Seen; It Has Golden Wings

Potential
Fly high with your creativity.

ARIES VICTORIES & CHALLENGES

ARIES NEW MOON MARCH 24TH

Say all of the statements in this section out loud. Then, underline the phrase that means the most to you. Use the phrase as your affirmation for manifesting throughout this moon phase.

I am the author of my life. I accept that I am a winner and, in so doing, all doors are open to me. I hold the world in the palm of my hand and I know that there is not a mountain that I cannot climb. My ability to respond to life is in operation today and I direct my intention to bring me to the next level of self-determined achievement. The world and its systems are available for me to use as tools for my success and I use them with true excellence. I am organized and all systems are in place for me to make my mark on the world. I accept that my structured ground state and my dynamic energy are ready to make headway using pure determination, action, planning, and power. I will manage this plan and know that the sequence of events provided support me to make a breakthrough today.

I am willing to make my plan and take action on it. I gather my support team together today to focus on the appropriate action and encourage each person in their area of excellence and production. I am a great leader and my dynamic power is a good resource for others to determine their own success formula. I am aware that all parts of my team are important and place value on all areas of performance required to manifest in the world. I know how to place people in their best areas of expertise, so they can experience their own unique talent manifesting. Today, I honor my father for what he taught me by what he did, or didn't do, to encourage my ability to perform. I am the producer. I am the protector. I am the provider. I am the promoter. I am power. I am the author of my life.

Aries Homework

Aries manifest best through sales and promotions, and as a professional athlete, personal trainer or coach, martial arts expert, military professional, demolition expert, fireworks manufacturer, or wardrobe consultant.

Merge your light and dark forces so balance can occur. Then, give shape to your feelings through creative forms and learn to live in the duality of your Soul and watch your spirit soar! The embodiment of this duality connects you to the Unity, a requirement for these times.

VICTORY LIST

Acknowledge what you have overcome. Keep this list active during this moon cycle. Honoring victory allows you to accept success.

TAROT

Ask the question out loud, then draw a card. You may wish to draw it or paste a copy of it here. Then write down what you feel it might be telling you, in response to the question. Use the glossary in the appendix and record here anything about the card that captures your attention. You may wish to come back throughout the moon cycle to meditate or journal more on the card.

How is my spirit supporting my manifesting?

MANIFESTING LIST

ARIES NEW MOON
MARCH 24TH

This or something better than this comes to me in an easy and pleasurable way, for the good of all concerned. Thank you, Universe!

Aries Manifesting Ideas

Now is the time to focus on manifesting personality power, leadership, strength, self-acceptance, winning, courage, personal appearance, and advancing to new frontiers.

New Moon in Aries

Your Personal Moon Experience

Fill in the Cosmic Check-In page. Then look up the degree of the Moon on the chart below. Take note of the "I" statement on the outside of the wheel where the Moon is located. Now, locate the same degree on your own chart and make a note of the house and corresponding "I" statement. Go back to the Cosmic Check-In page and circle the two statements from the charts and read what you wrote. This will give you an idea about what to expect from this moon phase on a personal level. For more information on personalizing your *Moon Book*, go to www.BlueMoonAcademy.com and look for *How to Use the Moon Book*.

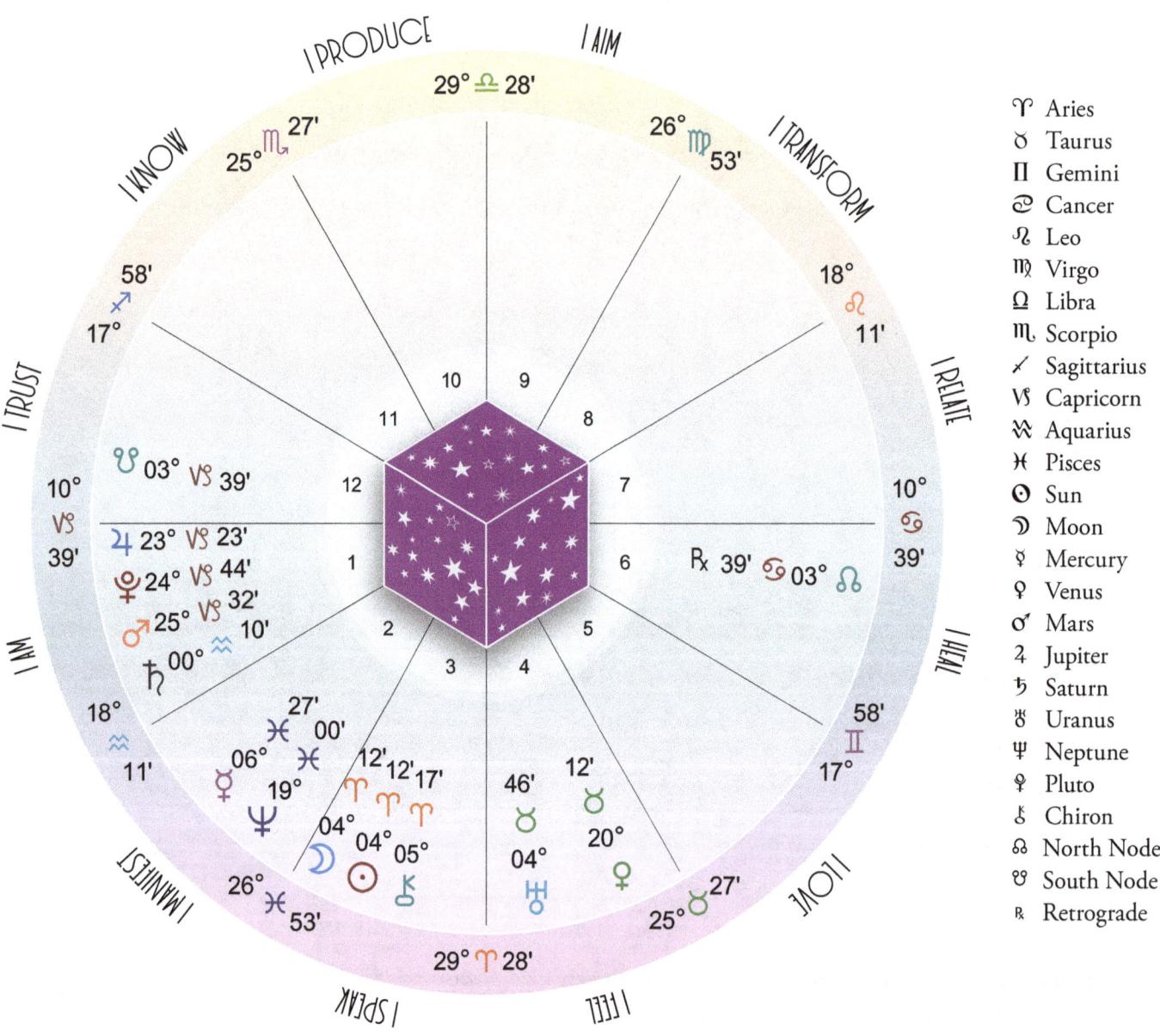

COSMIC CHECK-IN

ARIES NEW MOON
MARCH 24TH

Take a moment to write a brief phrase for each "I" statement. This activates all areas of your life for this creative cycle.

♈ I Am

♉ I Manifest

♊ I Speak

♋ I Feel

♌ I Love

♍ I Heal

♎ I Relate

♏ I Transform

♐ I Aim

♑ I Produce

♒ I Know

♓ I Trust

APRIL

April 3rd Venus moves into Gemini

Time to flirt. You will love the results of your bright mind and wit as the results create total fun on many levels.

April 5th Mars and Saturn coupled in Aquarius for a few days

Expect delays in most action, especially in travel. Don't try to go fast, it may slow you down and make you accident prone. Time to slow down and smell the roses. Keep a good watch on your technology, breakdowns could happen. Please remember to save and back up your files. This is not a good time to take your car to be fixed, wait a week. Avoid travel if possible.

April 7th Full Moon in Libra

Release the times when you felt wrongly accused.

April 7th Pluto and Jupiter conjunct in Capricorn throughout the year

This promotes a major drive for success that forms an alliance with your spiritual connection and makes the rewards of your success benefit all those with whom you come in contact. Expect to be and feel generous.

April 10th Mercury enters Aries

You may find you're talking too much about yourself.

April 19th The Sun enters Taurus

Time to feel beauty returning to nature as the flowers bloom all over, filling the earth with color and fragrance. Abundance is advancing and your ability to manifest will surface. Time to fill yourself with beauty and experience luxury.

April 22nd New Moon in Taurus

Optimum manifesting power is yours today. Spend time writing your wish list, without limiting beliefs. The magnetic field is working overtime; be willing to receive and your dreams could come true!

April 22nd Uranus, Moon, and Sun are dancing in Taurus

Tempers could fly. Your emotions may be super sensitive. Try not to take things personally. Stay in your own lane and you will be okay.

April 25th Pluto retrograde in Capricorn until October 4th

There is a big-time focus on business and wealth preservation. Visit a money manager and form a new plan. Expect old debts owed you to be paid off. It's time to pay your old debts as well.

April 27th Mercury enters Taurus

If you can't make a decision in three minutes, don't make one.

Low Vitality April 1st, 27th and 28th

Keep yourself energized by having a drumming circle. Earth changes are possible; get rest and stay close to home.

Super Sensitivity April 12th and 13th

The atmosphere is filled with chaotic fields of energy. Stay close to your body. Avoid daydreaming and meditating so that negative thinking and depression stay away from you.

SUNDAY	MONDAY	TUESDAY	WEDNESDAY	THURSDAY	FRIDAY	SATURDAY
			1▼ **April Fools' Day** 7. Use discernment before deciding.	2 ☽ V/C 9:48 AM ☽→♌ 11:26 AM 8. Let prosperity become you.	3 ☽ V/C 12:28 PM ♀→♊ 10:10 AM 9. Support a worthy cause.	4 ☽→♍ 2:19 PM 10. You are so close, get it done.
5 **Easter** 11. Share your Divine knowing.	6 ☽ V/C 6:28 AM ☽→♎ 2:17 PM 3. Invite friends to go dancing.	7 ○ 18° ♎ 44' 7:36 PM 4. A project needs a practical answer.	8 ☽ V/C 5:49 AM ☽→♏ 1:17 PM 5. Feeling stuck? Go for a walk.	9 6. Let's let Love go viral.	10 ☽ V/C 12:34 PM ☽→♐ 1:36 PM ☿→♈ 9:48 PM 7. Share a book with a friend.	11 8. Gratitude advances your abundance.
12▲ ☽ V/C 4:45 AM ☽→♑ 5:06 PM 9. Spirit knows no limits; be unlimited.	13▲ 10. Act like the future is yours.	14 ☽ V/C 4:47 PM 11. Feel the bigger picture in action.	15 ☽→♒ 12:38 PM 3. If it's not fun don't do it.	16 4. Bring stability to a situation.	17 ☽ V/C 7:34 AM ☽→♓ 11:30 AM 5. Don't wait, go now!	18 6. Create harmony, live love.
19 ☽ V/C 4:30 PM ☉→♉ 7:45 AM 7. Lessons learned bear fruit.	20 ☽→♈ 12:01 AM 8. Manifestation happens in the now!	21 9. Honor all spiritual beliefs.	22 ☽ V/C 5:31 AM ☽→♉ 12:36 PM ● 3° ♉ 24' 7:26 PM 10. Share your visionary thoughts.	23 11. Complete a project today!	24 ☽ V/C 5:42 PM 3. Create a happy music playlist.	25♇℞ ♇℞ 24° ♑ 00' 11:54 AM ☽→♊ 12:20 AM 4. Your patience is valued today.
26♇℞ 5. Take the path of least resistance.	27♇℞▼ ☽ V/C 9:59 AM ☽→♋ 10:28 AM ☿→♉ 12:52 PM 6. Burn incense to set the stage for love.	28♇℞▼ 7. Share your wisdom.	29♇℞ ☽ V/C 12:29 PM ☽→♌ 6:06 PM 8. Give your desire direction.	30♇℞ 9. Join a prayer group.		

♈ Aries	♍ Virgo	♒ Aquarius	♀ Venus	♆ Neptune	V/C Void-of-Course	2. Balance	7. Learning
♉ Taurus	♎ Libra	♓ Pisces	♂ Mars	♇ Pluto	℞ Retrograde	3. Fun	8. Money
♊ Gemini	♏ Scorpio	☉ Sun	♃ Jupiter	⚷ Chiron	§ Stationary Direct	4. Structure	9. Spirituality
♋ Cancer	♐ Sagittarius	☽ Moon	♄ Saturn	→ Enters	▲ Super Sensitivity	5. Action	10. Visionary
♌ Leo	♑ Capricorn	☿ Mercury	♅ Uranus		▼ Low Vitality	6. Love	11. Completion

Full Moon in Libra

April 7th, 7:36 PM

When the Sun is Opposite the Moon

Full moons are always in opposition to the Sun. This creates a feeling of tension between where you want to shine and how your feelings are flowing on a sensory level about the Sun's directive. The two forces seem like they are working against each other, yet they are on the same team displaying different techniques to obtain the same mission. The Libra/Aries polarity creates tension between the idea of "We" versus "Me."

Libra Goddess

Ostara, Goddess of the Spring Equinox, walks into your life creating a carpet of fragrant flowers in her wake with each step upon the Earth. Freed from the ice and snow of Winter, she bathes in the moonlight and breathes out warmer breezes to turn up the temperatures. This moon is the harbinger, a rebirth of the Earth to fresh growth and abundance.

What is blooming new in your life? What do your seeds need to shed and break through to bask in the bright Spring sunlight? Take Ostara's blessing of jasmine or rose fragrance into the bath or shower and allow the warm water to wash away the old.

Build Your Altar

Colors	Pink, green
Numerology	4 – A project needs a practical answer
Tarot Card	Justice – Positive and negative uses of karma
Gemstones	Rose quartz, jade
Plant remedy	Olive trees – Stamina
Fragrance	Eucalyptus – Clarity of breath

Moon Notes

Full Moon 18° Libra 44' 7:36 PM
Full Moons are about moving beyond blocks and setting yourself free.

Element
Air – The breath of life that allows the mind to achieve new insights and fresh perspectives, abstract dreaming, freedom from attachments, codes of intelligence, and academic applications.

Statement I Relate
Body Kidneys
Mind Social
Spirit Peace

12th House Moon
I Trust/I Relate

Umbrella Energy
Determines how you deal with your karma.

Choice Points
Opportunity   Robin Hood
Challenge   Subversive

Sabian Symbol
A Gang Of Robbers In Hiding

Potential
Stay open to integrity.

CLEARING THE SLATE

**LIBRA FULL MOON
APRIL 7TH**

Sixty hours before the full moon negative traits connected to the astro-sign might become activated to trigger what needs to be released during the full moon phase. You may notice an unusual need to defend, an over-shadowing guilt, or a need to justify. Make a list, look in the mirror, and for each negative trait, tell yourself *I am sorry, I forgive you, thank you for your awareness,* and *I love you.*

LIBRA VICTORIES & CHALLENGES

Say all of the statements in this section out loud. Then, underline the phrase that means the most to you. Use the phrase as your affirmation for releasing throughout this moon phase.

I am awakened to the reality of the Law of Cause and Effect. I take time out today to see what is coming back to me. I know my actions, my words, and my thoughts have life and manifest in a pattern that returns to me. Today, I am in a place where I can clearly see the results of my words, my actions, and my thoughts. I am aware that it is time for a review and, in so doing, I am given the opportunity to balance, integrate and redistribute these results in a more productive way. When I truly know and experience the Law of Cause and Effect (what I send out comes back to me), I can take responsibility for my actions, words, and thoughts, and set myself free of blame. When blame is gone from my thought pattern (self-inflicted or circumstantial), I am able to benefit from my review rather than wasting energy justifying or defending my position. I now accept the idea that I am free to reconcile with whatever I have labeled as an injustice in my life. I take the time to re-route my thinking towards making life a beneficial experience. Today, I accept that in changing my language I can change my life. Today, I prepare to take actions toward beneficial experiences. Today, I release the need to be right and accept the right to be. Today, I stop judging life and start living life.

Libra Homework

Let the fresh air blow away mental stagnation related to times when you let others' interests supersede your own. Drink an excess amount of water to alert your kidneys that the recalibration process has commenced. It's time to deepen your intention to be one with the light, promoting restoration on Earth.

GRATITUDE LIST

Keep this list active throughout the moon cycle. This will bring you to a level of completion so that a new cycle of opportunity can occur in your life. Be prepared for miracles!

TAROT

Ask the question out loud, then draw a card. You may wish to draw it or paste a copy of it here. Then write down what you feel it might be telling you, in response to the question. Use the glossary in the appendix and record here anything about the card that captures your attention. You may wish to come back throughout the moon cycle to meditate or journal more on the card.

How is my mind supporting my releasing?

RELEASING LIST

**LIBRA FULL MOON
APRIL 7TH**

Say this statement out loud three times before writing your list:

I am a free spiritual being and it is my desire to be free to think and to express myself fully.

I hereby fully and completely free my mind from all adhesions to outdated philosophies, habits, relationships, groups of people, man-made laws, moral codes, all rules, set ideas and set ways of thinking, traditions, organizations, duty-motivated activities, guilt, judgment, and being misunderstood!

Libra Freedom Ideas

Now is the time to activate a game change in my life, and give up situations that are not balanced, people-pleasing and the need to be liked, sorrow over past relationships, unsupportive relationships, the need to be right, false accusations, and being misunderstood.

Full Moon in Libra

Your Personal Moon Experience

Fill in the Cosmic Check-In page. Then look up the degree of the Moon on the chart below. Take note of the "I" statement on the outside of the wheel where the Moon is located. Now, locate the same degree on your own chart and make a note of the house and corresponding "I" statement. Go back to the Cosmic Check-In page and circle the two statements from the charts and read what you wrote. This will give you an idea about what to expect from this moon phase on a personal level. For more information on personalizing your *Moon Book*, go to www.BlueMoonAcademy.com and look for *How to Use the Moon Book*.

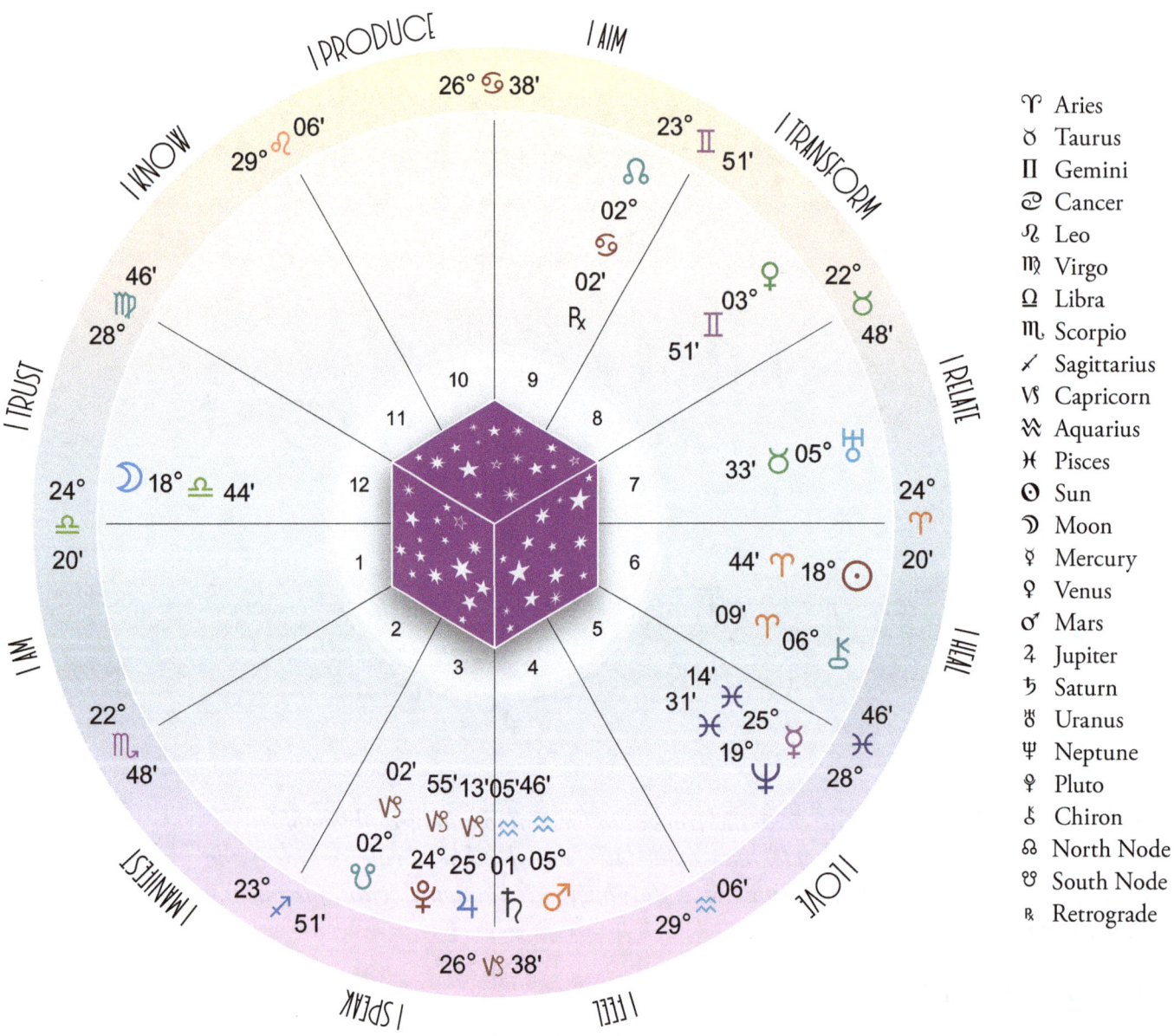

COSMIC CHECK-IN

LIBRA FULL MOON
APRIL 7ᵀᴴ

Take a moment to write a brief phrase for each "I" statement. This activates all areas of your life for this creative cycle.

♎ I Relate

♏ I Transform

♐ I Aim

♑ I Produce

♒ I Know

♓ I Trust

♈ I Am

♉ I Manifest

♊ I Speak

♋ I Feel

♌ I Love

♍ I Heal

New Moon in Taurus

April 22nd, 7:26 PM

When the Sun is in Taurus

Taurus is the time when we see the true manifesting power, as the plants move to a higher aspiration of life and bloom. Once again, we become connected to the essence of beauty as a symbol of our divinity. Taurus is the connection between humanity and divinity. Taurus' job is to infuse matter with light through accumulating layers of substance. This is why they are such good shoppers and collectors. The more they accumulate, the more divinity they experience. This process brings about a sense of self-value which is directly commensurate to the amount of money they manifest. Personal resources are part of the pattern. Discover your value at this time.

Taurus Goddess

Today, Lakshmi, the Hindu Goddess of Abundance, walks into your life bearing gifts. She joyously showers you with success, wealth, well-being, luck, happiness, and fulfillment. Her blessings also include forgiveness and the generosity of spirit that allows you to reap the recognition for good work well done.

Working with feng shui, place a statue of Lakshmi in the left-hand corner of your room (looking in from the entrance) to honor her and to signal your receptivity. Are your hands and heart open and ready to receive? Make space for the new. Step confidently into the flow of abundance! Take Lakshmi's lead and shower everyone you meet with kindness and generosity!

Build Your Altar

Colors   Green, pink, deep red, earth tones
Numerology   10 – Share your visionary thoughts
Tarot Card   Hierophant – The interpreter of life
Gemstones   Topaz, agate, smoky quartz, jade, rose quartz
Plant Remedy   Angelica – Connecting Heaven and Earth
Fragrance   Rose – Opening the heart

Moon Notes

New Moon 3° Taurus 24' 7:26 PM
New Moons are about opening new pathways for prosperity.

Element
Earth – Practical, determined, structured, enduring, stubborn, traditional, stable, and stuck inside the box.

Statement I Manifest
Body Neck
Mind Collector
Spirit Accumulation

6th House Moon
I Heal/I Manifest

Umbrella Energy
The way you manage your body and its appearance.

Choice Points
Opportunity   Seeking
Challenge   Pipe Dreams

Sabian Symbol
The Pot Of Gold At The End Of The Rainbow

Potential
Fabulous future and prosperity ahead.

Taurus Victories & Challenges

Taurus New Moon April 22nd

Say all of the statements in this section out loud. Then, underline the phrase that means the most to you. Use the phrase as your affirmation for manifesting throughout this moon phase.

Everything is possible for me today. My possibilities are endless. I have the power within me to make all of my dreams come true. I have the tools to make my talent a reality. I have the power to identify with my talent. Today, I focus my attention and intention on manifesting with my talent and, in so doing, I transform my ideas into reality. I recognize the part of me that is connected to the cosmic source of ideas and I express that source within me to manifest my creative power. I see my possibilities and act on them today. I am the creative power. I am all-knowing. I am an individual. There is no one else like me. I can manifest anything I desire. I intend it, I allow it, so be it.

Rules for Manifesting

Know what you want. Write it down. Say it out loud. Recognize that because you thought it, it can be so. Release your limiting beliefs. Override your limiting beliefs with power statements. Act as if you have already manifested your idea. Lastly, value yourself!

Taurus Homework

Taureans manifest best when buying, selling, and owning real estate, gardening and landscaping, selling and collecting art, manufacturing and selling fine furniture, singing or acting, and as a restaurateur, antique dealer, or interior designer.

The Taurus moon asks us to infuse light into form and, in so doing, the bridge between humanity and divinity is actualized and we can assume our stewardship in the physical world. When we release Spirit into matter, we become open to the idea that accumulation and actualization set us free to experience the abundance available to us here on Earth. Go shopping!

VICTORY LIST

Acknowledge what you have overcome. Keep this list active during this moon cycle. Honoring victory allows you to accept success.

TAROT

Ask the question out loud, then draw a card. You may wish to draw it or paste a copy of it here. Then write down what you feel it might be telling you, in response to the question. Use the glossary in the appendix and record here anything about the card that captures your attention. You may wish to come back throughout the moon cycle to meditate or journal more on the card.

How is my body supporting my manifesting?

MANIFESTING LIST

**TAURUS NEW MOON
APRIL 22ND**

This or something better than this comes to me in an easy and pleasurable way, for the good of all concerned. Thank you, Universe!

Taurus Manifesting Ideas
Now is the time to focus on manifesting success, money, property, luxury, beauty, personal value, and pleasure.

New Moon in Taurus

Your Personal Moon Experience

Fill in the Cosmic Check-In page. Then look up the degree of the Moon on the chart below. Take note of the "I" statement on the outside of the wheel where the Moon is located. Now, locate the same degree on your own chart and make a note of the house and corresponding "I" statement. Go back to the Cosmic Check-In page and circle the two statements from the charts and read what you wrote. This will give you an idea about what to expect from this moon phase on a personal level. For more information on personalizing your *Moon Book*, go to www.BlueMoonAcademy.com and look for *How to Use the Moon Book*.

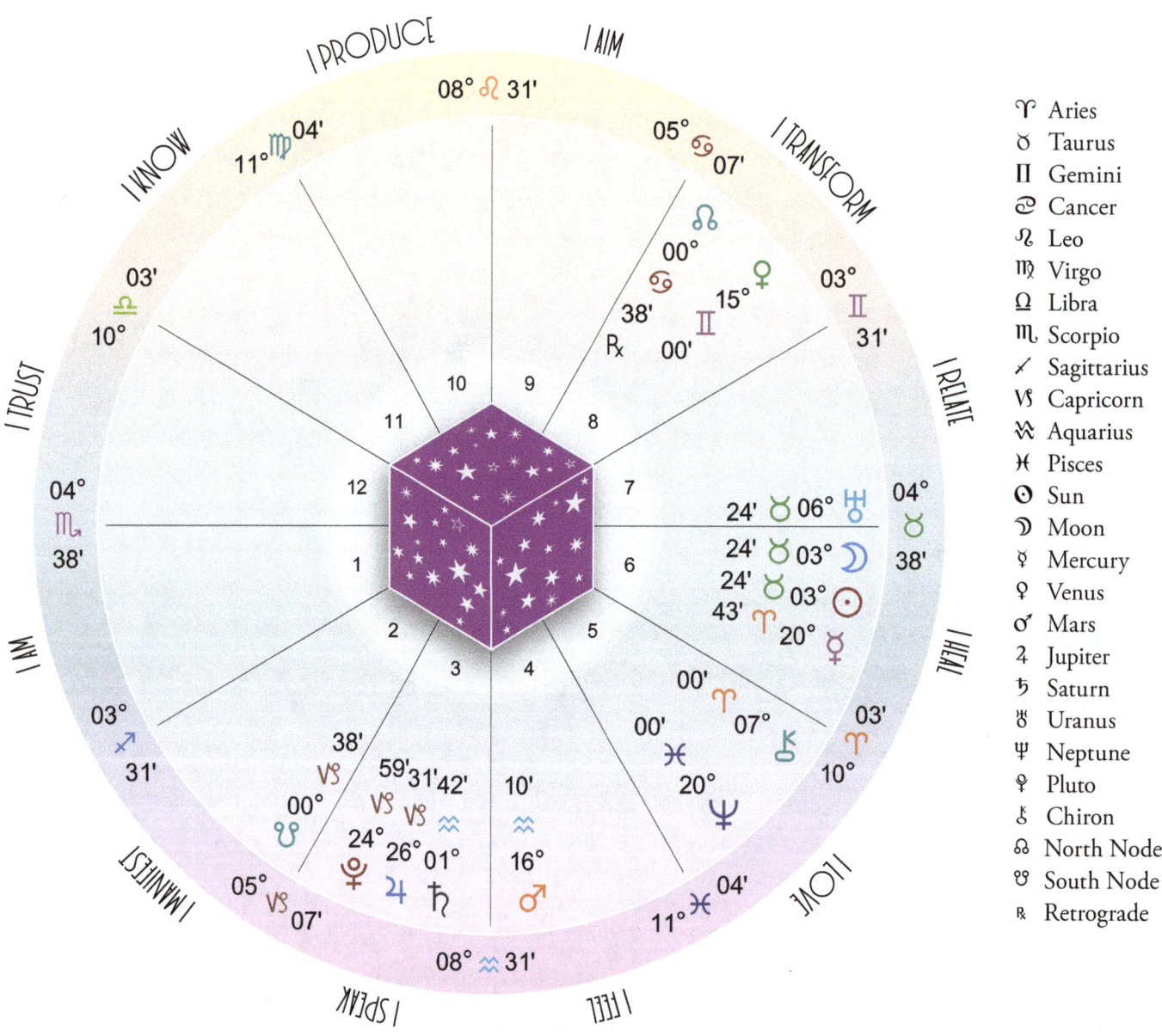

COSMIC CHECK-IN

**TAURUS NEW MOON
APRIL 22ND**

Take a moment to write a brief phrase for each "I" statement. This activates all areas of your life for this creative cycle.

♉ I Manifest

♊ I Speak

♋ I Feel

♌ I Love

♍ I Heal

♎ I Relate

♏ I Transform

♐ I Aim

♑ I Produce

♒ I Know

♓ I Trust

♈ I Am

81

MAY

May 1st throughout the month Pluto and Jupiter coupled in Capricorn

If you are willing to accept success, this is a great combination. Remember that Pluto rules wealth; Jupiter rules good fortune and blessings; and Capricorn rules accomplishment of goals. Trust the Universe in making your choices beyond survival. Aim for happiness.

May 1st throughout the entire month North and South Node at 29° in Gemini and Sagittarius

The fragile energy field sets up turning points in your life. It's time to release your obligation to your past, in this life or past lives. You may feel a deep need to explore your inner truth. Spiritual development comes into the foreground.

May 7th Full Moon in Scorpio

Set yourself free from resentment issues that turned into revenge. Recognize where sexual indiscretions or jealousy took you away from your focus.

May 7th the Sun is dancing with Mercury in Taurus

Share your love for beauty, art, abundance, and luxury. It is time to accept the power of being magnetic. The earth welcomes you talking about what you want to manifest. Remember, nothing happens on this earth without sound. Give voice to your manifest list.

May 10th Saturn retrograde in Aquarius through the Summer, goes direct in Capricorn September 28th

It's a good time to review and research your projects, inventions, and ideas. In other words, go deeper.

May 12th Venus retrograde in Gemini until June 24th

Your flirting may backfire. Your love nature might be misunderstood if a brat attack has been part of your expression.

May 12th Mars enters Pisces

Your emotional body will get a steam cleaning. Pay attention to what comes up. It is time to bring what you have buried into the light. Healing is the name of the game. It is also time to face an addiction and be done with it.

May 14th Jupiter retrograde in Capricorn until September 12th

Go back 12 years to 2008. Expect emotional regression in the areas of home, health, and love.

May 20th The Sun enters Gemini

This is a great time to focus on your message and how to get your message out. Is it blogging, video, newsletter, discussion group, or marketing? Remember the marketplace is your playground. Go play!

May 22nd New Moon in Gemini

Your gift for gab is front and center.

May 22nd Mercury dancing with Venus in Gemini

Your love for life manifests. Tell it like it is and dance on the tabletops. You can be the life of the party right now. Enjoy!

May 28th Mercury enters Cancer

Time to express yourself in your family. Have a family reunion and tell it like it is for you.

Super Sensitivity May 10th and 11th

Extra fragility is in the atmosphere right now. This energy is extreme so you can motivate a turning point for yourself.

Low Vitality May 24th, 25th and 27th-30th

Now is the time to awaken new beginnings by completing emotional loyalty to the past.

SUNDAY	MONDAY	TUESDAY	WEDNESDAY	THURSDAY	FRIDAY	SATURDAY
					1 ♇℞ ☽ V/C 9:04 AM ☽→♍ 10:35 PM 10. A new beginning is here ... Go Now!	2 ♇℞ 11. Act on the intuitive feeling.
3 ♇℞ ☽ V/C 7:24 PM 3. Optimism opens many doors.	4 ♇℞ ☽→♎ 12:10 AM 4. Apply what you know.	5 ♇℞ ☽ V/C 7:30 PM 5. Relax and enjoy the ride.	6 ♇℞ ☽→♏ 12:04 AM 6. Light a candle, time for romance.	7 ♇℞ ○ 17° ♏ 20' 3:45 AM ☽ V/C 7:38 PM 7. Be ready to help solve a problem.	8 ♇℞ ☽→♐ 12:15 AM 8. It takes courage to say yes or no.	9 ♇℞ ☽ V/C 11:10 PM 9. Spirit is waiting, just ask.
10 ♄♇℞▲ **Mother's Day** ♄℞ 1° ♒ 57' 9:09 PM ☽→♑ 2:39 AM 10. Having a goal fulfills your dreams.	11 ♄♇℞▲ ☿→♊ 2:57 PM 11. Accept yourself as victorious.	12 ♀♄♇℞ ♀℞ 21° ♊ 50' 11:45 PM ☽ V/C 3:29 AM ☽→♒ 8:38 AM ♂→♓ 9:17 PM 3. Base your choices on fun today.	13 ♀♄♇℞ 4. Logic is a go-to tool this year.	14 ♀♃♄♇℞ ☽ V/C 7:02 AM ♃℞ 27° ♑ 14' 7:32 AM ☽→♓ 6:25 PM 5. Multiple options are open today.	15 ♀♃♄♇℞ 6. Let's let love go viral. Live Love!	16 ♀♃♄♇℞ 7. Research gets you everything today!
17 ♀♃♄♇℞ ☽ V/C 12:59 AM ☽→♈ 6:36 AM 8. Follow the way towards success.	18 ♀♃♄♇℞ 9. Generosity breeds more abundance.	19 ♀♃♄♇℞ ☽ V/C 1:32 PM ☽→♉ 7:11 PM 10. Innovation makes the future.	20 ♀♃♄♇℞ ☉→♊ 6:49 AM 11. Stand tall in the mysteries today.	21 ♀♃♄♇℞ 3. Kindness fills the world with joy.	22 ♀♃♄♇℞ ☽ V/C 1:00 AM ☽→♊ 6:36 AM ● 2° ♊ 05' 10:39 AM 4. A solid foundation is critical.	23 ♀♃♄♇℞ 5. Try a new and different way.
24 ♀♃♄♇℞▼ ☽ V/C 4:09 AM ☽→♋ 4:08 PM 6. Reformat your health regime.	25 ♀♃♄♇℞▼ **Memorial Day** 7. Silence speaks volumes today.	26 ♀♃♄♇℞ ☽ V/C 6:06 PM ☽→♌ 11:34 PM 8. Create success by taking the lead.	27 ♀♃♄♇℞▼ 10. See your future as fulfilled.	28 ♀♃♄♇℞▼ ☽ V/C 6:30 AM ☿→♋ 11:09 AM 11. Intuitive connections are strong.	29 ♀♃♄♇℞▼ ☽→♍ 4:41 AM 3. It's easy to be optimistic today.	30 ♀♃♄♇℞▼ 4. A no-nonsense, practical day.
31 ♀♃♄♇℞ ☽ V/C 2:16 AM ☽→♎ 7:37 AM 5. Things may change on a dime.						

♈ Aries
♉ Taurus
♊ Gemini
♋ Cancer
♌ Leo
♍ Virgo
♎ Libra
♏ Scorpio
♐ Sagittarius
♑ Capricorn
♒ Aquarius
♓ Pisces
☉ Sun
☽ Moon
☿ Mercury
♀ Venus
♂ Mars
♃ Jupiter
♄ Saturn
♅ Uranus
♆ Neptune
♇ Pluto
⚷ Chiron
→ Enters
V/C Void-of-Course
℞ Retrograde
S/D Stationary Direct
▲ Super Sensitivity
▼ Low Vitality
2. Balance
3. Fun
4. Structure
5. Action
6. Love
7. Learning
8. Money
9. Spirituality
10. Visionary
11. Completion

Full Moon in Scorpio

May 7th, 3:45 AM

When the Sun is Opposite the Moon

Full moons are always in opposition to the Sun. This creates a feeling of tension between where you want to shine and how your feelings are flowing on a sensory level about the Sun's directive. The two forces seem like they are working against each other, yet they are on the same team displaying different techniques to obtain the same mission. The Scorpio/Taurus polarity creates tension between sharing resources and living abundantly for yourself.

Scorpio Goddess

The concept of web thinking, in which all is intrinsically interconnected and related to the whole, comes to us through the creator myths of the Pueblo and Hopi people, as Grandmother Spider. She spun a sparkling dew-dropped web and threw it up into the night sky to create the stars.

Her interdependent web of light reminds us to promote the power of community and band together to take action when important issues affect the whole. Grandmother Spider can help you appreciate your own and others' unique contributions and talents, and show you how to combine them to create a strong and sustainable web of action.

Build Your Altar

Colors	Indigo, deep purple, scarlet
Numerology	7 – Be ready to help solve a problem
Tarot Card	Death – Change or die
Gemstones	Topaz, tanzanite, onyx, obsidian
Plant remedy	Manzanita – Prepares the body for transformation
Fragrance	Sandalwood – Awakens your sensuality

Moon Notes

Full Moon 17° Scorpio 20' 3:45 AM
Full Moons are about moving beyond blocks and setting yourself free.

Element
Water – Taking the line of least resistance, going with the flow, creativity at its best, secretive, sensual, glamorous, psychic, magnetic, escaping reality, a healer, an actor/actress.

Statement I Transform
Body Reproductive Organs
Mind Investigation
Spirit Transformation
8th House Moon
I Transform/I Transform

Umbrella Energy
How you share money and other resources, what you keep hidden regarding sex, death, taxes and regeneration.

Choice Points
Opportunity   Successful Harvest
Challenge   Disintegration

Sabian Symbol
A Quiet Path Through Woods, Brilliant In Autumn Coloring

Potential
Accept the power of change.

Clearing the Slate

Scorpio Full Moon May 7th

Sixty hours before the full moon negative traits connected to the astro-sign might become activated to trigger what needs to be released during the full moon phase. You may notice a deep desire to be secretive, resist sharing money, a feeling of revenge, or the need to create control dramas. Make a list, look in the mirror, and for each negative trait, tell yourself *I am sorry, I forgive you, thank you for your awareness,* and *I love you.*

Scorpio Victories & Challenges

Say all of the statements in this section out loud. Then, underline the phrase that means the most to you. Use the phrase as your affirmation for releasing throughout this moon phase.

I will not compromise myself today. I know that transformation occurs when I stand tall in my truth, even if everything around me needs to die. I see death as a new beginning and know that in death comes new aliveness. I am willing to embrace transformation and open to the idea that change is in my favor. I know that in letting go, I give new life to myself. I am willing to accept that life is ever-changing and in a constant state of renewal; one cannot occur without the other.

Releasing is easy when I offer myself something new. When I allow for the motion of change to stay alive, I let go with one hand and receive with the other hand. The ever-present flow and motion keeps me alive and connected to the revitalizing power of Nature. When the power of Nature becomes apparent to me, I become aware that Nature abhors a vacuum. Rejuvenation is mine when I embrace change.

Scorpio Homework

The Scorpio moon creates the urge within us to make life happen. Pay attention to these urges so you can prepare yourself for greater action, intention, and purpose.

GRATITUDE LIST

Keep this list active throughout the moon cycle. This will bring you to a level of completion so that a new cycle of opportunity can occur in your life. Be prepared for miracles!

TAROT

Ask the question out loud, then draw a card. You may wish to draw it or paste a copy of it here. Then write down what you feel it might be telling you, in response to the question. Use the glossary in the appendix and record here anything about the card that captures your attention. You may wish to come back throughout the moon cycle to meditate or journal more on the card.

How is my heart supporting my releasing?

RELEASING LIST

SCORPIO FULL MOON
MAY 7TH

Say this statement out loud three times before writing your list:

I am a free spiritual being and it is my desire to be free to think and to express myself fully.

I am now free and ready to make choices beyond survival!

Scorpio Freedom Ideas

Now is the time to activate a game change in my life, and give up resentment, jealousy, revenge, vendettas, betrayals, blocks to transformation, destructive relationships, unhealthy joint financial situations, obstacles to having a healthy sex life, resistance to changing paradigms, and karma relating to all issues of power.

Full Moon in Scorpio

Your Personal Moon Experience

Fill in the Cosmic Check-In page. Then look up the degree of the Moon on the chart below. Take note of the "I" statement on the outside of the wheel where the Moon is located. Now, locate the same degree on your own chart and make a note of the house and corresponding "I" statement. Go back to the Cosmic Check-In page and circle the two statements from the charts and read what you wrote. This will give you an idea about what to expect from this moon phase on a personal level. For more information on personalizing your *Moon Book*, go to www.BlueMoonAcademy.com and look for *How to Use the Moon Book*.

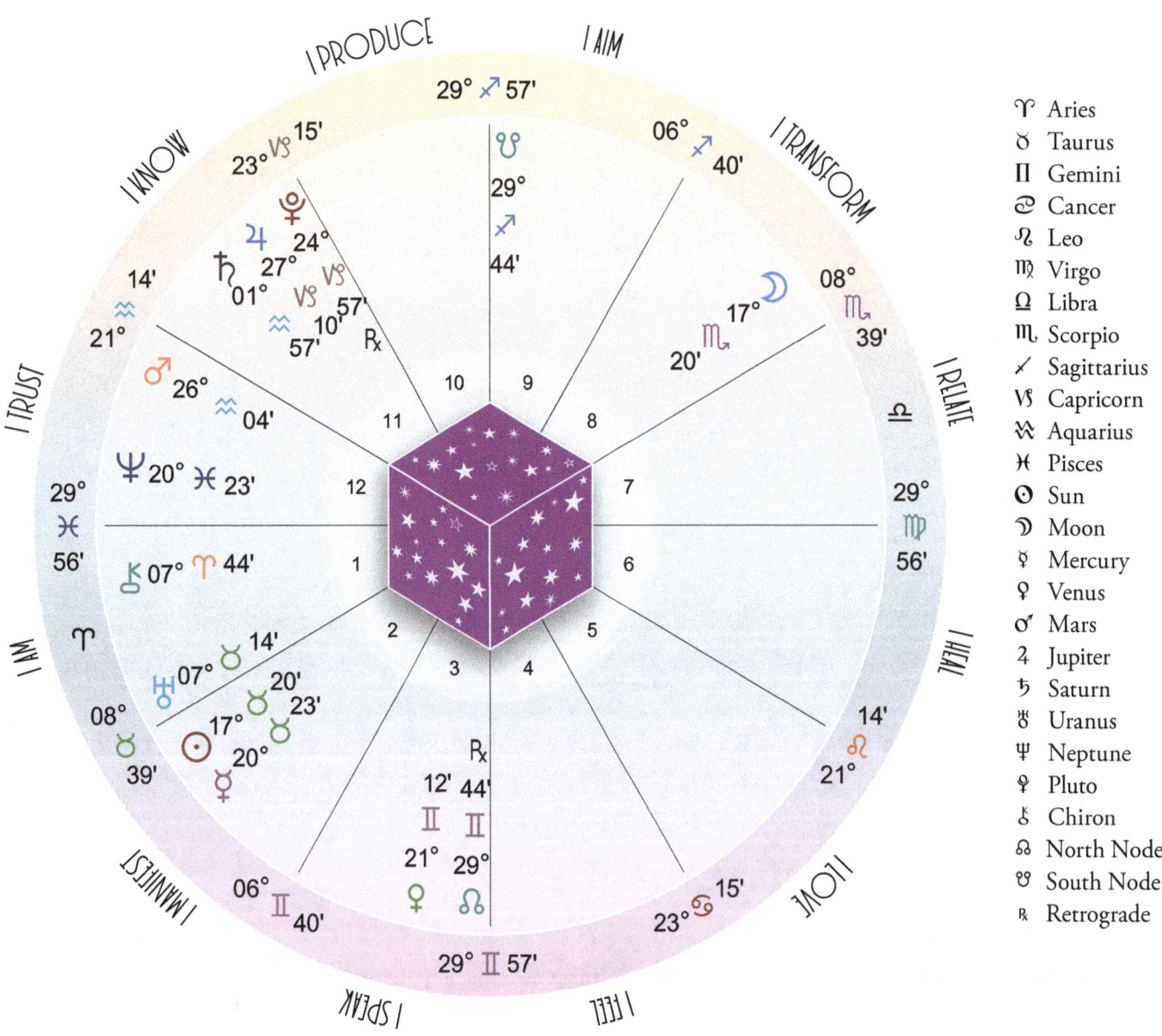

COSMIC CHECK-IN

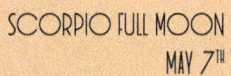
SCORPIO FULL MOON
MAY 7TH

Take a moment to write a brief phrase for each "I" statement. This activates all areas of your life for this creative cycle.

♏ I Transform

♐ I Aim

♑ I Produce

♒ I Know

♓ I Trust

♈ I Am

♉ I Manifest

♊ I Speak

♋ I Feel

♌ I Love

♍ I Heal

♎ I Relate

91

New Moon in Gemini

May 22nd, 10:39 AM

When the Sun is in Gemini

This is a time when the ability to communicate is at the top of the priority list. Allow your thoughts to lead you to a formula for success so you can put your thoughts into action. Then, find the appropriate soapbox to stand on so your message can be heard. Right now is the time to make your message clear, enlightening, witty, and thought-provoking. Your bright mind is on its high throne and waiting for an audience. Try blogging, do a show on YouTube, join Toastmasters, write that screenplay, film yourself doing a travel show, start a discussion group, or write a newsletter for your neighborhood. Most of all, put your bright mind to work!

Gemini Goddess

Some of Zeus's favorite consorts were the nymphs who lived on Mount Kithairon. One in particular, Echo, incurred Zeus' wife Hera's wrath. As punishment for trying to protect Zeus, Hera cursed Echo with only being able to speak the last few words spoken to her. In love with Narcissus, Echo was unable to speak her own truth, and watched as Narcissus fell in love with himself, abetted by the words he spoke that Echo was forced to repeat back to him. After he died, Echo physically wasted away, leaving only the sound of her voice.

During this Gemini full moon, attend to your communications! What reverberates and repeats? Is it your truth?

Build Your Altar

- **Colors** — Bright yellow, orange, multi-colors
- **Numerology** — 4 – A solid foundation is critical
- **Tarot Card** — The Lovers – Integrate, don't separate
- **Gemstones** — Yellow diamond, citrine
- **Plant Remedy** — Morning Glory – Thinking with your heart.
- **Fragrance** — Iris – The ability to focus the mind

Moon Notes

New Moon 2° Gemini 05' 10:39 AM
New Moons are about opening new pathways for prosperity.

Element
Air – The breath of life that allows the mind to achieve new insights and fresh perspectives, abstract dreaming, freedom from attachments, codes of intelligence, and academic applications.

Statement I Speak
Body Lungs and Hands
Mind Intellect
Spirit Intelligence

10th House Moon
I Produce/I Speak

Umbrella Energy
Your approach to status, career, honor, prestige, and why you chose your father.

Choice Points
Opportunity   Affluence
Challenge   Coerce

Sabian Symbol
The Charming Court Life At The Garden Of The Tuileries In Paris

Potential
To cultivate beauty.

GEMINI VICTORIES & CHALLENGES

GEMINI NEW MOON MAY 22ND

Say all of the statements in this section out loud. Then, underline the phrase that means the most to you. Use the phrase as your affirmation for manifesting throughout this moon phase.

I am dark. I am light. I am day. I am night. The extremes in life exist within me, completing themselves in reality. The "I" that is "we" lives within me. I am one in the same. I am both.

I know that flow comes from accepting my opposite natures. Today, I accept my opposites and get into the flow. I am aware today of how my judgments separate me from people, events, experiences, and, most of all, from myself. Today, I am going to see where I have separated all of the parts of myself and begin to integrate into wholeness through acceptance and understanding. I begin by breathing. I breathe in wholeness and breathe out separation. I understand that breath is life and that life includes all facets of my experience to gain awareness. I know that I am Heaven. I know that I am Earth. I know that I am masculine. I know that I am feminine. Today, I become unified. Today, I integrate into wholeness. I breathe into all of these aspects of myself, knowing that in my totality I am connected to Oneness. The "I" that is "we" lives within me. I am one in the same. I am both.

Gemini Homework

Geminis manifest best through broadcasting and journalism, as a speech coach, comedian, political satirist, gossip columnist, negotiator, media specialist, manicurist, salesperson, teacher, or travel consultant.

Expect to awaken your will on seven levels…

- The will to direct – through the power of your original intention.
- The will to love – stimulating goodwill among humankind through cooperation.
- The will to act – by laying foundations for a happier world.
- The will to cooperate – the desire and demand for right relationships.
- The will to know – to think correctly and creatively so that every man/woman can find their outstanding characteristics.
- The will to persist – to be one with your light and represent the ideal standard for living.
- The will to organize – to carry forward direct inspiration through groups of goodwill.

VICTORY LIST

Acknowledge what you have overcome. Keep this list active during this moon cycle. Honoring victory allows you to accept success.

TAROT

Ask the question out loud, then draw a card. You may wish to draw it or paste a copy of it here. Then write down what you feel it might be telling you, in response to the question. Use the glossary in the appendix and record here anything about the card that captures your attention. You may wish to come back throughout the moon cycle to meditate or journal more on the card.

How is my mind supporting my manifesting?

MANIFESTING LIST

**GEMINI NEW MOON
MAY 22ND**

This or something better than this comes to me in an easy and pleasurable way, for the good of all concerned. Thank you, Universe!

Gemini Manifesting Ideas

Now is the time to focus on manifesting communications, a promotion, technology, ideas, non-judgmental communication, thinking outside of duality, a quiet mind, charisma and charm, and flirting.

New Moon in Gemini

Your Personal Moon Experience

Fill in the Cosmic Check-In page. Then look up the degree of the Moon on the chart below. Take note of the "I" statement on the outside of the wheel where the Moon is located. Now, locate the same degree on your own chart and make a note of the house and corresponding "I" statement. Go back to the Cosmic Check-In page and circle the two statements from the charts and read what you wrote. This will give you an idea about what to expect from this moon phase on a personal level. For more information on personalizing your *Moon Book*, go to www.BlueMoonAcademy.com and look for *How to Use the Moon Book*.

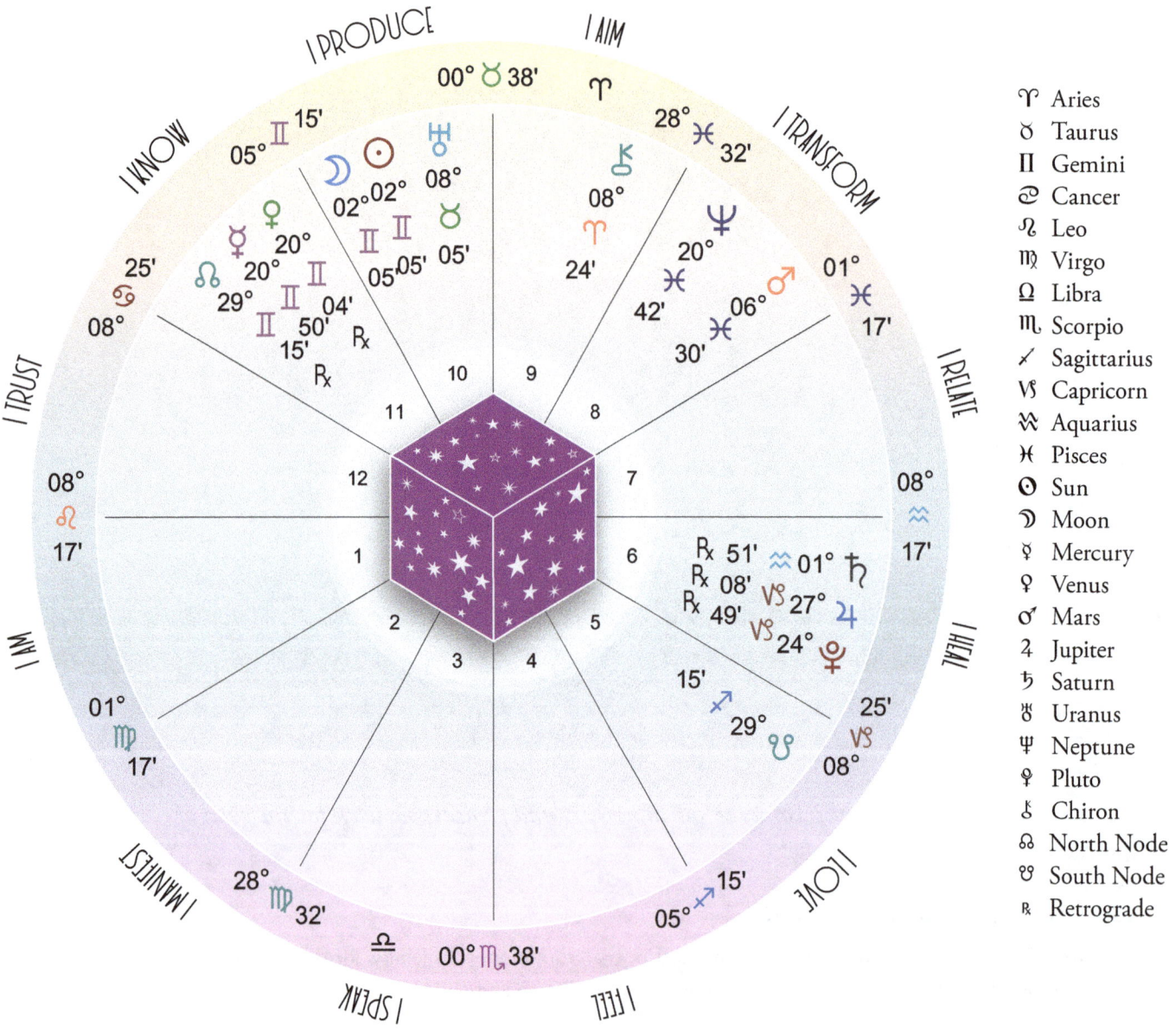

COSMIC CHECK-IN

GEMINI NEW MOON
MAY 22ND

Take a moment to write a brief phrase for each "I" statement. This activates all areas of your life for this creative cycle.

♊ I Speak

♋ I Feel

♌ I Love

♍ I Heal

♎ I Relate

♏ I Transform

♐ I Aim

♑ I Produce

♒ I Know

♓ I Trust

♈ I Am

♉ I Manifest

JUNE

June 1st Pluto and Jupiter in Capricorn coupled through the entire month

This produces the need to accomplish something spectacular. Keep an eye on balance so that you are not overwhelmed with obsession.

June 5th Full Moon in Sagittarius – Lunar Eclipse

Let go of an old pattern relating to a ritual or habit that is no longer useful to you or the planet. Ask yourself, "What was going on in my life 19 years ago?" Whatever the answer, it will be automatically released.

June 5th-9th Venus and the Sun dancing in Gemini

It's happy days and party time! Get together with friends and dance on the tabletops! Play your favorite music.

June 17th Mercury goes retrograde in Cancer until July 12th

Time to make amends with the family around miscommunications. Be aware, complaining does not work; self-pity is outdated; and misery is optional.

June 20th New Moon in Cancer – Solar Eclipse

Make a wish list for updating your home.

June 20th the Sun moves into Cancer – Summer Solstice

The Sun is high in the sky. It's time to reach your potential and shine! Prepare to manifest your wildest dreams.

June 20th until the end of the month Neptune and Mars conjunct in Pisces

Don't promise something you cannot deliver, or you will end up in a smoke-and-mirrors deception.

June 22nd Neptune goes retrograde in Pisces until November 28th

If your nature is addictive, now is the time when you may get into trouble. Make sure that you stay close to reality. If there is something rumbling inside you, now is the time to check in with a group. Better yet, one-on-one therapy.

June 24th Venus goes direct in Gemini

Time to go dancing, have a party, and celebrate life! Know that your flirting will return, and you can expect great results. Expect a blast of creative juices to inspire new endeavors. A shopping spree is in order to express the new, invigorated you! This is a great time to take a creative writing class.

June 27th Mars enters Aries

Full speed ahead. You will feel like you are on steroids, so pace yourself to avoid accidents. You will need to be first and fast and you will act like a self-cleaning oven if it does not happen fast enough.

June 27th North and South Node are on a very fragile degree through September

Expect the possibility of your mind working overtime and physical exhaustion. Do what you can to pace yourself; pushing the envelope is not an option.

Super Sensitivity June 6th and 7th

Take care. Chaos is in the air and you don't want to fall down the rabbit hole.

Low Vitality June 19th and 20th

Earth changes are possible. Stay safe and stay close to home!

SUNDAY	MONDAY	TUESDAY	WEDNESDAY	THURSDAY	FRIDAY	SATURDAY
	1 ♀♃♄♇℞ 6. Listen to your body's messages.	2 ♀♃♄♇℞ ☽ V/C 3:39 AM ☽→♏ 9:06 AM 7. A good problem-solving day.	3 ♀♃♄♇℞ 8. Prosperity pathways open today.	4 ♀♃♄♇℞ ☽ V/C 4:36 AM ☽→♐ 10:17 AM 9. Donate your time.	5 ♀♃♄♇℞ ○ 15° ♐ 34' 12:13 PM **Lunar Eclipse** 15° ♐ 42' 12:25 PM ☽ V/C 9:10 PM 10. The future is now.	6 ♀♃♄♇℞▲ ☽→♑ 12:45 PM 11. Let vastness imprint on your mind.
7 ♀♃♄♇℞▲ 3. Make a colorful mandala.	8 ♀♃♄♇℞ ☽ V/C 11:05 AM ☽→♒ 5:54 PM 4. High producers use unity for success.	9 ♀♃♄♇℞ 5. Get in the car and go!	10 ♀♃♄♇℞ ☽ V/C 7:34 AM 6. Express your love nature when talking.	11 ♀♃♄♇℞ ☽→♓ 2:32 AM 7. Trust that you know the answer.	12 ♀♃♄♇℞ 8. Let creativity guide you to success.	13 ♀♃♄♇℞ ☽ V/C 5:44 AM ☽→♈ 2:03 PM 9. For answers, talk to the angels.
14 ♀♃♄♇℞ **Flag Day** 10. Opportunities need direction.	15 ♀♃♄♇℞ ☽ V/C 5:49 PM 11. Be open to a mystical experience.	16 ♀♃♄♇℞ ☽→♉ 2:36 AM 3. It's all fun and games today.	17 ☿♀♃♄♇℞ ☿℞ 14° ♋ 46' 9:59 PM 4. Add order to your day.	18 ☿♀♃♄♇℞ ☽ V/C 5:02 AM ☽→♊ 2:00 PM 5. So many options to choose from.	19 ☿♀♃♄♇℞▼ 6. Use music to fill the soul.	20 ☿♀♃♄♇℞▼ **Summer Solstice** ☉→♋ 2:43 PM ☽ V/C 2:47 PM ☽→♋ 11:01 PM **Solar Eclipse** 0° ♋ 21' 11:40 PM ● 0° ♋ 21' 11:42 PM 7. Dream big.
21 ☿♀♃♄♇℞ **Father's Day** 8. Spend money, open the flow.	22 ☿♀♃♄♇♆℞ ♆℞ 20° ♓ 58' 9:32 PM 9. Being generous is rewarding.	23 ☿♀♃♄♇♆℞ ☽ V/C 12:20 AM ☽→♌ 5:33 AM ☽ V/C 10:34 PM 10. What perception can be updated?	24 ☿♃♄♇♆℞ ♀SD 5° ♊ 20' 11:48 PM 11. Be a pioneer in your field.	25 ☿♃♄♇♆℞ ☽→♍ 10:04 AM 3. Kindness makes life joyful.	26 ☿♃♄♇♆℞ 4. Logic is your friend today.	27 ☿♃♄♇♆℞ ☽ V/C 1:01 PM ☽→♎ 1:17 PM ♂→♈ 6:45 PM 5. Know that today brings change.
28 ☿♃♄♇♆℞ 6. Sharing love is healing.	29 ☿♃♄♇♆℞ ☽ V/C 6:01 AM ☽→♏ 3:48 PM 7. Research is the answer.	30 ☿♃♄♇♆℞ 8. Acknowledge your victories.				

♈ Aries
♉ Taurus
♊ Gemini
♋ Cancer
♌ Leo
♍ Virgo
♎ Libra
♏ Scorpio
♐ Sagittarius
♑ Capricorn
♒ Aquarius
♓ Pisces
☉ Sun
☽ Moon
☿ Mercury
♀ Venus
♂ Mars
♃ Jupiter
♄ Saturn
♅ Uranus
♆ Neptune
♇ Pluto
⚷ Chiron
→ Enters
V/C Void-of-Course
℞ Retrograde
SD Stationary Direct
▲ Super Sensitivity
▼ Low Vitality
2. Balance
3. Fun
4. Structure
5. Action
6. Love
7. Learning
8. Money
9. Spirituality
10. Visionary
11. Completion

Full Moon in Sagittarius

June 5th, 12:13 PM

When the Sun is Opposite the Moon

Full moons are always in opposition to the Sun. This creates a feeling of tension between where you want to shine and how your feelings are flowing on a sensory level about the Sun's directive. The two forces seem like they are working against each other, yet they are on the same team displaying different techniques to obtain the same mission. The Sagittarius/Gemini polarity creates tension between the quest for higher knowledge and the need for academic accolades.

Sagittarius Goddess

Pythia was the title bestowed upon the priestess who channeled the Oracle of Delphi at the Temple of Apollo. The rambling prophecies she spoke were induced by breathing the vapors rising out of the chasm in the rocks, at a site formerly dedicated to the great Earth Goddess, Gaia.

Allow yourself quiet meditation time with your favorite divination tool (Tarot cards, pendulum, automatic writing) and give yourself over to messages you receive. Remember that Pythia calls forth her art through the magic of breathwork, which operates without hallucinogenic vapors! Seek the messages she delivers from the wisdom and stored history of the Earth. Find a rock to sit on and breathe!

Build Your Altar

Colors	Deep purple, turquoise, royal blue
Numerology	10 - The future is now
Tarot Card	Temperance – Balancing the present with the past, updating yourself
Gemstone	Turquoise
Plant remedy	Madia – Seeing and hitting the target
Fragrance	Magnolia – Expanded beauty

Moon Notes

Lunar Eclipse

Full Moon 15° Sagittarius 34' 12:13 PM
Full Moons are about moving beyond blocks and setting yourself free.

Element
Fire – Igniting, dissolving, accelerating, cleansing, advancing awareness, impatience, leadership, passion, and vitality.

Statement I Aim
Body Thighs
Mind Philosophical
Spirit Optimism

4th House Moon
I Feel/I Aim

Umbrella Energy
The way your early environmental training was and how that set your foundation for living, and why you chose your mother.

Choice Points
Opportunity Watchfulness
Challenge Excitability

Sabian Symbol
Seagulls Fly Around A Ship Looking For Food

Potential
Shortcuts don't work.

CLEARING THE SLATE

Sagittarius Full Moon — June 5th

Sixty hours before the full moon negative traits connected to the astro-sign might become activated to trigger what needs to be released during the full moon phase. You may notice a sudden urge to be excessive, to resist reality by exaggerating, to speak before thinking, to be blunt, or to use unfiltered language. Make a list, look in the mirror, and for each negative trait, tell yourself *I am sorry, I forgive you, thank you for your awareness,* and *I love you.*

SAGITTARIUS VICTORIES & CHALLENGES

Say all of the statements in this section out loud. Then, underline the phrase that means the most to you. Use the phrase as your affirmation for releasing throughout this moon phase.

Today, I blend my old self with my new self, my physical reality with my spiritual awareness, my positive thoughts with my negative thoughts, my past with my present, my feminine with my masculine, my rewards with my losses, my ups with my downs, and my higher self with my lower self. It is a day for me to refine and fine tune my life by looking at my extremes. I recognize what inspires me and what keeps me stuck. I find my center today by acknowledging my extremes. I am aware that balance comes to those who are able to locate the space in the center of these opposite energy fields. When I am in my center, my polarities are in motion. Healing cannot occur unless my polarities are moving and I know that healing is motion.

I am ready for a healing today and know that by visiting my opposites and determining their vast opposition to each other, I can find the paradoxes that I have chosen for myself and begin to heal. I am willing to experiment with this blending of opposites and become the alchemist of my own life. When I blend all aspects of myself, rather than separating them, I can truly become whole. Today is a day to integrate, rather than separate, in order to release the spark of light that stays prisoner when my polarities are in operation. When I find balance, motion occurs and the Law of Harmony takes over, putting paradoxical energies to rest, thus breaking the crystallization of polarity. The Law of Harmony is beauty in motion, promoting the flow of color, light, sound, and movement into form. Balance is a condition that keeps my spark in motion. I become the vertical line in the center of polarity today and carry the secret of balance. Balance cannot be my goal, motion is my goal today. When I am in motion, I can take action to evolve and to express all of myself freely.

Sagittarius Homework

Now is the time to use your physical body to release the feeling of being caged in by people or circumstances. Choose an activity that burns away confinement and allows you to feel the power of your passion.

The Sagittarius moon awakens us to know the spark of light that lives in our heart, thus elevating love in ourselves and in our world. This is when we come to realize what is in our highest and best good and we can begin to recalibrate all that is not lovable in our lives.

GRATITUDE LIST

Keep this list active throughout the moon cycle. This will bring you to a level of completion so that a new cycle of opportunity can occur in your life. Be prepared for miracles!

TAROT

Ask the question out loud, then draw a card. You may wish to draw it or paste a copy of it here. Then write down what you feel it might be telling you, in response to the question. Use the glossary in the appendix and record here anything about the card that captures your attention. You may wish to come back throughout the moon cycle to meditate or journal more on the card.

How is my spirit supporting my releasing?

RELEASING LIST

**SAGITTARIUS FULL MOON
JUNE 5TH**

Say this statement out loud three times before writing your list:

I am a free spiritual being and it is my desire to be free to think and to express myself fully.

I am now free and ready to make choices beyond survival!

Sagittarius Freedom Ideas

Now is the time to activate a game change in my life, and give up belief systems that no longer apply, attitudes that are not uplifting to me, addiction to excess and risk, the need to exaggerate based on low self-esteem, dishonesty, being too blunt, staying in the future and avoiding the NOW, overriding fear by being too optimistic, and preaching.

Full Moon in Sagittarius

Your Personal Moon Experience

Fill in the Cosmic Check-In page. Then look up the degree of the Moon on the chart below. Take note of the "I" statement on the outside of the wheel where the Moon is located. Now, locate the same degree on your own chart and make a note of the house and corresponding "I" statement. Go back to the Cosmic Check-In page and circle the two statements from the charts and read what you wrote. This will give you an idea about what to expect from this moon phase on a personal level. For more information on personalizing your *Moon Book*, go to www.BlueMoonAcademy.com and look for *How to Use the Moon Book*.

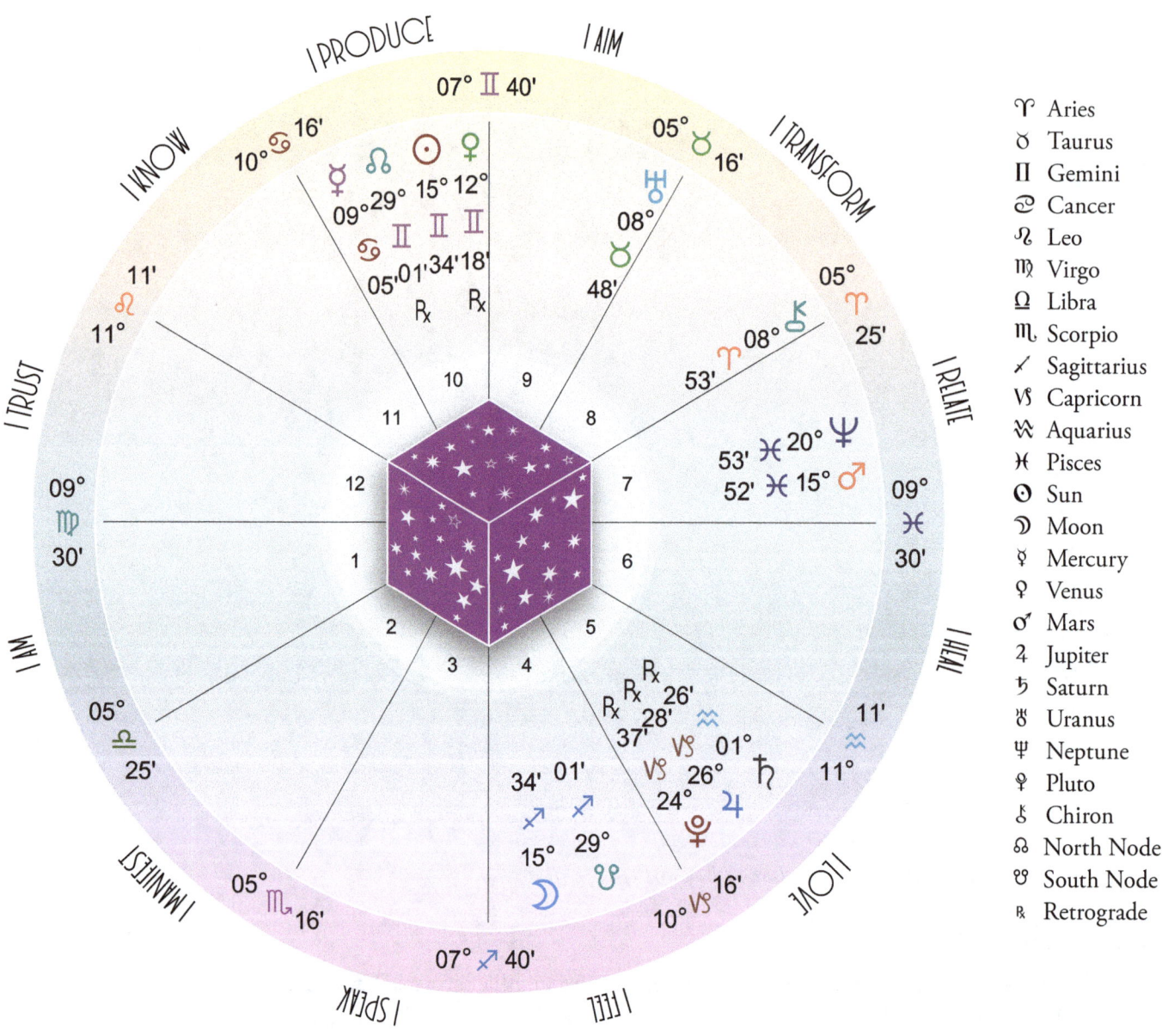

COSMIC CHECK-IN

**SAGITTARIUS FULL MOON
JUNE 5TH**

Take a moment to write a brief phrase for each "I" statement. This activates all areas of your life for this creative cycle.

♐ I Aim

♑ I Produce

♒ I Know

♓ I Trust

♈ I Am

♉ I Manifest

♊ I Speak

♋ I Feel

♌ I Love

♍ I Heal

♎ I Relate

♏ I Transform

109

New Moon in Cancer

June 20th, 11:42 PM

When the Sun is in Cancer

It is now time to build our structure and foundation. Cancer holds the wisdom of the Great Cosmic Architect. Her statement is, "I build a lighted house and therein I dwell." The key is to use the materials of light, love, and wisdom to build your house and become the creator of form. Look within to see what lights your home and your body. Also check security systems, early environmental training, and mother/child relationships to see what materials you are using to build the structure for your life. Use this creating moon to build the structure you want.

Cancer Goddess

Artemis, "The Shining One," Goddess of the Moon and the Hunt, is called upon by all creatures laboring to create new life, animal and human. She provides protection for both mothers and the children being born. Renowned as a powerful sorceress, she appears in darkened forest groves at the new moon to bless her creatures and to call down the Moon to begin its journey to fullness.

Find a crescent moon pendant you can wear to honor Artemis. Let her bless it in a water-filled bowl on a new moon night to assist you in birthing your creative endeavors. Think of her crescent as a cradle that holds your newborn dreams safely, as they emerge from the darkness in the first quarter phase. Let Artemis be the midwife of your dreams!

Build Your Altar

Colors	Shades of gray, milky/creamy colors
Numerology	7 – Think big
Tarot Card	Chariot – Victory through action
Gemstones	Pearl, moonstone, ruby
Plant Remedy	Shooting Star – The ability to move straight ahead
Fragrance	Peppermint – The essence of the Great Mother

Moon Notes

Solar Eclipse

New Moon 0° Cancer 21' 11:42 PM
New Moons are about opening new pathways for prosperity.

Element
Water – Taking the line of least resistance, going with the flow, creativity at its best, secretive, sensual, glamorous, psychic, magnetic, escaping reality, a healer, an actor/actress.

Statement I Feel
Body Stomach
Mind Worried
Spirit Nurturing

4th House Moon
I Feel/I Feel

Umbrella Energy
The way your early environmental training was and how that set your early foundation for living and why you chose your Mother.

Choice Points
Opportunity   Adaptability
Challenge   Instability

Sabian Symbol
On A Ship, Sailors Lower An Old Flag And Raise A New One

Potential
Moving and claiming a new opportunity.

CANCER VICTORIES & CHALLENGES

**CANCER NEW MOON
JUNE 20TH**

Say all of the statements in this section out loud. Then, underline the phrase that means the most to you. Use the phrase as your affirmation for manifesting throughout this moon phase.

Today I take advantage of my ability to take action and position myself for success. I clearly know that the road to success is before me, and all I need to do is move forward. I am aware that when I take action and move forward, the Universe fills in the dots. Whether I move left, right, or straight ahead doesn't matter—what matters is movement. Today, I release the indecisiveness that keeps me stuck. Today, I let go of vacillation that exhausts my mind. Today, I take my foot off of the brakes and find the gas pedal. I allow movement to occur, even if I don't know where I am going. When I take action, I trust that guideposts will appear. I am aware that action leads me to my new direction. So, today I know and GO! I remember that karma comes to the space of non-action, while success comes through action. Action brings me to my victory. Standing still leads to regret, resentment, and chaos. I am aware that action can be as simple as taking a walk on the beach, buying fresh flowers to add a new dimension to my home, or simply going to a new restaurant for lunch. I take action today to break up a crystallized pattern and, in so doing, my life begins to show me newfound awareness and light to guide me.

Cancer Homework

Cancers manifest best when catering, writing cookbooks, in marriage and family counseling, providing childcare, giving massage, or when engaged in genealogy, arts and crafts, architecture, and home-building.

During the Cancer new moon cycle, we are asked to turn light into form, and then turn it into beauty on four levels. Physically, we must feel nurtured and protected. Emotionally, we must set safe boundaries for the expression of our feelings. Mentally, we must release self-pity and embrace rightful thinking. Spiritually, we must hold the space for the infusion of light to shine inside all bodies on Earth.

VICTORY LIST

Acknowledge what you have overcome. Keep this list active during this moon cycle. Honoring victory allows you to accept success.

TAROT

Ask the question out loud, then draw a card. You may wish to draw it or paste a copy of it here. Then write down what you feel it might be telling you, in response to the question. Use the glossary in the appendix and record here anything about the card that captures your attention. You may wish to come back throughout the moon cycle to meditate or journal more on the card.

How is my heart supporting my manifesting?

MANIFESTING LIST

CANCER NEW MOON
JUNE 20TH

This or something better than this comes to me in an easy and pleasurable way, for the good of all concerned. Thank you, Universe!

Cancer Manifesting Ideas

Now is the time to focus on manifesting being a good mother, new ways to be a mom, nurturing and self-love, the ability to see joy, a clutter-free home, your dream home, and inner and outer security.

New Moon in Cancer

Your Personal Moon Experience

Fill in the Cosmic Check-In page. Then look up the degree of the Moon on the chart below. Take note of the "I" statement on the outside of the wheel where the Moon is located. Now, locate the same degree on your own chart and make a note of the house and corresponding "I" statement. Go back to the Cosmic Check-In page and circle the two statements from the charts and read what you wrote. This will give you an idea about what to expect from this moon phase on a personal level. For more information on personalizing your *Moon Book*, go to www.BlueMoonAcademy.com and look for *How to Use the Moon Book*.

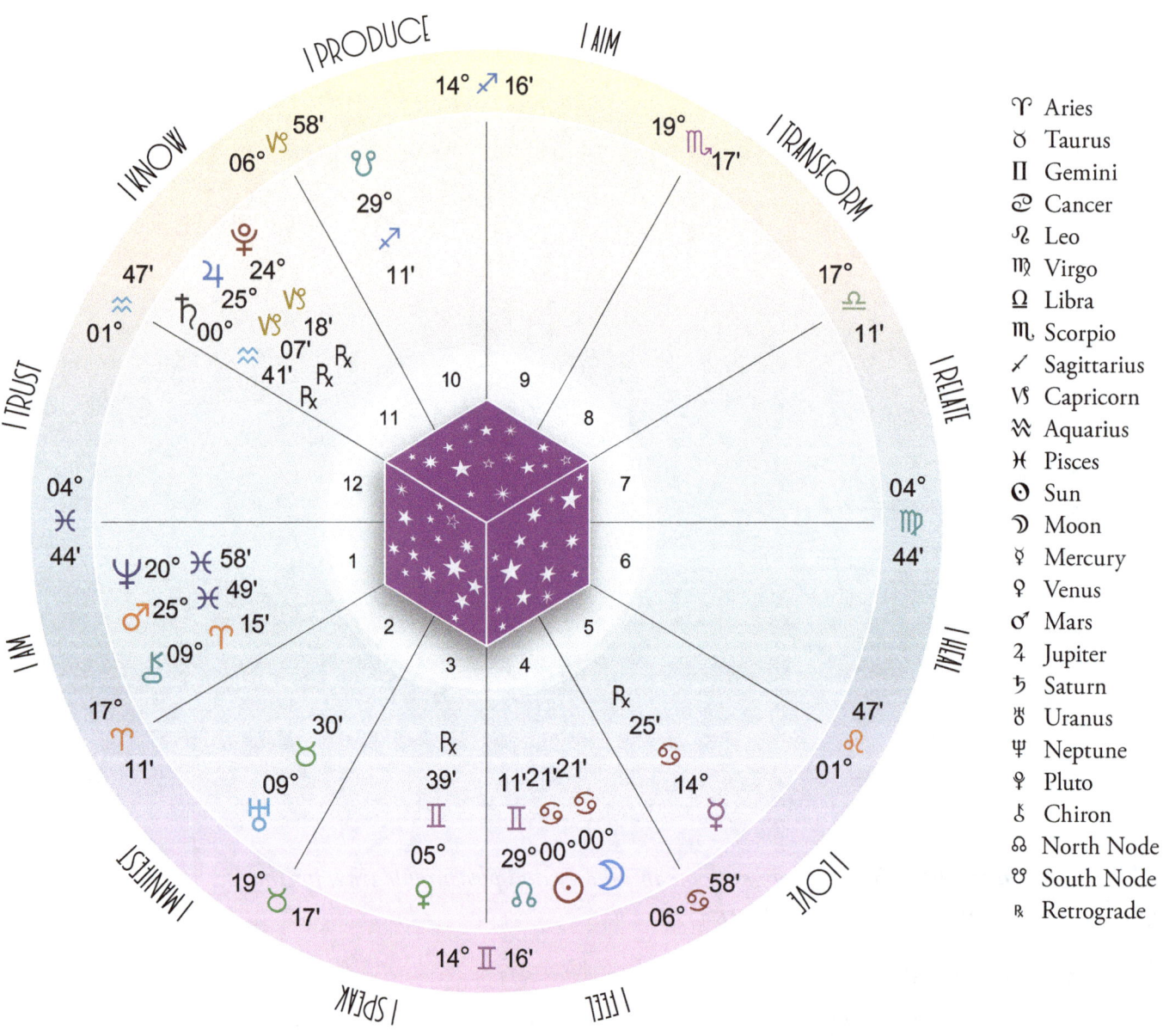

COSMIC CHECK-IN

**CANCER NEW MOON
JUNE 20TH**

Take a moment to write a brief phrase for each "I" statement. This activates all areas of your life for this creative cycle.

♋ I Feel

♌ I Love

♍ I Heal

♎ I Relate

♏ I Transform

♐ I Aim

♑ I Produce

♒ I Know

♓ I Trust

♈ I Am

♉ I Manifest

♊ I Speak

117

JULY

July 1st Pluto and Jupiter in Capricorn coupled through the entire month

This produces the need to accomplish something spectacular. Keep an eye on balance so you aren't overwhelmed with an obsession to get to the top of the mountain first.

July 1st until the end of September

North and South Node are challenged, giving us an opportunity to flush out what is no longer important to you now. It allows us to see if our future focus really matches our original intention.

July 1st Saturn retrograde returns to Capricorn until September 28th

This provides us a chance to see if our previous ambitions still fit our present situation.

July 4th Full Moon in Capricorn – Lunar Eclipse

This brings us to a place where what we have held onto for the last 19 years is no longer relevant. Time to give up our emotional loyalty to the past.

July 4th Mars and Chiron coupled in Aries

This releases issues relating to feeling like an underdog and sets you free from the irritations relating to self-identity.

July 12th Mercury goes direct in Cancer

Feel the power of emotional freedom.

July 20th New Moon in Cancer

Celebrate your heritage by having a family party. Don't forget to write your wish list about what you want to manifest for your home and for your family.

July 22nd Sun enters Leo

Party time! Pay attention to the light of the sun. It knows where you should go to achieve your brightest potential. Play full out. Now is the time!

Super Sensitivity July 3rd, 4th and 31st

The doorway to the galaxy is open, so expect a major download to occur. Keep a paper and pen handy to take notes to help you remember. Avoid thinking too much. Slow down and smell the roses.

Low Vitality July 18th and 19th

The earth is very fragile. Avoid any extreme action. If you experience an ending coming into play, let it end. Take a nap when you feel tired.

SUNDAY	MONDAY	TUESDAY	WEDNESDAY	THURSDAY	FRIDAY	SATURDAY
			1 ☿♃♄♀♆℞ ♄℞→♑ 4:36 PM ☽ V/C 6:20 PM ☽→♐ 6:21 PM 9. We are all Divinely blessed.	2 ☿♃♄♀♆℞ 10. Update your attitude.	3 ☿♃♄♀♆℞▲ ☽ V/C 6:05 AM ☽→♑ 9:48 PM 11. Use breath to connect to spirit.	4 ☿♃♄♀♆℞▲ **Independence Day** **Lunar Eclipse** 13° ♑ 30' 9:30 PM ○ 13° ♑ 38' 9:44 PM 3. Behold joy in the moment.
5 ☿♃♄♀♆℞ 4. Organize with a "to-do" list.	6 ☿♃♄♀♆℞ ☽ V/C 2:35 AM ☽→♒ 3:09 AM ☽ V/C 9:37 PM 5. It's okay to take a different path.	7 ☿♃♄♀♆℞ 6. Take time out to be with a loved one.	8 ☿♃♄♀♆℞ ☽→♓ 11:13 AM 7. You have wisdom to share.	9 ☿♃♄♀♆℞ 8. Seek the advice of a money manager.	10 ☿♃♄♀♆℞ ☽ V/C 8:48 PM ☽→♈ 10:06 PM 9. Meditate by water.	11 ☿♃♄♀♆℞ 10. Gather ideas from a visionary.
12 ♃♄♀♆℞ ☿ SD 5° ♋ 30' 1:26AM 11. As above, so below = wholeness.	13 ♃♄♀♆℞ ☽ V/C 8:54 AM ☽→♉ 10:33 AM 3. Get creative! Dance on tabletops.	14 ♃♄♀♆℞ 4. Be a team player.	15 ♃♄♀♆℞ ☽ V/C 8:21 PM ☽→♊ 10:20 PM 5. Be ready for plans to change.	16 ♃♄♀♆℞ 6. Find a place to watch the sunset.	17 ♃♄♀♆℞ ☽ V/C 2:14 PM 7. Spend the day in bookstores.	18 ♃♄♀♆℞▼ ☽→♋ 7:25 AM 8. Use courage to accept your power.
19 ♃♄♀♆℞▼ 9. Join a cause and make a difference.	20 ♃♄♀♆℞ ● 28° ♋ 27' 10:33 AM ☽ V/C 10:54 AM ☽→♌ 1:16 PM 10. Search the web for new inventions.	21 ♃♄♀♆℞ ☽ V/C 5:27 PM 2. Gather facts, then decide.	22 ♃♄♀♆℞ ☉→♌ 1:36 AM ☽→♍ 4:40 PM 3. Lighten up, make time to play.	23 ♃♄♀♆℞ 4. Organize, things work more smoothly.	24 ♃♄♀♆℞ ☽ V/C 4:07 PM ☽→♎ 6:54 PM 5. Follow your curiosity.	25 ♃♄♀♆℞ 6. Take time to relate from the heart.
26 ♃♄♀♆℞ ☽ V/C 6:08 PM ☽→♏ 9:11 PM 7. Don't overthink the details.	27 ♃♄♀♆℞ 8. Make a wish list and manifest!	28 ♃♄♀♆℞ ☽ V/C 9:01 PM 9. All things are in Divine right order.	29 ♃♄♀♆℞ ☽→♐ 12:25 AM 10. Every minute the future begins.	30 ♃♄♀♆℞ ☽ V/C 5:07 PM 2. In the quiet, intuition speaks.	31 ♃♄♀♆℞▲ ☽→♑ 4:59 AM 3. Creative energy is empowering.	

♈ Aries	♍ Virgo	♒ Aquarius	♀ Venus	♆ Neptune	V/C Void-of-Course	2. Balance	7. Learning
♉ Taurus	♎ Libra	♓ Pisces	♂ Mars	♇ Pluto	℞ Retrograde	3. Fun	8. Money
♊ Gemini	♏ Scorpio	☉ Sun	♃ Jupiter	⚷ Chiron	SD Stationary Direct	4. Structure	9. Spirituality
♋ Cancer	♐ Sagittarius	☽ Moon	♄ Saturn	→ Enters	▲ Super Sensitivity	5. Action	10. Visionary
♌ Leo	♑ Capricorn	☿ Mercury	♅ Uranus		▼ Low Vitality	6. Love	11. Completion

Full Moon in Capricorn

July 4th, 9:44 PM

When the Sun is Opposite the Moon

Full moons are always in opposition to the Sun. This creates a feeling of tension between where you want to shine and how your feelings are flowing on a sensory level about the Sun's directive. The two forces seem like they are working against each other, yet they are on the same team displaying different techniques to obtain the same mission. The Capricorn/Cancer polarity creates tension between the quest for status and the need to feel secure.

Capricorn Goddess

The Goddess of hearth and home, Hestia, was once known as Chief of the Goddesses, and Hestia, the First and Last. Representing the central source, she embodies the virtues of a calm, stable, supportive, and well-centered mother and loving home-base. Hestia's symbols are the sacred flame and the circle. Choosing to stay home on Mount Olympus, she manages the estate and dependably provides a safe haven of unconditional love for all, even strangers. Connected by an umbilical cord at Delphi to the molten core of the Earth, Hestia's hearth flame will never be extinguished.

Allow your energy to tap into that root, running directly to the center of the Earth, and energize your ability to source and sustain your vision of your home, your community, and the Earth as sacred sanctuary.

Build Your Altar

Colors	Forest green, earth tones
Numerology	3 – Celebrate joy in the moment
Tarot Card	Devil – Time to look at the broader view
Gemstones	Smoky quartz, topaz, garnet
Plant remedy	Rosemary – Activates appropriate memory
Fragrance	Frankincense – Assists the Soul's entry into the body

Moon Notes

Lunar Eclipse

Full Moon 13° Capricorn 30' 9:44 PM
Full Moons are about moving beyond blocks and setting yourself free.

Element
Earth – Practical, determined, structured, enduring, stubborn, traditional, stable, and stuck inside the box.

Statement I Produce
Body Knees
Mind Authority Issues
Spirit Accepting Success

11th House Moon
I Know/I Produce

Umbrella Energy
Your approach to friends, social consciousness, teamwork, community service, and the future.

Choice Points
Opportunity   Infrastructure Grid
Challenge   Old Guard Static

Sabian Symbol
An Ancient Bas-Relief Carved In Granite Remains A Witness To A Long-Forgotten Culture

Potential
Time to move beyond old traditions.

CLEARING THE SLATE

**CAPRICORN FULL MOON
JULY 4TH**

Sixty hours before the full moon negative traits connected to the astro-sign might become activated to trigger what needs to be released during the full moon phase. You may notice a sudden burden of responsibility taking over your experience of life, of paying too much attention to status and position, of no time to feel compassionate, and of challenging authorities. Make a list, look in the mirror, and for each negative trait, tell yourself *I am sorry, I forgive you, thank you for your awareness,* and *I love you.*

CAPRICORN VICTORIES & CHALLENGES

Say all of the statements in this section out loud. Then, underline the phrase that means the most to you. Use the phrase as your affirmation for releasing throughout this moon phase.

I feel limited. I feel confined. I feel stuck. I feel there is no way out. Perhaps I am the target of someone's envy or jealousy, or perhaps I am jealous or I am envious. Maybe I am spending too much time in the outer world and putting too much value on material rewards, things, and possessions. Maybe I am trying to possess someone or limit their view or choice. I may feel there are no choices. Maybe I am living by someone else's rules and beliefs and forgot how to think for myself. I could also be overcome by fear and too terrorized to look at anything at all.

Today, I see and feel the limits of placing the source of love outside myself. I have tunnel vision and I seem to have forgotten to look at my options. I must ask myself today, "How many ways can I look at my life, my situation, or my perceived problems?" Today, I must expand my view to encompass 360-degrees instead of only 180-degrees. I begin by acknowledging to myself that today is the worst it is going to get. I know deep within me that if I allow myself to truly experience my bottom, the top will become visible to me. It is time to look at the brighter side. Begin by identifying the problem by writing it down on a piece of paper. Start with the phrase, "The problem is_____." Fill in the blank. Then, list as many solutions to the problem as you can. List at least three. Then, say these solutions out loud every day until the answer comes to you through a person, an idea, an event, or a choice.

Capricorn Homework

Put on a good pair of walking shoes and get ready to walk your blues away. It is time to get outside and feel the loving power of Mother Earth. The green of the trees refreshes your stagnant energy while you exhaust yourself to a point of vulnerability. Then, and only then, will you feel freedom. Give yourself permission to throw your watch away and learn to live in the moment.

The Capricorn moon is the reincarnation of Spirit emerging from the dark waters of our past emotions releasing us from our fear of change and our fear of loss. Awaken your powerful and positive spiritual connection to be open to new possibilities. Ask yourself to release your emotional loyalty to the past. We are reminded of our need for material and emotional security at this time. In order to ensure this, we must learn to build a foundation for ourselves that is lit from within, made from the materials of love, goodwill, and intelligence.

GRATITUDE LIST

Keep this list active throughout the moon cycle. This will bring you to a level of completion so that a new cycle of opportunity can occur in your life. Be prepared for miracles!

TAROT

Ask the question out loud, then draw a card. You may wish to draw it or paste a copy of it here. Then write down what you feel it might be telling you, in response to the question. Use the glossary in the appendix and record here anything about the card that captures your attention. You may wish to come back throughout the moon cycle to meditate or journal more on the card.

How is my body supporting my releasing?

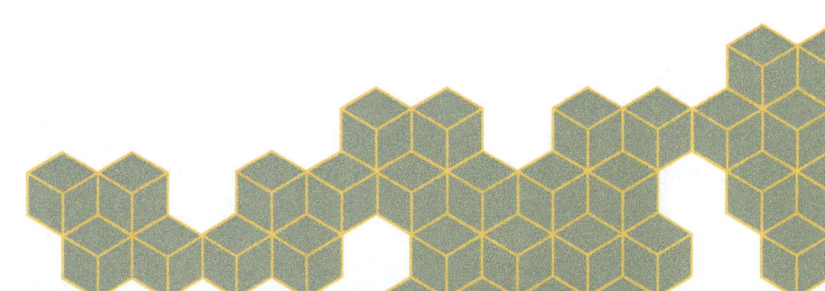

RELEASING LIST

**CAPRICORN FULL MOON
JULY 4ᵀᴴ**

Say this statement out loud three times before writing your list:

I am a free spiritual being and it is my desire to be free to think and to express myself fully.

I am now free and ready to make choices beyond survival!

Capricorn Freedom Ideas

Now is the time to activate a game change in my life, and give up obstacles to success, authority issues, sorrow and sadness, fear that blocks me, arrogance, irritability, limitations of time, priorities that are no longer valid, control and domination, the need to do it all alone, and taking on excessive responsibility.

Full Moon in Capricorn

Your Personal Moon Experience

Fill in the Cosmic Check-In page. Then look up the degree of the Moon on the chart below. Take note of the "I" statement on the outside of the wheel where the Moon is located. Now, locate the same degree on your own chart and make a note of the house and corresponding "I" statement. Go back to the Cosmic Check-In page and circle the two statements from the charts and read what you wrote. This will give you an idea about what to expect from this moon phase on a personal level. For more information on personalizing your *Moon Book*, go to www.BlueMoonAcademy.com and look for *How to Use the Moon Book*.

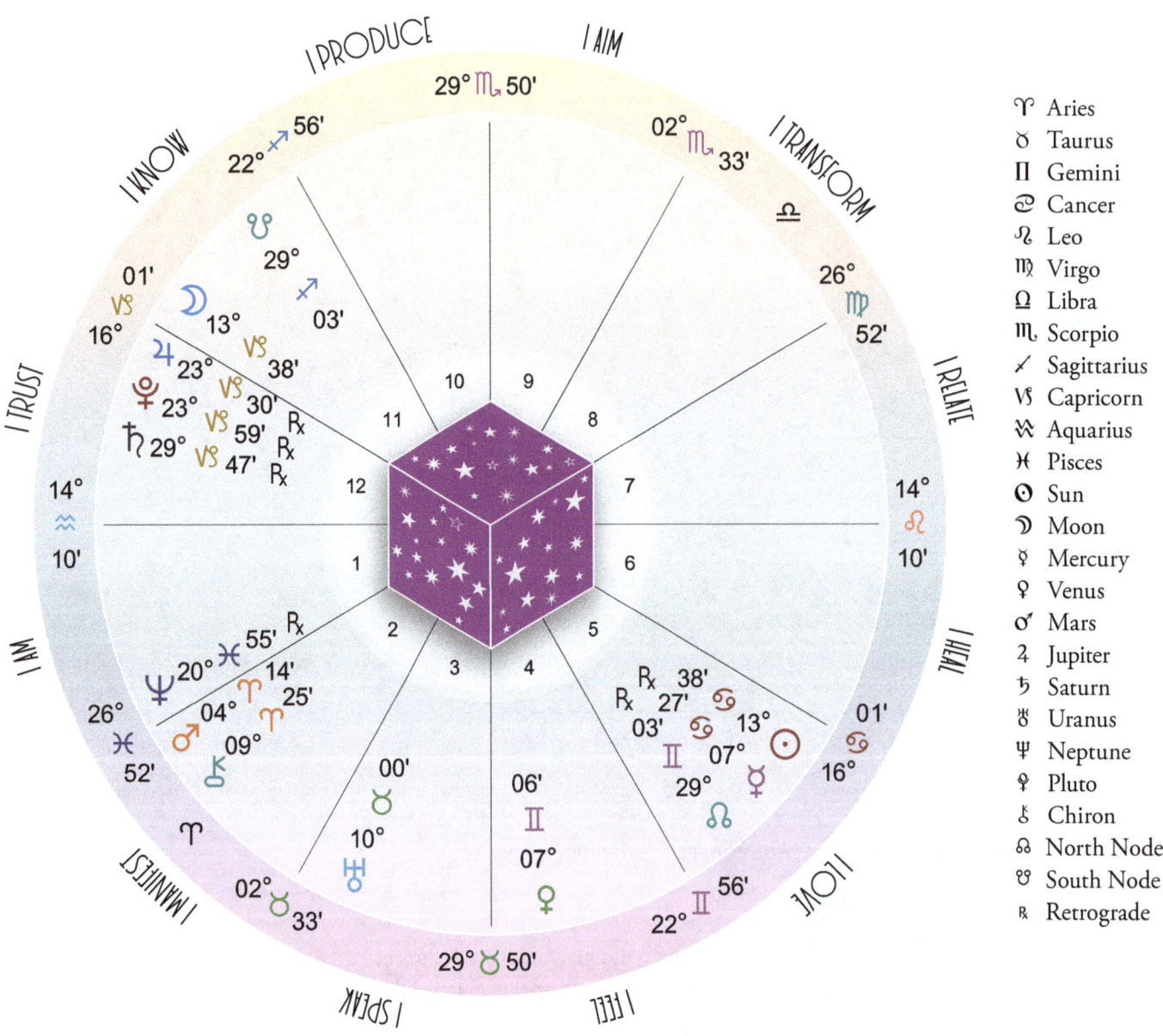

COSMIC CHECK-IN

CAPRICORN FULL MOON
JULY 4TH

Take a moment to write a brief phrase for each "I" statement. This activates all areas of your life for this creative cycle.

♑ I Produce

♒ I Know

♓ I Trust

♈ I Am

♉ I Manifest

♊ I Speak

♋ I Feel

♌ I Love

♍ I Heal

♎ I Relate

♏ I Transform

♐ I Aim

New Moon in Cancer

July 20th, 10:33 AM

When the Sun is in Cancer

It is now time to build our structure and foundation. Cancer holds the wisdom of the Great Cosmic Architect. Her statement is, "I build a lighted house and therein I dwell." The key is to use the materials of light, love, and wisdom to build your house and become the creator of form. Look within to see what lights your home and your body. Also check security systems, early environmental training, and mother/child relationships to see what materials you are using to build the structure for your life. Use this creating moon to build the structure you want.

Cancer Goddess

Hecate is a household goddess who assists people at times of transitions, such as childbirth and death. She is depicted as holding a torch to light the way when you reach major crossroads in life. Associated with the Underworld and the bridge into death and rebirth, Hecate is often shown with three heads and a loyal dog at her side. Her ability to see through the veil of illusion allowed her to assist Demeter in her search for Persephone, because Hecate could see into Hades. She rules over the earth, sea, and sky.

Are you, or someone in your household, feeling restless or aimless? Call upon Hecate's ability to clear the pathway through discernment, the wisdom that comes with age, and the knowledge of cycles.

Build Your Altar

Colors	Shades of gray, milky/creamy colors
Numerology	10 – Set your goals with gusto
Tarot Card	Chariot – Victory through action
Gemstones	Pearl, moonstone, ruby
Plant Remedy	Shooting Star – The ability to move straight ahead
Fragrance	Peppermint – The essence of the Great Mother

Moon Notes

New Moon 28° Cancer 27' 10:33 AM
New Moons are about opening new pathways for prosperity.

Element
Water – Taking the line of least resistance, going with the flow, creativity at its best, secretive, sensual, glamorous, psychic, magnetic, escaping reality, a healer, an actor/actress.

Statement I Feel
Body Stomach
Mind Worried
Spirit Nurturing

11th House Moon
I Know/I Feel

Umbrella Energy
Your approach to friends, social consciousness, teamwork, community service, and the future.

Choice Points
Opportunity Beneficial Choices
Challenge   Out of Balance

Sabian Symbol
A Greek Muse Weighing New Born Twins In Golden Scales

Potential
Look for a double opportunity coming your way.

CANCER VICTORIES & CHALLENGES

**CANCER NEW MOON
JULY 20TH**

Say all of the statements in this section out loud. Then, underline the phrase that means the most to you. Use the phrase as your affirmation for manifesting throughout this moon phase.

Today I take advantage of my ability to take action and position myself for success. I clearly know that the road to success is before me, and all I need to do is move forward. I am aware that when I take action and move forward, the Universe fills in the dots. Whether I move left, right, or straight ahead doesn't matter—what matters is movement. Today, I release the indecisiveness that keeps me stuck. Today, I let go of vacillation that exhausts my mind. Today, I take my foot off of the brakes and find the gas pedal. I allow movement to occur, even if I don't know where I am going. When I take action, I trust that guideposts will appear. I am aware that action leads me to my new direction. So, today I know and GO! I remember that karma comes to the space of non-action, while success comes through action. Action brings me to my victory. Standing still leads to regret, resentment, and chaos. I am aware that action can be as simple as taking a walk on the beach, buying fresh flowers to add a new dimension to my home, or simply going to a new restaurant for lunch. I take action today to break up a crystallized pattern and, in so doing, my life begins to show me newfound awareness and light to guide me.

Cancer Homework

Cancers manifest best when catering, writing cookbooks, in marriage and family counseling, providing childcare, giving massage, or when engaged in genealogy, arts and crafts, architecture, and home-building.

During the Cancer new moon cycle, we are asked to turn light into form, and then turn it into beauty on four levels. Physically, we must feel nurtured and protected. Emotionally, we must set safe boundaries for the expression of our feelings. Mentally, we must release self-pity and embrace rightful thinking. Spiritually, we must hold the space for the infusion of light to shine inside all bodies on Earth.

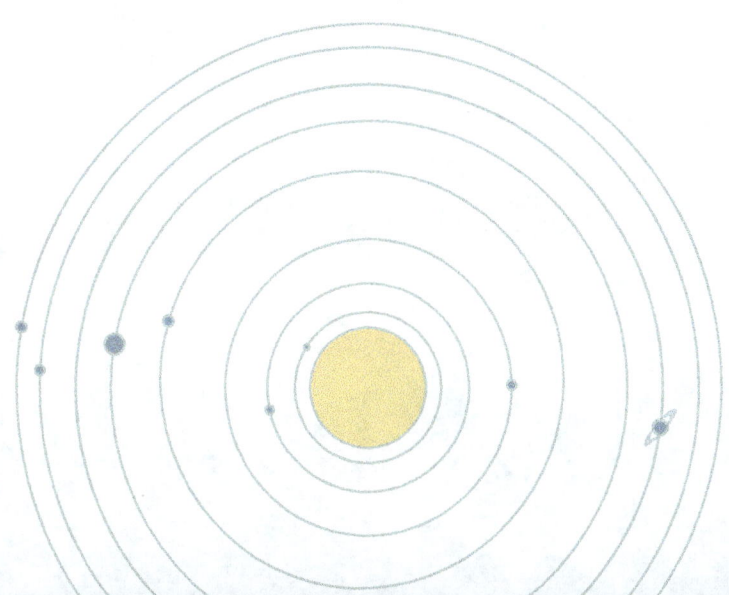

VICTORY LIST

Acknowledge what you have overcome. Keep this list active during this moon cycle. Honoring victory allows you to accept success.

TAROT

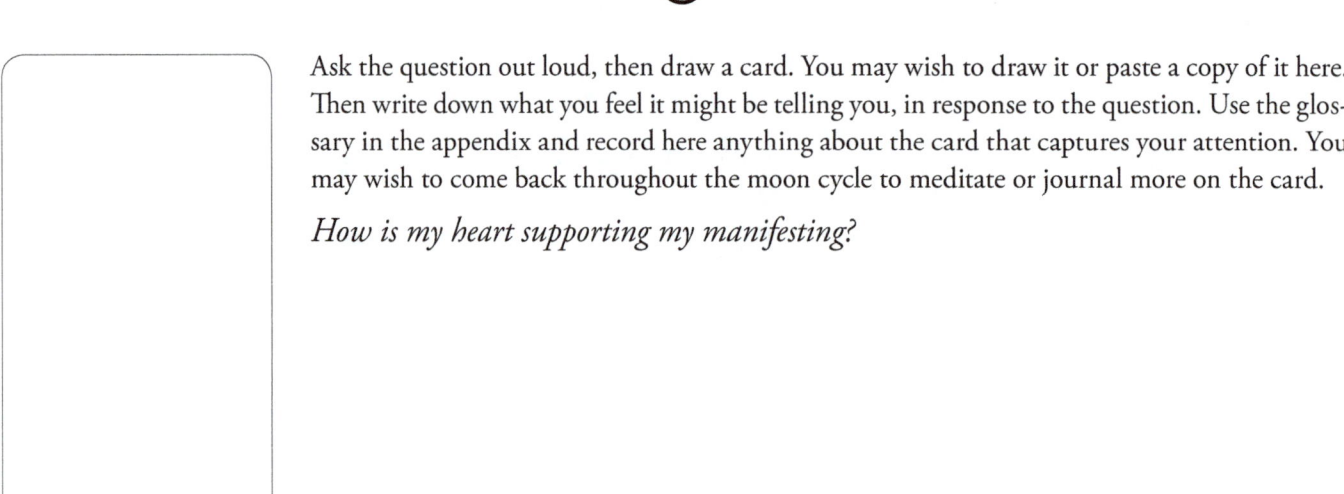

Ask the question out loud, then draw a card. You may wish to draw it or paste a copy of it here. Then write down what you feel it might be telling you, in response to the question. Use the glossary in the appendix and record here anything about the card that captures your attention. You may wish to come back throughout the moon cycle to meditate or journal more on the card.

How is my heart supporting my manifesting?

MANIFESTING LIST

CANCER NEW MOON
JULY 20TH

This or something better than this comes to me in an easy and pleasurable way, for the good of all concerned. Thank you, Universe!

Cancer Manifesting Ideas

Now is the time to focus on manifesting being a good mother, new ways to be a mom, nurturing and self-love, the ability to see joy, a clutter-free home, your dream home, and inner and outer security.

New Moon in Cancer

Your Personal Moon Experience

Fill in the Cosmic Check-In page. Then look up the degree of the Moon on the chart below. Take note of the "I" statement on the outside of the wheel where the Moon is located. Now, locate the same degree on your own chart and make a note of the house and corresponding "I" statement. Go back to the Cosmic Check-In page and circle the two statements from the charts and read what you wrote. This will give you an idea about what to expect from this moon phase on a personal level. For more information on personalizing your *Moon Book*, go to www.BlueMoonAcademy.com and look for *How to Use the Moon Book*.

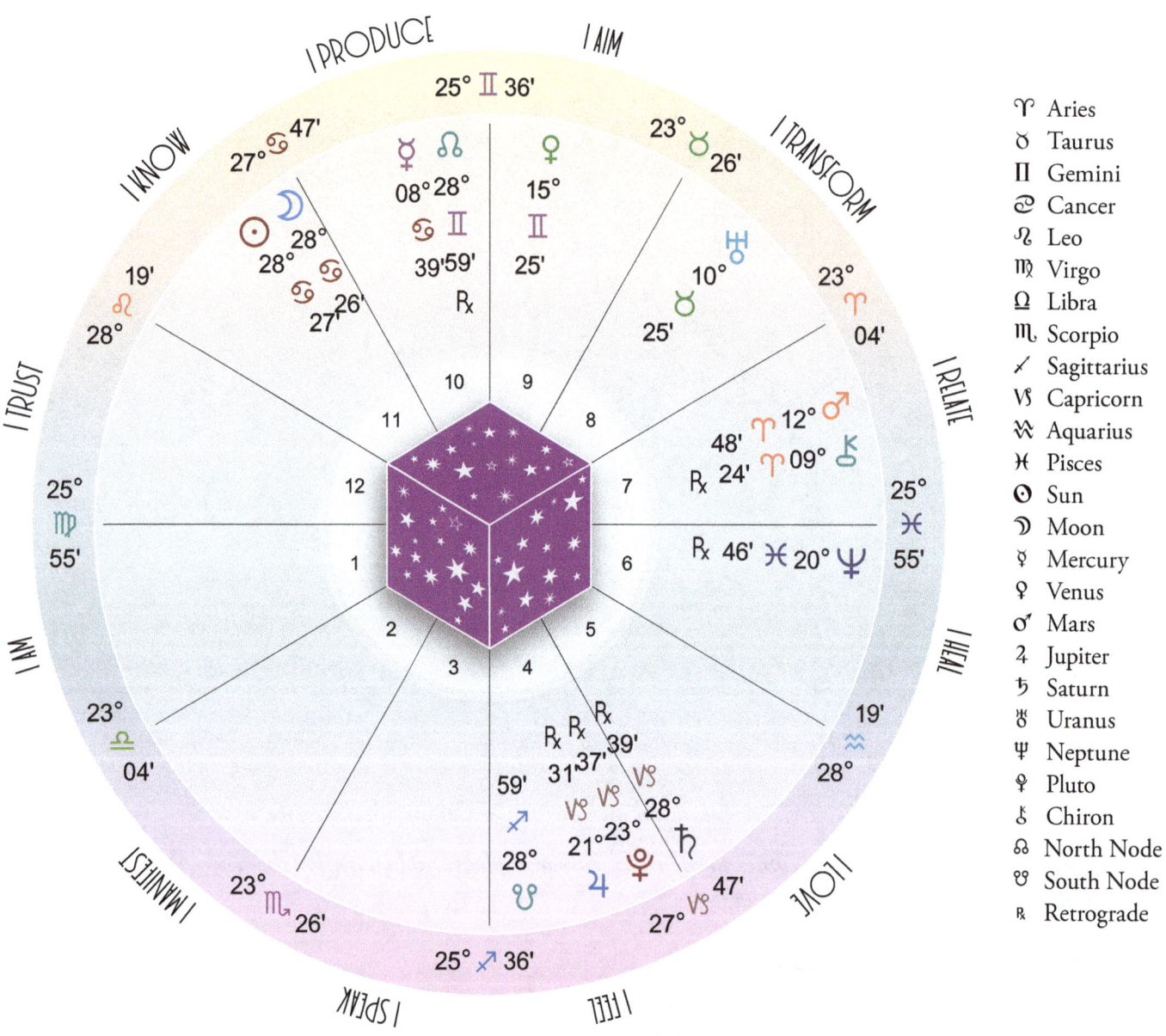

COSMIC CHECK-IN

CANCER NEW MOON
JULY 20TH

Take a moment to write a brief phrase for each "I" statement. This activates all areas of your life for this creative cycle.

♋ I Feel

♌ I Love

♍ I Heal

♎ I Relate

♏ I Transform

♐ I Aim

♑ I Produce

♒ I Know

♓ I Trust

♈ I Am

♉ I Manifest

♊ I Speak

AUGUST

August 1st-10th Venus is conjunct North Node in Gemini

Expect a new way of loving to come forward. Love attraction will be karmic, so romance could be a different experience.

August 1st through the entire month Pluto, Jupiter, and Saturn are tripled in Capricorn

The distribution of power and resources comes together in a new way, bringing the teacher of perfection aboard. Your quest for good fortune and advancement will come across some new options to add to your project. Be willing to extend your energy this way and you won't regret it.

August 3rd Full Moon in Aquarius

Expect the unexpected from your mind. Use your curiosity to discover a new version of life for yourself. Unwind your mind from the usual spiral and come up with something new!

August 4th Mercury enters Leo

Time to let your love nature out and speak from your heart.

August 7th Venus moves into Cancer

Your love nature will be going to your family right now. Time to keep what you love in your home and get rid of what you don't love. Have a family party and make delicious food so everyone feels nurtured.

August 15th Uranus retrograde in Taurus until next year

Time to review your value system. Look into your own version of self-worth. Self-esteem is coming forward; begin by remembering the good you have done.

August 18th New Moon in Leo

Make a list to manifest experiences that you love.

August 18th through the end of the month North and South Nodes are in a fragile alignment in Gemini and Sagittarius

Earth and sky power need to stay together. Wear Turquoise and Tiger Eye to assist with the alignment. Body/Mind connection is very important.

August 18th the Sun, Moon, and Mercury tripled in Leo

Express your inner and outer reality in a way that allows you to be known. It's your time to shine!

August 19th Mercury moves into Virgo

Time to let your mind go a little and find Divinity in the details. A great time to clean out your closets, file cabinets, and all the places needing an upgrade in your life. Keep your judgmental self out of the matrix.

August 22nd the Sun moves into Virgo

Time to find a happy version of yourself. Let the healer in you come alive and go into service. You will experience great gratitude for being you.

Super Sensitivity August 1st, 2nd, 27th and 28th

Chaos is in the atmosphere. It doesn't belong to you.

Low Vitality August 6th-10th, 14th and 15th

Earth changes are possible; stay close to home.

SUNDAY	MONDAY	TUESDAY	WEDNESDAY	THURSDAY	FRIDAY	SATURDAY
						1 ♃♄♇♆℞▲ 4. Orderly patterns make it easy.
2 ♃♄♇♆℞▲ ☽ V/C 6:59 AM ☽→♒ 11:11 AM 5. Expect twists and turns today, Enjoy!	3 ♃♄♇♆℞ ○ 11° ♒ 46' 8:59 AM 6. Make room for romance today!	4 ♃♄♇♆℞ ☽ V/C 2:45 PM ☽→♓ 7:28 PM ☿→♌ 8:31 PM 7. Mental alertness is stimulated today.	5 ♃♄♇♆℞ 8. Be willing to accept victory.	6 ♃♄♇♆℞▼ 9. Say extra prayers for a friend.	7 ♃♄♇♆℞▼ ☽ V/C 5:53 AM ☽→♈ 6:05 AM ♀→♋ 8:21 AM 10. Meet a goal, set a new goal.	8 ♃♄♇♆℞▼ 3. It's easy to be optimistic today.
9 ♃♄♇♆℞▼ ☽ V/C 12:49 PM ☽→♉ 6:28 PM 4. Acknowledge your team.	10 ♃♄♇♆℞▼ 5. Change a repeating pattern.	11 ♃♄♇♆℞ 6. Make a date to go dancing.	12 ♃♄♇♆℞ ☽ V/C 12:54 AM ☽→♊ 6:46 AM 7. Wisdom brings on understanding.	13 ♃♄♇♆℞ 8. Add to your manifestation list.	14 ♃♄♇♆℞▼ ☽ V/C 4:19 AM ☽→♋ 4:36 PM 9. Where can you be of service?	15 ♃♄♅♇♆℞▼ ♅℞ 10° ♉ 42' 7:26 AM 10. Increase opportunities with a goal.
16 ♃♄♅♇♆℞ ☽ V/C 4:58 PM ☽→♌ 10:38 PM 11. Trust your intuitive knowing.	17 ♃♄♅♇♆℞ 3. Become fulfilled through playfulness.	18 ♃♄♅♇♆℞ ● 26° ♌ 35' 7:41 PM ☽ V/C 10:38 PM 4. More gets done with a plan.	19 ♃♄♅♇♆℞ ☽→♍ 1:21 AM ☿→♍ 6:29 PM 5. Be prepared for a game-changer	20 ♃♄♅♇♆℞ ☽ V/C 8:36 PM 6. Be willing to share love.	21 ♃♄♅♇♆℞ ☽→♎ 2:15 AM 7. The quiet voice within speaks truth.	22 ♃♄♅♇♆℞ ☉→♍ 8:44 AM ☽ V/C 9:19 PM 8. Be a winner today and accept yourself.
23 ♃♄♅♇♆℞ ☽→♏ 3:16 AM 9. Grow spiritually by sharing.	24 ♃♄♅♇♆℞ ☽ V/C 11:27 PM 10. Where can you be innovative?	25 ♃♄♅♇♆℞ ☽→♐ 5:49 AM 11. You are universally connected.	26 ♃♄♅♇♆℞ 3. Turn your work into play.	27 ♃♄♅♇♆℞▲ ☽ V/C 4:59 AM ☽→♑ 10:36 AM 4. Use your organizing skills.	28 ♃♄♅♇♆℞▲ 5. Variety is the spice of life.	29 ♃♄♅♇♆℞ ☽ V/C 12:30 PM ☽→♒ 5:36 PM 6. Celebrate beauty, bring flowers home!
30 ♃♄♅♇♆℞ 7. Advance your knowledge.	31 ♃♄♅♇♆℞ ☽ V/C 9:56 PM 8. Your success brings celebration!					

♈ Aries	♍ Virgo	♒ Aquarius	♀ Venus	♆ Neptune	V/C Void-of-Course	2. Balance	7. Learning
♉ Taurus	♎ Libra	♓ Pisces	♂ Mars	♇ Pluto	℞ Retrograde	3. Fun	8. Money
♊ Gemini	♏ Scorpio	☉ Sun	♃ Jupiter	⚷ Chiron	§ Stationary Direct	4. Structure	9. Spirituality
♋ Cancer	♐ Sagittarius	☽ Moon	♄ Saturn	→ Enters	▲ Super Sensitivity	5. Action	10. Visionary
♌ Leo	♑ Capricorn	☿ Mercury	♅ Uranus		▼ Low Vitality	6. Love	11. Completion

Full Moon in Aquarius

August 3rd, 8:59 AM

When the Sun is Opposite the Moon

Full moons are always in opposition to the Sun. This creates a feeling of tension between where you want to shine and how your feelings are flowing on a sensory level about the Sun's directive. The two forces seem like they are working against each other, yet they are on the same team displaying different techniques to obtain the same mission. The Aquarian/Leo polarity creates tension between the quest for group interaction and the recognition of self.

Aquarius Goddess

The Egyptian Goddess Maat ushers in a time of discovery about who you are at the core, as your most balanced and beneficent self, and about the work you came here to do in this lifetime. According to the Egyptian Book of the Dead, Maat is the goddess you visit upon your death. She places her single ostrich feather on the scale to be weighed against your heart. If you have lived a virtuous life, and reached your highest potential as a kind and decent human being, your heart will be as light as Maat's feather, and you would cross over. If not, you will be devoured by the Goddess Ammit and would be reborn into duality for another lifetime.

Let this moon show you your potential and re-orient yourself to your life's highest work and purpose. The Egyptian word for heart was "ib." Ask yourself, who will "I be" in this lifetime?

Build Your Altar

Colors Electric colors, neon, multi-colors, pearl white

Numerology 6 – Make room for romance today

Tarot Card The Star – Follow your light, it knows where to go

Gemstones Aquamarine, amethyst, opal

Plant remedy Queen of the Night Cactus – Ability to see in the dark

Fragrance Myrrh – Healing the nervous system

Moon Notes

Full Moon 11° Aquarius 46' 8:59 AM
Full Moons are about moving beyond blocks and setting yourself free.

Element
Air – The breath of life that allows the mind to achieve new insights and fresh perspectives, abstract dreaming, freedom from attachments, codes of intelligence, and academic applications.

Statement I Know
Body Ankles
Mind Genius
Spirit Innovation

5th House Moon
I Love/I Know

Umbrella Energy
The way you love and how you want to be loved.

Choice Points
Opportunity Progressive
Challenge Social Climbing

Sabian Symbol
People On A Vast Staircase, Graduated Upwards

Potential
Be open to new opportunities.

CLEARING THE SLATE

**AQUARIUS FULL MOON
AUGUST 3RD**

Sixty hours before the full moon negative traits connected to the astro-sign might become activated to trigger what needs to be released during the full moon phase. You may notice yourself becoming stubborn, escaping reality by living in the future, and the need to be rebellious if you feel frenzied or chaotic. Make a list, look in the mirror, and for each negative trait, tell yourself *I am sorry, I forgive you, thank you for your awareness,* and *I love you.*

AQUARIUS VICTORIES & CHALLENGES

Say all of the statements in this section out loud. Then, underline the phrase that means the most to you. Use the phrase as your affirmation for releasing throughout this moon phase.

Today my true potential can be realized. All I have to do is take a risk and know that my faith is in operation. My future is very bright and offers me a promise of things to come. Today is a day of destiny. I have chosen this day to determine a DESTINY PROMISE I MADE TO MYSELF BEFORE I CAME INTO THIS LIFE. All that is required of me is to move out of my comfort zone and take a risk. I am aware that faith cannot be determined without risk. I take the risk to move into the next space of creation in my life. I release fear and move into faith, knowing full well that my logic and reason are part of the fear that keeps me stuck.

I am reminded that the kingdom of heaven is open to the child. I find the child within me today to embrace what life has for me with open arms and a spirit of adventure. I know my true potential lives inside my magical child and she/he is willing to play and go for the gusto. I am here in this life to fulfill my promise to experience life to the fullest and to release the fear of judgment that has hounded me and kept me from playing full-out. I remember that when I experience, I gather a knowledge base within my Soul and keep my agreement with myself and the Universe. I connect to my super-consciousness and take on the bigger view of my life and all that it has to offer me when I risk reason and take a leap of faith. I know in the depth of my awareness that, if I jump off the diving board, there will be water in the pool. I am willing to risk reason for an experience. Everything I ever wanted is one step outside my comfort zone. I go for the GUSTO today! I release my fear today and turn it into faith. I trust in the promise of things to come. I know my potential is realized today, and that all I have to do is say "YES!" to life!

Aquarius Homework

The Aquarius moon reminds us of our connection to solar fire (the heart of the Sun) also known as the Heart of the Cosmos. During this time, we get our vitality recharged and our potent power comes into play motivating the masses to receive more energy to transmute into the new world. Voice all that you know to be true to the point of self-realization where your authentic purpose can be revealed to you. This is the moment where you have released all that has kept you from your true sense of freedom. Remember to replenish all the electrolytes in your system.

GRATITUDE LIST

Keep this list active throughout the moon cycle. This will bring you to a level of completion so that a new cycle of opportunity can occur in your life. Be prepared for miracles!

TAROT

Ask the question out loud, then draw a card. You may wish to draw it or paste a copy of it here. Then write down what you feel it might be telling you, in response to the question. Use the glossary in the appendix and record here anything about the card that captures your attention. You may wish to come back throughout the moon cycle to meditate or journal more on the card.

How is my mind supporting my releasing?

RELEASING LIST

**AQUARIUS FULL MOON
AUGUST 3RD**

Say this statement out loud three times before writing your list:

I am a free spiritual being and it is my desire to be free to think and to express myself fully.

Aquarius Releasing Ideas

Now is the time to activate a game change in my life, and give up resistance to authority figures, blocks to living in the moment, unnecessary rebellion, non-productive frenzy and fantasy, the need to be spontaneous, and people who aren't team players.

Full Moon in Aquarius

Your Personal Moon Experience

Fill in the Cosmic Check-In page. Then look up the degree of the Moon on the chart below. Take note of the "I" statement on the outside of the wheel where the Moon is located. Now, locate the same degree on your own chart and make a note of the house and corresponding "I" statement. Go back to the Cosmic Check-In page and circle the two statements from the charts and read what you wrote. This will give you an idea about what to expect from this moon phase on a personal level. For more information on personalizing your *Moon Book*, go to www.BlueMoonAcademy.com and look for *How to Use the Moon Book*.

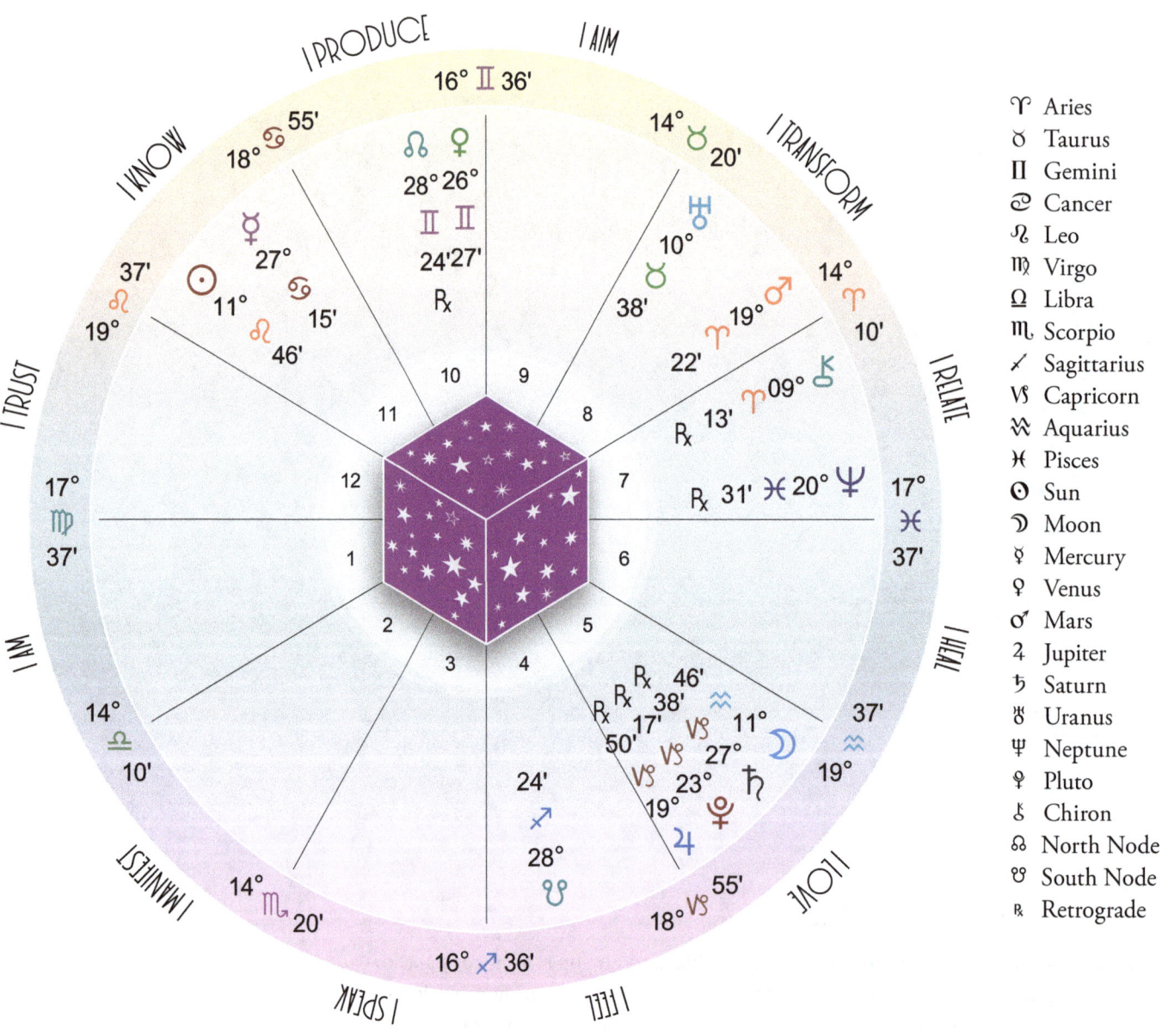

COSMIC CHECK-IN

AQUARIUS FULL MOON
AUGUST 3RD

Take a moment to write a brief phrase for each "I" statement. This activates all areas of your life for this creative cycle.

♒ I Know

♓ I Trust

♈ I Am

♉ I Manifest

♊ I Speak

♋ I Feel

♌ I Love

♍ I Heal

♎ I Relate

♏ I Transform

♐ I Aim

♑ I Produce

New Moon in Leo

August 18th, 7:41 PM

When the Sun is in Leo

This is the time when you feel the power from the Sun, the heart of the Cosmos. Leo has a direct relationship with the Sun's heart. The Sun rules your identity. Now is the time to shine and stand tall in the center of your life. Allow yourself to feel the power of your individual conscious Self. When you align with the power of the Sun, you become radiant. This radiance gives you the power to transmit energy into life. Personal fulfillment becomes a reality when you align your will with love. Remember to live love every day!

Leo Goddess

Aphrodite sashays into the Summer party, full of moxie and ready to flirt! The Goddess of Beauty and Love is enlivening all aspects of your life with joyful play!

Get into your Feminine Light. Giggle, dance, and sing! What a great time for a girl's night out or karaoke on the beach beside a roaring bonfire! Work it! Swish your skirts and strut your stuff! Tap into Aphrodite's inner light for fun and frolic. Aphrodite reminds us that play is also our spiritual work. Bring some joy and fun into it!

Build Your Altar

Colors	Royal purple, royal blue, orange
Numerology	4 – More gets done with a plan
Tarot Card	Sun – Accept abundance and the ability to have it all
Gemstones	Peridot, emerald, amber
Plant Remedy	Sunflower – Standing tall in the center of your garden
Fragrance	Jasmine – Remembering your Soul's original intention

Moon Notes

New Moon 26° Leo 35' 7:41 PM
New Moons are about opening new pathways for prosperity.

Element
Fire – Igniting, dissolving, accelerating, cleansing, advancing awareness, impatience, leadership, passion, and vitality.

Statement I Love
Body Heart
Mind Self-confidence
Spirit Generosity

6th House Moon
I Heal/I Love

Umbrella Energy
The way you manage your body and its appearance.

Choice Points
Opportunity   Quickening
Challenge   Illusion

Sabian Symbol
Daybreak – The Luminescence Of Dawn In The Eastern Sky

Potential
Widen your horizons, something new is coming.

LEO VICTORIES & CHALLENGES

LEO NEW MOON AUGUST 18TH

Say all of the statements in this section out loud. Then, underline the phrase that means the most to you. Use the phrase as your affirmation for manifesting throughout this moon phase.

Today, I am at the center of bliss, happiness, abundance, and total celebration. It is my time to shine and feel the power of my true self blasting the Universe, the entire planet, and all of life with the light of my awareness. There is nothing that can stop me today, because I am free to be me. When I am free to be me, I can stand naked in the daylight and have nothing to hide. I truly know that all of life loves me and I love all of life. I feel the radiance and vibration of my being activating me with aliveness, vitality, and charisma. I know that I can make a difference because I celebrate life by infusing, sparking, and igniting matter with light. I am open and ready to embrace all that comes to me with joy. I say "YES!" to all opportunities today; knowing that today is my day. I am in the flow of abundance and I let abundance flow through me.

The child within me is open and ready to play full out; there is not a cloud in the sky today that can eclipse me or place a shadow on me and keep me from my true level of power. I am aware that the child state of being within me simply says yes to action and action is power. When I take action today, my possibilities are endless because they are generated from my true self and motivated by happiness, joy, and freedom. The child within me is able to play full out because I have birthed myself beyond my old perception of blocks. I know that in taking this true power, to be motivated by happiness, pathways on all levels and in all dimensions can open to the empowerment of joy. Empowerment is mine today because I am shining from within myself and I know my deepest self is connected to the source. Empowerment occurs when I live from the inside out. Today, I wave the banner of my being from within, feel the glow, and go.

Leo Homework

Leos manifest best through fashion and jewelry design, glamour, politics, super-modeling, movie stardom, child advocacy, fundraising, toy and game design, image consulting, authoring children's books, sales, and cardiology.

Leo gets you closer to your essential self, reminding you of your Soul's original intention. You become ready to receive the benefits of reflective light and radiating light at the same time, so that you can see your personality and your Soul connecting to love which constitutes a new level of fulfillment. Expect purification, transmutation, communication, and mastery to be part of your personal experience.

VICTORY LIST

Acknowledge what you have overcome. Keep this list active during this moon cycle. Honoring victory allows you to accept success.

TAROT

Ask the question out loud, then draw a card. You may wish to draw it or paste a copy of it here. Then write down what you feel it might be telling you, in response to the question. Use the glossary in the appendix and record here anything about the card that captures your attention. You may wish to come back throughout the moon cycle to meditate or journal more on the card.

How is my spirit supporting my manifesting?

MANIFESTING LIST

> LEO NEW MOON
> AUGUST 18TH

This or something better than this comes to me in an easy and pleasurable way, for the good of all concerned. Thank you, Universe!

Leo Manifesting Ideas

Now is the time to focus on manifesting new love or new ways of loving, new creative ways of expressing myself, bonding with those I love, quality time with those I love, knowledge of my Soul's intention, fun with my children, being a bright beaming light, and connecting to the hearts of humanity.

New Moon in Leo

Your Personal Moon Experience

Fill in the Cosmic Check-In page. Then look up the degree of the Moon on the chart below. Take note of the "I" statement on the outside of the wheel where the Moon is located. Now, locate the same degree on your own chart and make a note of the house and corresponding "I" statement. Go back to the Cosmic Check-In page and circle the two statements from the charts and read what you wrote. This will give you an idea about what to expect from this moon phase on a personal level. For more information on personalizing your *Moon Book*, go to www.BlueMoonAcademy.com and look for *How to Use the Moon Book*.

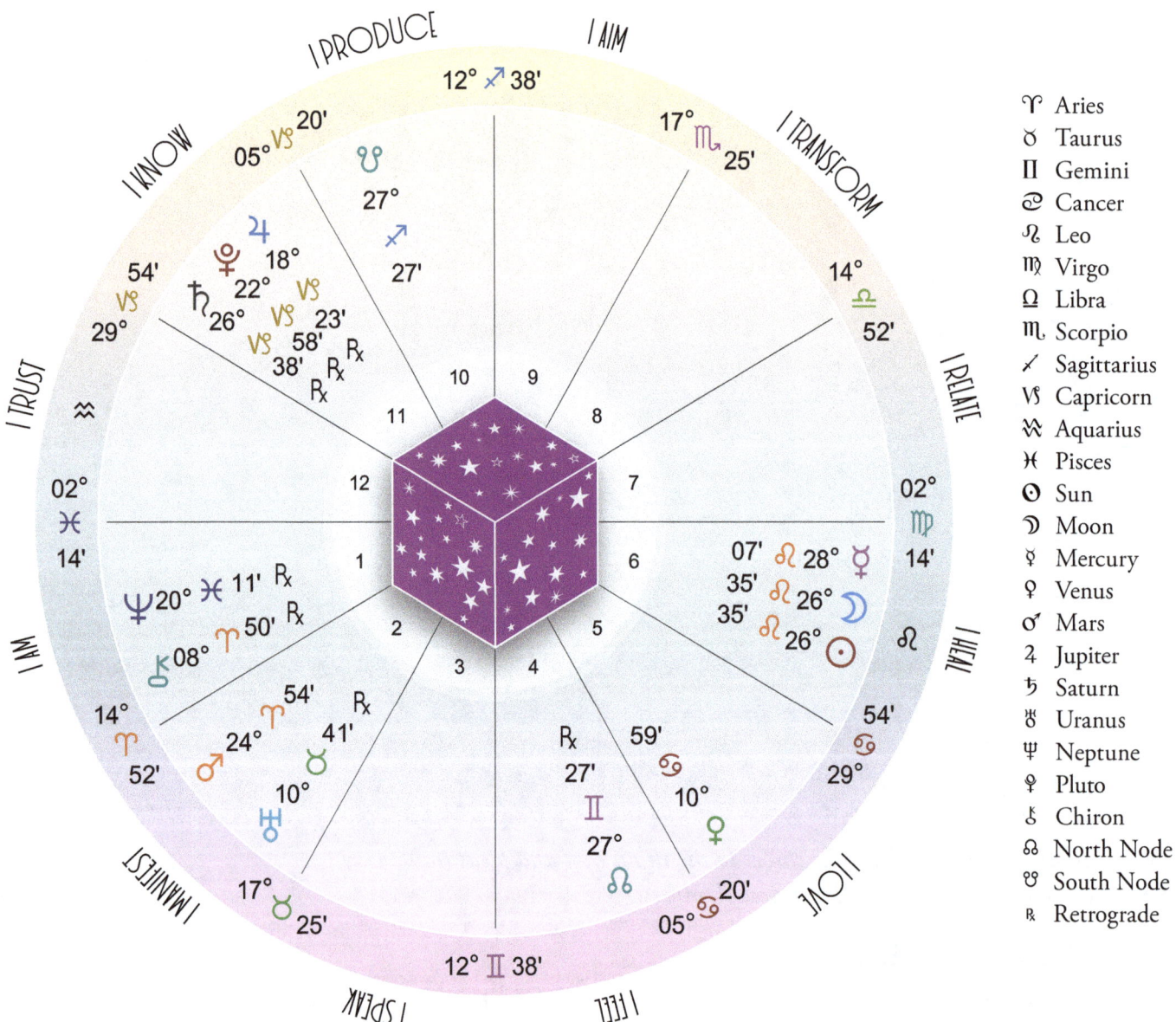

COSMIC CHECK-IN

LEO NEW MOON
AUGUST 18ᵀᴴ

Take a moment to write a brief phrase for each "I" statement. This activates all areas of your life for this creative cycle.

♌ I Love

♍ I Heal

♎ I Relate

♏ I Transform

♐ I Aim

♑ I Produce

♒ I Know

♓ I Trust

♈ I Am

♉ I Manifest

♊ I Speak

♋ I Feel

SEPTEMBER

September 1st through the end of the month Pluto and Saturn in Capricorn

They dance the dance of power and perfection. Pluto desires power as it relates to the beginning and end of things. Saturn desires to know what governs and underlies the order of structure. Let's set the intention to let fear from this power play motivate us into renovation rather than destruction.

September 1st-17th North and South Nodes in Gemini and Sagittarius

Begin to release from fragility and notice, at last, some flexibility arriving.

September 1st Full Moon in Pisces

Set yourself free from addictions. Release disappointments from dreams that didn't come true, this will help you make space for new dreams. Find a group that meditates on the full-moon phase so you can connect your spiritual self to a routine.

September 5th Mercury enters Libra

Do what it takes to express the importance of PEACE.

September 6th Venus enters Leo

This is a great time for love and romance. The deep desire to connect is huge right now, Let it happen; it is time to let love heal the earth. It starts with you living love!

September 9th Mars retrograde in Aries until Nov. 13th

Expect impatience, personally and politically, to lead to brat attacks that could have a lasting, regrettable impact. Warring tendencies are way too close to the surface; walking on eggshells could be your daily experience.

September 12th Jupiter goes direct in Capricorn

Blessings abound. All your hard work and focus can now complete itself and you could experience some rewards. You are now clear from the year 2008. Relationships, health, and home issues are now in check. Enjoy.

September 17th New Moon in Virgo

Remember to write your new manifest list. Set new boundaries. Start a new health regime. Do something that raises the standard of excellence in your world.

September 22nd the Sun enters Libra – Autumnal Equinox

Get ready to harvest your year's blessings. Time to celebrate the fruit on the trees.

September 27th Mercury goes into Scorpio

Time to let your mind go deep to discover what has been hidden and needs to be brought to the surface. Let your shadow side find the light. Now is the time!

September 28th Saturn goes direct in Capricorn

The testing period is over! You may experience some relief, mentally.

Low Vitality September 10th and 11th

Time to honor the earth; have a drumming circle. Earth changes may be in order. Stay safe, and get rest.

Super Sensitivity September 23rd and 24th

Chaos is in the air. It is not personal, so it can be easily avoided. The gateway to all there is downloads new information, so stay out of the way. You can glean what you need when it settles after the 24th.

SUNDAY	MONDAY	TUESDAY	WEDNESDAY	THURSDAY	FRIDAY	SATURDAY
		1 ♃♄♅♀♆℞ ☽→♓ 2:35 AM ○ 10° ♓ 12' 10:22 PM 9. Spiritual help is there, just ask.	2 ♃♄♅♀♆℞ 10. See your aspirations thriving.	3 ♃♄♅♀♆℞ ☽ V/C 7:34 AM ☽→♈ 1:22 PM 11. You are more than you think.	4 ♃♄♅♀♆℞ 3. Call friends, time for a party.	5 ♃♄♅♀♆℞ ☿→♎ 12:46 PM 4. Your practical side wins today.
6 ♃♄♅♀♆℞ ♀→♌ 12:21 AM ☽→♉ 1:44 AM ☽ V/C 9:45 AM 5. Plan a trip to see the fall leaves.	7 ♃♄♅♀♆℞ 6. Embrace love in all its forms.	8 ♃♄♅♀♆℞ ☽ V/C 5:46 AM ☽→♊ 2:28 PM 7. Solutions are likely to be found.	9 ♂♃♄♅♀♆℞ ♂℞ 28° ♈ 09' 3:22 PM 8. Intend that money works for you.	10 ♂♃♄♅♀♆℞ ▼ ☽ V/C 9:45 PM 9. Listen; Spirit is speaking today.	11 ♂♃♄♅♀♆℞ ▼ ☽→♋ 1:23 AM 10. Learn about a new technology.	12 ♂♄♅♀♆℞ ♃SD 17° ♑ 24' 5:41 PM 11. Breathe in the power of *allness.*
13 ♂♄♅♀♆℞ ☽ V/C 5:05 AM ☽→♌ 8:33 AM 3. Bring in joy, go dancing.	14 ♂♄♅♀♆℞ 4. Organize your options.	15 ♂♄♅♀♆℞ ☽ V/C 8:09 AM ☽→♍ 11:38 AM 5. Take a different route to work.	16 ♂♄♅♀♆℞ 6. Let's let love go viral.	17 ♂♄♅♀♆℞ ● 25° ♍ 01' 4:00 AM ☽ V/C 4:42 AM ☽→♎ 11:55 AM 7. Go to an intriguing lecture.	18 ♂♄♅♀♆℞ 8. Celebrate abundance!	19 ♂♄♅♀♆℞ ☽ V/C 7:29 AM ☽→♏ 11:32 AM 9. Be generous with your time.
20 ♂♄♅♀♆℞ 10. Try a new innovative technique.	21 ♂♄♅♀♆℞ ☽ V/C 11:13 AM ☽→♐ 12:32 PM 2. Look for more than two options.	22 ♂♄♅♀♆℞ **Autumnal Equinox** ☉→♎ 6:30 AM 3. There is joy in sharing the fun.	23 ♂♄♅♀♆℞ ▲ ☽ V/C 10:31 AM ☽→♑ 4:17 PM 4. Before leaving, ground your energy.	24 ♂♄♅♀♆℞ ▲ 5. Plan your dream vacation.	25 ♂♄♅♀♆℞ ☽ V/C 8:36 PM ☽→♒ 11:08 PM 6. Romance is in the air, time for love.	26 ♂♄♅♀♆℞ 7. Think outside the box today.
27 ♂♄♅♀♆℞ ☿→♏ 12:40 AM 8. Ask and you shall receive.	28 ♂♅♀♆℞ ☽ V/C 12:17 AM ☽→♓ 8:34 AM ♄SD 25° ♑ 20' 10:11 PM 9. Notice the Divine blessings.	29 ♂♅♀♆℞ 10. A new beginning starts now.	30 ♂♅♀♆℞ ☽ V/C 10:29 AM ☽→♈ 7:48 PM 11. A mystical and magical day.			

♈ Aries
♉ Taurus
♊ Gemini
♋ Cancer
♌ Leo
♍ Virgo
♎ Libra
♏ Scorpio
♐ Sagittarius
♑ Capricorn
♒ Aquarius
♓ Pisces
☉ Sun
☽ Moon
☿ Mercury
♀ Venus
♂ Mars
♃ Jupiter
♄ Saturn
♅ Uranus
♆ Neptune
♇ Pluto
⚷ Chiron
→ Enters
V/C Void-of-Course
℞ Retrograde
SD Stationary Direct
▲ Super Sensitivity
▼ Low Vitality
2. Balance
3. Fun
4. Structure
5. Action
6. Love
7. Learning
8. Money
9. Spirituality
10. Visionary
11. Completion

Full Moon in Pisces

September 1st, 10:22 PM

When the Sun is Opposite the Moon

Full moons are always in opposition to the Sun. This creates a feeling of tension between where you want to shine and how your feelings are flowing on a sensory level about the Sun's directive. The two forces seem like they are working against each other, yet they are on the same team displaying different techniques to obtain the same mission. The Pisces/Virgo polarity creates tension between addiction and perfection.

Pisces Goddess

Lady Change'e, the Chinese Moon Goddess, is honored at the full moon closest to the Autumnal Equinox, with the sharing of moon cakes, whose round shape symbolizes completeness and togetherness. She ascended to the Moon after drinking the Elixir of Immortality. It had been gifted to her husband after he saved the Earth. If she and her husband had split the elixir, they would each be immortal, but her mistake in drinking it all (or her sacrifice, depending on the telling) means she will spend eternity on the Moon.

Depicted with a companion rabbit, a magical potion maker, Change'e is beneficent, and will grant your wishes. Remember she favors those who are careful what they wish for, and who take initiative towards working to make their own dreams a reality.

Build Your Altar

Colors	Greens, blues, amethyst, aquamarine
Numerology	9 – Spiritual help is there, just ask
Tarot Card	The Hanged Man – Learning to let go
Gemstones	Opal, turquoise, amethyst
Plant remedy	Passion flower – The ability to live in the here and now
Fragrance	White lotus – Connect to the Divine

Moon Notes

Full Moon 10° Pisces 12' 10:22 PM
Full Moons are about moving beyond blocks and setting yourself free.

Element
Water – Taking the line of least resistance, going with the flow, creativity at its best, secretive, sensual, glamorous, psychic, magnetic, escaping reality, a healer, an actor/actress.

Statement I Trust
Body Feet
Mind Super-sensitive
Spirit Mystical

11th House Moon
I Know/I Trust

Umbrella Energy
Your approach to friends, social consciousness, teamwork, community service, and the future.

Choice Points
Opportunity   Devotion
Challenge   Hypocrisy

Sabian Symbol
Men Traveling A Narrow Path, Seeking Illumination

Potential
Make sure that your belief system matches your reality.

CLEARING THE SLATE

**PISCES FULL MOON
SEPTEMBER 1ST**

Sixty hours before the full moon negative traits connected to the astro-sign might become activated to trigger what needs to be released during the full moon phase. You may notice a sudden urge to escape into unrealistic attitudes or addictive habits that bring a feeling of aimlessness. Make a list, look in the mirror, and for each negative trait, tell yourself *I am sorry, I forgive you, thank you for your awareness,* and *I love you.*

PISCES VICTORIES & CHALLENGES

Say all of the statements in this section out loud. Then, underline the phrase that means the most to you. Use the phrase as your affirmation for releasing throughout this moon phase.

The best thing I can do for myself today is to get out of the way, so life can take its own course without the interference of my control drama. I take time out to let go and let things be. I have become too involved in the details and have lost sight of the vastness of the Universe, and the infinite possibilities that are available to me at all times and in every moment. I am aware that all I need is a different way of seeing what I have perceived as a problem, and that my view is limited by my needs, rather than by accepting things as they are. I trust that, when I get out of the way and give space to the power of NOW, all is in Divine Order and everything works out for the good of all concerned. This is the day when doing nothing gets me everything. I allow myself to experience the void. I empty myself of my rigidity, small-mindedness, racing thoughts, the need to be right, and to control outcomes. I know that non-action will present me with right action. I give the Universe a chance and trust the view to be larger than mine. When I accept myself as I am, I learn what I can become. I remove myself from all of the mind chatter and allow for silence to do its work. I am aware that a quiet mind brings me peace (the absence of conflict). In turning upside down, I see how right-side-up things really are. Acceptance brings me perspective. Acceptance sets me free. Acceptance brings me wholeness. Acceptance widens my mind.

Pisces Homework

Get a foot massage to bring your energy back to the ground. Feel the power of your path on the bottom of your feet. Now that you are back to your body, it is time to make a list of the ways your boundaries get breached. After the completion of your list, read it out loud and then throw it in the ocean.

GRATITUDE LIST

Keep this list active throughout the moon cycle. This will bring you to a level of completion so that a new cycle of opportunity can occur in your life. Be prepared for miracles!

TAROT

Ask the question out loud, then draw a card. You may wish to draw it or paste a copy of it here. Then write down what you feel it might be telling you, in response to the question. Use the glossary in the appendix and record here anything about the card that captures your attention. You may wish to come back throughout the moon cycle to meditate or journal more on the card.

How is my heart supporting my releasing?

RELEASING LIST

**PISCES FULL MOON
SEPTEMBER 1ST**

Say this statement out loud three times before writing your list:

I am a free spiritual being and it is my desire to be free to think and to express myself fully.

From this day forward I resolve to be true – first to myself and my highest self, and then to the highest self in me which is the Source of Love That I Am.

Pisces Releasing Ideas

Now is the time to activate a game change in my life, and give up addictions, illusions and fantasy, escape dramas, martyrdom, victimhood, and mental chaos.

Full Moon in Pisces

Your Personal Moon Experience

Fill in the Cosmic Check-In page. Then look up the degree of the Moon on the chart below. Take note of the "I" statement on the outside of the wheel where the Moon is located. Now, locate the same degree on your own chart and make a note of the house and corresponding "I" statement. Go back to the Cosmic Check-In page and circle the two statements from the charts and read what you wrote. This will give you an idea about what to expect from this moon phase on a personal level. For more information on personalizing your *Moon Book*, go to www.BlueMoonAcademy.com and look for *How to Use the Moon Book*.

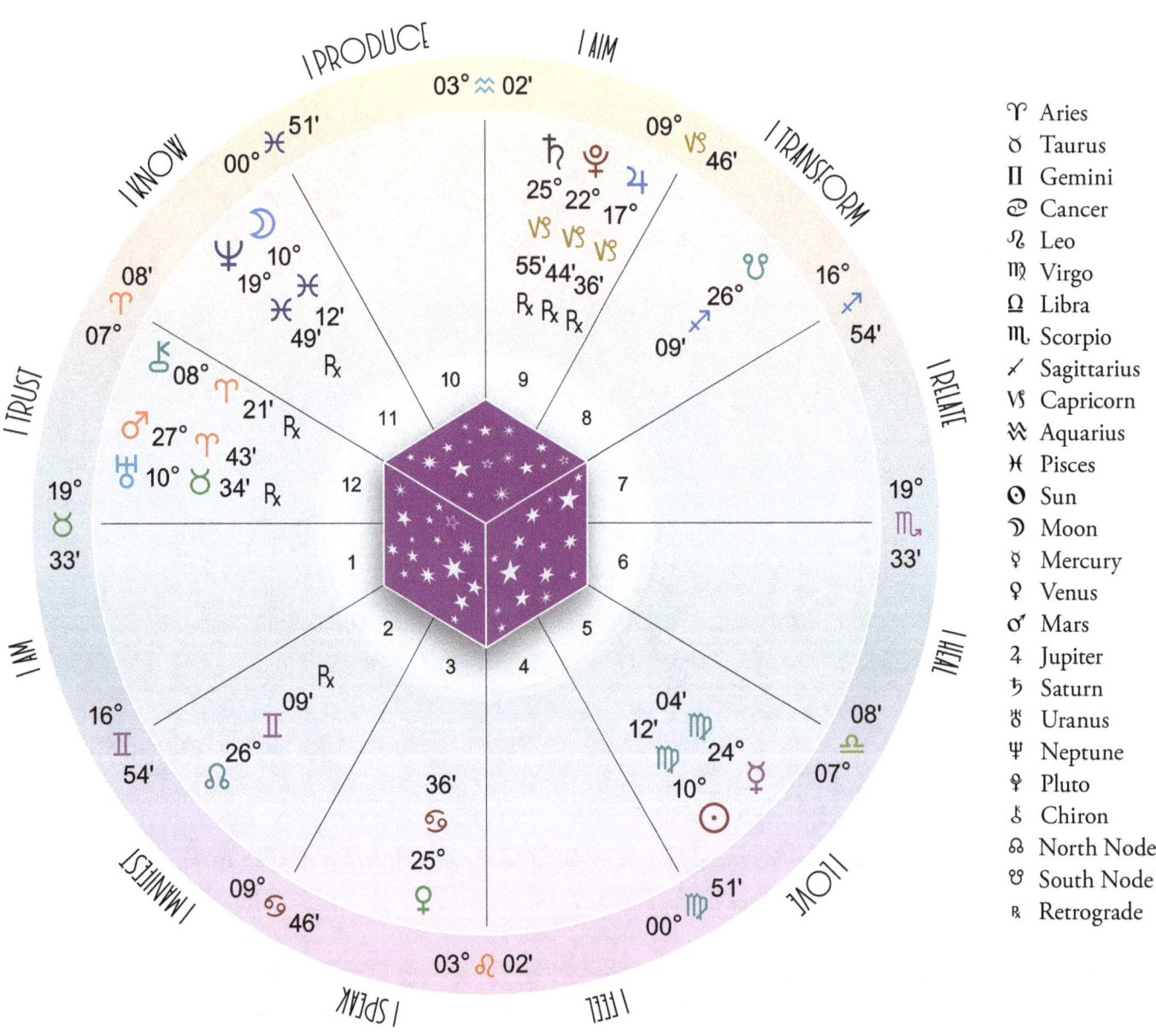

COSMIC CHECK-IN

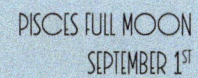

PISCES FULL MOON
SEPTEMBER 1ST

Take a moment to write a brief phrase for each "I" statement. This activates all areas of your life for this creative cycle.

♓ I Trust

♈ I Am

♉ I Manifest

♊ I Speak

♋ I Feel

♌ I Love

♍ I Heal

♎ I Relate

♏ I Transform

♐ I Aim

♑ I Produce

♒ I Know

New Moon in Virgo

September 17th, 4:00 AM

When the Sun is in Virgo

Virgo is called the "Womb of Time" in which the seeds of great value are planted, shielded, nourished, and revealed. It is the labor of Virgo that brings the Christ Principle into manifestation within individuals and humanity. This unification occurs when we feel the power within us to serve. When we serve, we give birth to Divinity. Virgo time is when we all have a chance to raise the standard of excellence in our lives and on the Earth. The Virgo intelligence stores and maintains light in a precise manner. Attention to detail is Virgo's great gift to life.

Virgo Goddess

Mayan Goddess of medicine and midwifery, Ixchel, enters quietly in her jaguar form, to sit and observe. How are you being healed and how are you assisting the healing of others? Jaguar medicine is powerful for clearing attachments and cords that no longer serve you.

Call upon Ixchel to help you find precision and clarity through your words. Let her help you end negative self-talk. Enlist her to walk your boundaries and protect you fiercely, as though you were her little cub. Locate a stone or amulet you can carry in your pocket to remind you of her power, just like shaman and physicians of old would carry in their medicine bundles. When Ixchel has your back, you can roar!

Build Your Altar

Colors	Earth tones, blue, green
Numerology	7 – Go to an intriguing lecture
Tarot Card	The Hermit – Be willing to get off the mountain top and go be of service
Gemstones	Emerald, malachite, sapphire
Plant Remedy	Sagebrush – The ability to hold and store light
Fragrance	Lavender – Management and storage of energy

Moon Notes

New Moon 25° Virgo 01' 4:00 AM
New Moons are about opening new pathways for prosperity.

Element
Earth – Practical, determined, structured, enduring, stubborn, traditional, stable, and stuck inside the box.

Statement I Heal

Body Intestines

Mind Critical

Spirit Divinity In Details

2nd House Moon
I Manifest/I Heal

Umbrella Energy
The way you make your money and the way you spend your money.

Choice Points
Opportunity   Apprenticeship
Challenge   A 'Yes' Person

Sabian Symbol
A Boy With A Censer Serves Near The Priest At The Altar

Potential
Bringing a new form to spirituality.

VIRGO VICTORIES & CHALLENGES

**VIRGO NEW MOON
SEPTEMBER 17TH**

Say all of the statements in this section out loud. Then, underline the phrase that means the most to you. Use the phrase as your affirmation for manifesting throughout this moon phase.

Today, I recognize what I love most about myself. I am the source of my love, my life, and my experience. I will set aside time today to nurture myself. I allow myself to receive these gifts and know in my heart that it is natural for me to love myself. I discover, deep within myself, the knowing that the love I give myself is commensurate to the love I am willing to receive from others. I am aware that what I expect from others cannot be truly expressed or experienced if I cannot give to myself first. I can never be disappointed when I know that love is a natural resource for me today.

Today, I honor the Earth by acknowledging what she has given me. I take time out to walk in the woods or on the beach, to feel the power of the creative pulse of the creative forces flowing through my body with the energy of being alive. I spend time in my garden and plant flowers to enhance the idea of beauty today. I honor my body today and get a massage. I spend quality time sharing joyful moments with those who love to connect from the heart and realize the blessings that come from living my life with love.

Virgo Homework

Virgos manifest best through working with herbology, folk medicine, environmental industries, organic farming, recycling, horticulture, acupuncture, healing arts, nutritional counseling, yoga instruction, and editing.

The Virgo moon cycle gives birth to Divinity in its own unique way, understanding the Soul's blueprint to be a temple of beauty. This creates what is known as the "crisis of perfection" within the minds of humankind during this time. We become aware of Spirit ascending and descending at the same time and must recognize that these contradicting energies are working within us in order to give birth to Divinity.

VICTORY LIST

Acknowledge what you have overcome. Keep this list active during this moon cycle. Honoring victory allows you to accept success.

TAROT

Ask the question out loud, then draw a card. You may wish to draw it or paste a copy of it here. Then write down what you feel it might be telling you, in response to the question. Use the glossary in the appendix and record here anything about the card that captures your attention. You may wish to come back throughout the moon cycle to meditate or journal more on the card.

How is my body supporting my manifesting?

MANIFESTING LIST

**VIRGO NEW MOON
SEPTEMBER 17TH**

This or something better than this comes to me in an easy and pleasurable way, for the good of all concerned. Thank you, Universe!

Virgo Manifesting Ideas

Now is the time to focus on manifesting a high standard of excellence, a healthy lifestyle, self-acceptance, discernment without judgment, healing abilities, a contribution to nature, and a healthy body.

New Moon in Virgo

Your Personal Moon Experience

Fill in the Cosmic Check-In page. Then look up the degree of the Moon on the chart below. Take note of the "I" statement on the outside of the wheel where the Moon is located. Now, locate the same degree on your own chart and make a note of the house and corresponding "I" statement. Go back to the Cosmic Check-In page and circle the two statements from the charts and read what you wrote. This will give you an idea about what to expect from this moon phase on a personal level. For more information on personalizing your *Moon Book*, go to www.BlueMoonAcademy.com and look for *How to Use the Moon Book*.

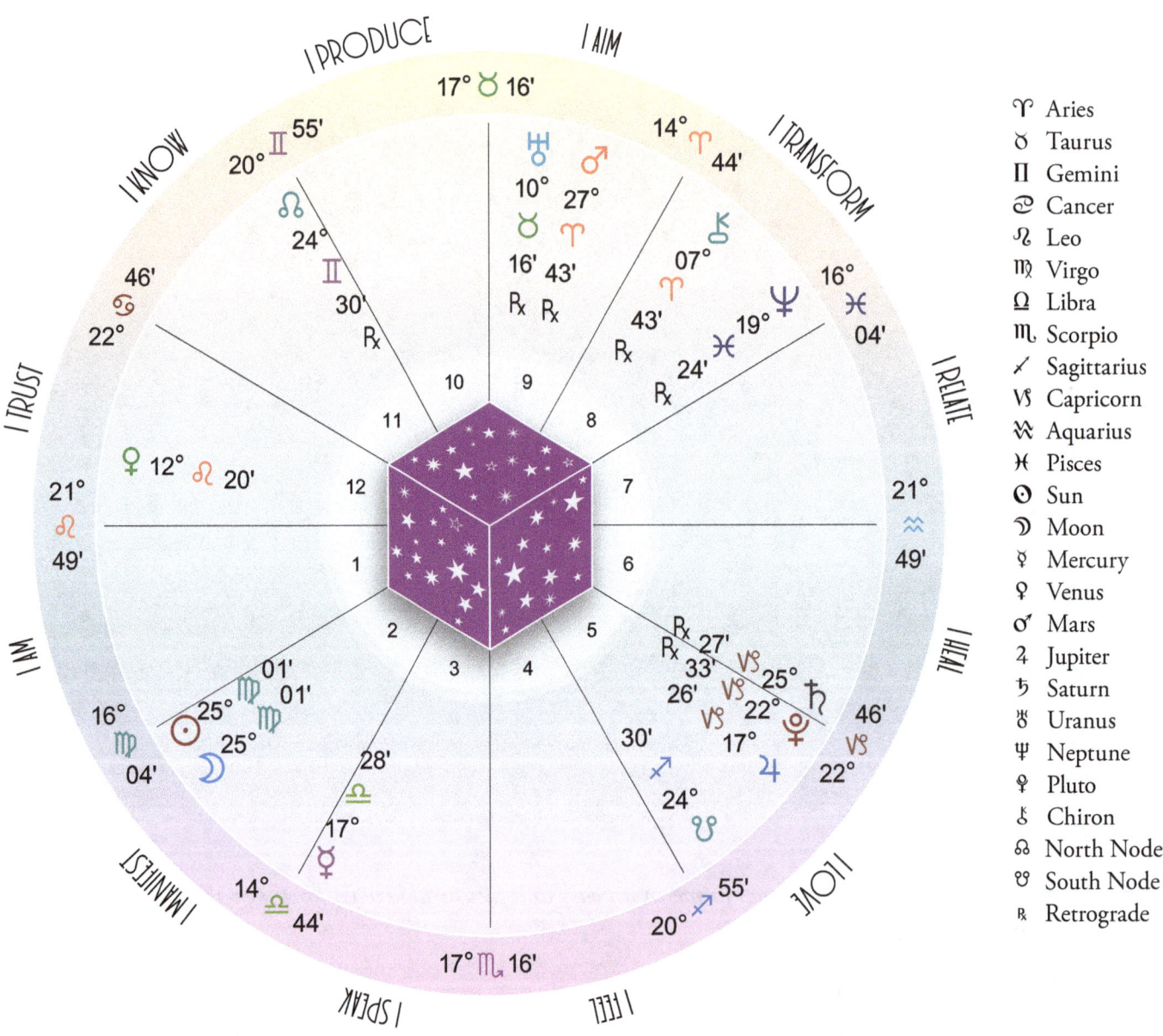

COSMIC CHECK-IN

VIRGO NEW MOON
SEPTEMBER 17TH

Take a moment to write a brief phrase for each "I" statement. This activates all areas of your life for this creative cycle.

♍ I Heal

♎ I Relate

♏ I Transform

♐ I Aim

♑ I Produce

♒ I Know

♓ I Trust

♈ I Am

♉ I Manifest

♊ I Speak

♋ I Feel

♌ I Love

OCTOBER

October 1st Full Moon in Aries

Time to release old patterns of anger, impatience, or impulsive brat attacks.

October 1st Pluto and Saturn in Capricorn are still in a power play

Here is where tradition meets transformation and creates uncertainty when a choice is necessary.

October 1st the Full Moon is conjunct Chiron in Aries

Expect a download of feelings to come forward ready to be healed, especially if you have incomplete mother issues (about your mother or being a mother.)

October 2nd Venus moves into Virgo

Make sure that you don't get overwhelmed by image management. It can become overwhelming and distract you from your focus.

October 4th Pluto goes direct in Capricorn

Time to shine in business again; forge forward now. The cleanup is over; it is now time to open pathways for new money to come your way.

October 13th Mercury goes retrograde in Scorpio for a couple of weeks

Time to face your indiscretions, resentments, or any other hidden issues. Let them find their way to the light; now is the time. It is no longer fashionable to be secretive.

October 16th New Moon in Libra

Time to write your love-interest wish list; remember to make it juicy and romantic.

October 16th Pluto and Saturn in Capricorn are asking you to define power for yourself

Time to remember that, in this moment, we are living two versions of power: The power of perfection, all about tradition and keeping things the same (Saturn); and the power of transformation, all about change and impermanence (Pluto).

October 22nd The Sun moves into Scorpio

Let the light guide you out of darkness.

October 27th Venus enters Libra

Love and relationship come into play here. Trust your attraction to lead you to a place where you may love without having to scotch-tape yourself to the person.

October 27th Mercury retrograde backs into Libra until Nov. 3rd

Do what you can to reconcile miscommunication with loved ones. Now is the time!

October 31st "Blue Moon" Full Moon in Taurus

According to Druid tradition, this is a time when a woman may ask her boyfriend to become her husband and he must say "yes!" Remember, it is Halloween, so make sure he is who you think he is; he could be wearing a mask! Uranus retrograde conjunct the Moon in Taurus, watch out for explosive feminine energy.

Low Vitality October 8th and 9th

Get rest; it's time to nurture yourself. Get a massage.

Super Sensitivity October 20th and 21st

Don't let yourself get caught up with mass-consciousness thinking. Stay in your own thoughts and all will be well!

SUNDAY	MONDAY	TUESDAY	WEDNESDAY	THURSDAY	FRIDAY	SATURDAY
				1 ♂♅♀♆℞ ○ 9° ♈ 08' 2:06 PM 3. Celebrate ... Go to a concert today.	2 ♂♅♀♆℞ ☽ V/C 10:47 PM ♀→♍ 1:47 PM 4. Re-organize your workspace.	3 ♂♅♀♆℞ ☽→♉ 8:13 AM 5. There is adventure to be had today.
4 ♂♅♆℞ ♇SD 22° ♑ 29' 6:32AM 6. Make your health a top priority.	5 ♂♅♆℞ ☽ V/C 10:40 AM ☽→♊ 9:03 PM 7. Share your wisdom today.	6 ♂♅♆℞ 8. Prosperity loves to go shopping.	7 ♂♅♆℞ ☽ V/C 6:56 PM 9. People may seem more sensitive.	8 ♂♅♆℞ ▼ ☽→♋ 8:46 AM 10. Recognize what good you have done.	9 ♂♅♆℞ ▼ 3. Gather friends to play a sport.	10 ♂♅♆℞ ☽ V/C 9:03 AM ☽→♌ 5:24 PM 4. Clear your space, set boundaries.
11 ♂♅♆℞ 5. A good day to get lots done.	12 ♂♅♆℞ ☽ V/C 7:29 AM ☽→♍ 9:55 PM 6. Are you feeling romantic today?	13 ☿♂♅♆℞ ☿℞ 11° ♏ 40' 6:05 PM 7. Find time for quiet introspection.	14 ☿♂♅♆℞ ☽ V/C 3:46 PM ☽→♎ 10:54 PM 8. Abundance is our birthright.	15 ☿♂♅♆℞ 9. Where can you be of service?	16 ☿♂♅♆℞ ● 23° ♎ 53' 12:31 PM ☽ V/C 3:11 PM ☽→♏ 10:06 PM 10. Practice self-reliance today.	17 ☿♂♅♆℞ 11. Breathe. Feel empowered.
18 ☿♂♅♆℞ ☽ V/C 2:42 PM ☽→♐ 9:43 PM 3. Live today with a childlike wonder.	19 ☿♂♅♆℞ 5. Change really is your friend.	20 ☿♂♅♆℞ ▲ ☽ V/C 8:37 PM ☽→♑ 11:44 PM 6. Share a smile, share love.	21 ☿♂♅♆℞ ▲ 7. Clear thinking = easy discernment.	22 ☿♂♅♆℞ ☉→♏ 3:59 PM ☽ V/C 9:34 PM 8. Accept your power and manifest.	23 ☿♂♅♆℞ ☽→♒ 5:16 AM 9. Say an extra prayer for the earth.	24 ☿♂♅♆℞ ☽ V/C 2:53 PM 10. Write a new goal list.
25 ☿♂♅♆℞ ☽→♓ 2:19 PM 2. A highly intuitive day. Trust it.	26 ☿♂♅♆℞ 3. Be imaginative, be creative.	27 ☿♂♅♆℞ ☽ V/C 5:45 PM ☿℞→♎ 6:33 PM ♀→♎ 6:41 PM 4. Apply what you know.	28 ☿♂♅♆℞ ☽→♈ 1:45 AM 5. Curiosity opens many pathways.	29 ☿♂♅♆℞ 6. Add beauty to your home.	30 ☿♂♅♆℞ ☽ V/C 9:12 AM ☽→♉ 2:19 PM 7. Mysteries may be unfolding today.	31 ☿♂♅♆℞ **Halloween** ○ 8° ♉ 38' 7:50 AM 8. Sound manifests prosperity.

♈ Aries
♉ Taurus
♊ Gemini
♋ Cancer
♌ Leo
♍ Virgo
♎ Libra
♏ Scorpio
♐ Sagittarius
♑ Capricorn
♒ Aquarius
♓ Pisces
☉ Sun
☽ Moon
☿ Mercury
♀ Venus
♂ Mars
♃ Jupiter
♄ Saturn
♅ Uranus
♆ Neptune
♇ Pluto
⚷ Chiron
→ Enters
V/C Void-of-Course
℞ Retrograde
SD Stationary Direct
▲ Super Sensitivity
▼ Low Vitality
2. Balance
3. Fun
4. Structure
5. Action
6. Love
7. Learning
8. Money
9. Spirituality
10. Visionary
11. Completion

Full Moon in Aries

October 1st, 2:06 PM

When the Sun is Opposite the Moon

Full moons are always in opposition to the Sun. This creates a feeling of tension between where you want to shine and how your feelings are flowing on a sensory level about the Sun's directive. The two forces seem like they are working against each other, yet they are on the same team displaying different techniques to obtain the same mission. The Aries/Libra polarity creates tension between "I Am" and "We Are".

Aries Goddess

Heqet, the Fertility Goddess of the early dynastic period of Egypt, is often depicted on the amulets of pregnant women as a frog sitting on a lotus. Associated with germination of corn following the flooding of the Nile (when frogs were most prolific), and with the final stages of childbirth, she is said to breathe the "breath of life" into the bodies of newborn children who are formed on the potter's wheel of her partner Khnum. It was she who breathed life into Horus, in the myth of Isis and Osiris.

The moonlight is now shining on you as you take your self-confidence and self-awareness to a new level. Is it time for you to take on a new role within your community? Have you developed new knowledge, skills, and qualities that you're ready to try out? Ask Heqet to assist you through the stages from tadpole to adult, as you lose your tail and develop your sea legs.

Build Your Altar

Colors	Red, black, coral
Numerology	3 – Time to celebrate and dance the dance of life
Tarot Card	Tower – Release from a stuck place, major breakthrough
Gemstones	Diamond, red jasper, coral, obsidian
Plant remedy	Oak, pomegranate – Planting and rooting new life
Fragrance	Ginger – The ability to ingest and digest life

Moon Notes

Full Moon 9° Aries 08' 2:06 PM
Full Moons are about moving beyond blocks and setting yourself free.

Element
Fire – Igniting, dissolving, accelerating, cleansing, advancing awareness, impatience, leadership, passion, and vitality.

Statement I Am
Body Head
Mind Impulsive
Spirit Leadership
3rd House Moon
I Speak/I Am

Umbrella Energy
How you get the word out and the message behind the words.

Choice Points
Opportunity   Reinvigorate
Challenge   Distortion

Sabian Symbol
A Teacher Gives New Symbolic Forms To Traditional Images

Potential
Moving outside of the box.

CLEARING THE SLATE

**ARIES FULL MOON
OCTOBER 1ST**

Sixty hours before the full moon negative traits connected to the astro-sign might become activated to trigger what needs to be released during the full moon phase. You may notice a sudden need to be first or impatience that could lead to anger or arrogance. Make a list, look in the mirror, and for each negative trait, tell yourself *I am sorry, I forgive you, thank you for your awareness,* and *I love you.*

ARIES VICTORIES & CHALLENGES

Say all of the statements in this section out loud. Then, underline the phrase that means the most to you. Use the phrase as your affirmation for releasing throughout this moon phase.

Today, I let go. I trust that whatever breaks down or breaks through is a blessing in disguise for me. I make a commitment to allow myself to be spontaneous and live in the moment. I know the unexpected is a blessing for me and a way for me to make a breakthrough out of my limitations. I am aware that I am resistant to change. I know I must make changes and am too stubborn to take the appropriate action myself to change. I have built many walls of false protection around me, guarding me and blocking me from the reality that change is a constant. I have freeze-framed my life and desire support to update myself. I have allowed my fear of change to become my false motto and my life is at a standstill. I am unwilling to use any more energy to perpetuate my resistance. I know that continuing to cling to the past is a waste of my energy. I can no longer put things off that delay my process. I feel the breaking down of form. I trust that all changes are in my favor. All changes lead me to golden opportunities. I release false pride. I release false foundations. I release false authorities. In so doing, I allow for everything to crumble around me so I can see that my true strength is within and I will build my life from the inside out.

I am ready for new experiences. I am ready for the unexpected. I am willing to have an event occur so I can become activated towards my breakthrough. I am ready for the power of now. I know being spontaneous will bring me to true joy. I know if I ride this carrier wave it will take me to a place far beyond my scope of limited thinking. I know the will of God works in my favor and knows more than I do in any given moment.

Aries Homework

Now you are ready to take a personal inventory on behaviors such as impatience, talking over people, brat attacks, and starting every sentence with "I."

This is a time when the light becomes a prisoner of polarized forces. This diminishing light begins its yearly sojourn beneath the surface, asking us to balance light and dark by mastering the concept of equilibrium. Equilibrium is the Law of Harmony, where we attempt to reach a state of achievement by combining paradoxical fields that break the crystallization of polarity. Spend time looking for increasing and decreasing fields of light around you.

GRATITUDE LIST

Keep this list active throughout the moon cycle. This will bring you to a level of completion so that a new cycle of opportunity can occur in your life. Be prepared for miracles!

TAROT

Ask the question out loud, then draw a card. You may wish to draw it or paste a copy of it here. Then write down what you feel it might be telling you, in response to the question. Use the glossary in the appendix and record here anything about the card that captures your attention. You may wish to come back throughout the moon cycle to meditate or journal more on the card.

How is my spirit supporting my releasing?

RELEASING LIST

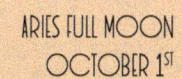
ARIES FULL MOON
OCTOBER 1ST

Say this statement out loud three times before writing your list:

I am a free spiritual being and it is my desire to be free to think and to express myself fully.

From this day forward I resolve to be true – first to myself and my highest self, and then to the highest self in me which is the Source of Love That I Am.

Aries Releasing Ideas

Now is the time to activate a game change in my life, and give up anger as a default, competition and comparison, irritation and struggle, the need to be first, overdoing it and not resting, impatience, impulsiveness, and hostility.

Full Moon in Aries

Your Personal Moon Experience

Fill in the Cosmic Check-In page. Then look up the degree of the Moon on the chart below. Take note of the "I" statement on the outside of the wheel where the Moon is located. Now, locate the same degree on your own chart and make a note of the house and corresponding "I" statement. Go back to the Cosmic Check-In page and circle the two statements from the charts and read what you wrote. This will give you an idea about what to expect from this moon phase on a personal level. For more information on personalizing your *Moon Book*, go to www.BlueMoonAcademy.com and look for *How to Use the Moon Book*.

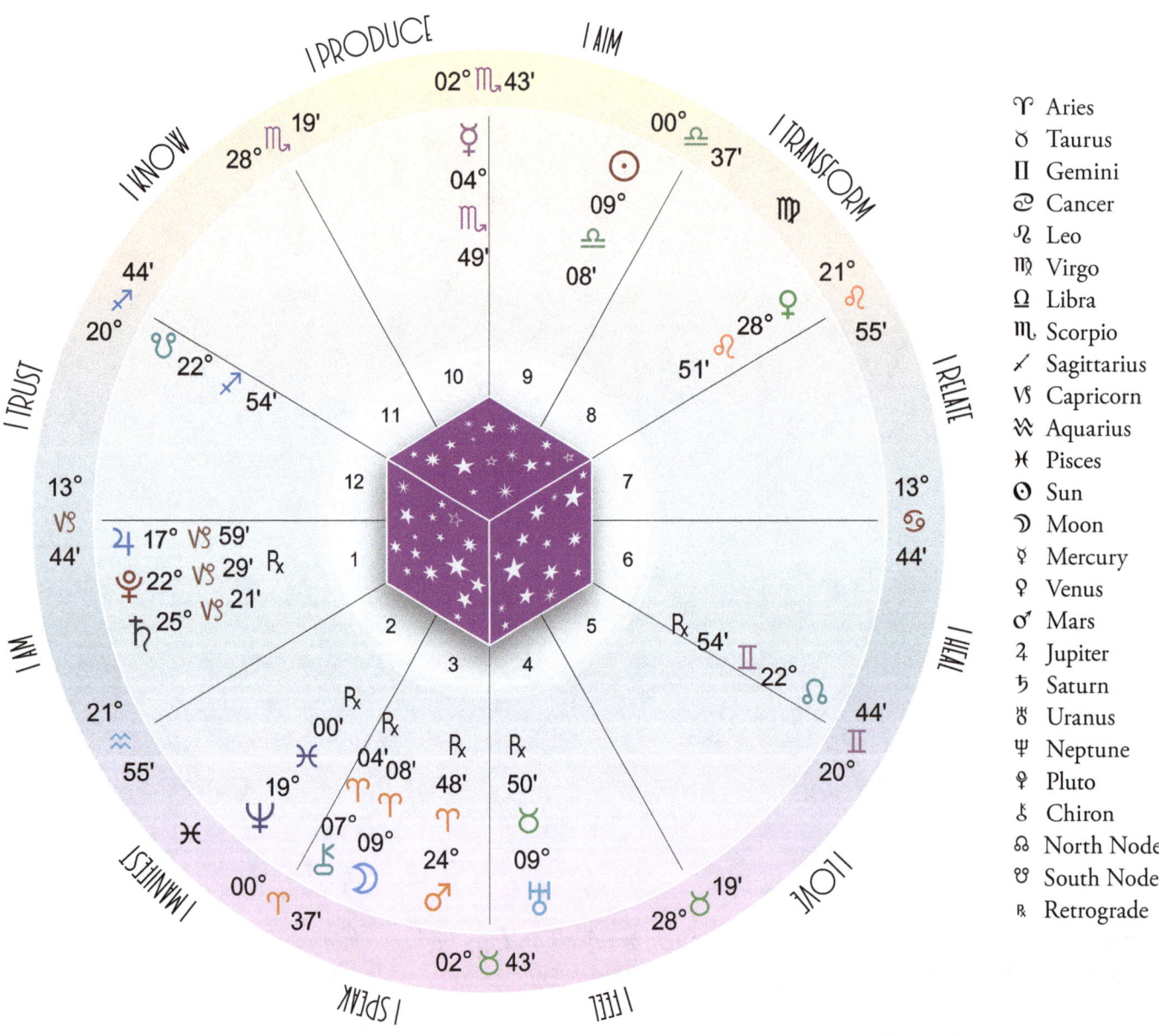

COSMIC CHECK-IN

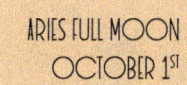
ARIES FULL MOON
OCTOBER 1ST

Take a moment to write a brief phrase for each "I" statement. This activates all areas of your life for this creative cycle.

♈ I Am

♉ I Manifest

♊ I Speak

♋ I Feel

♌ I Love

♍ I Heal

♎ I Relate

♏ I Transform

♐ I Aim

♑ I Produce

♒ I Know

♓ I Trust

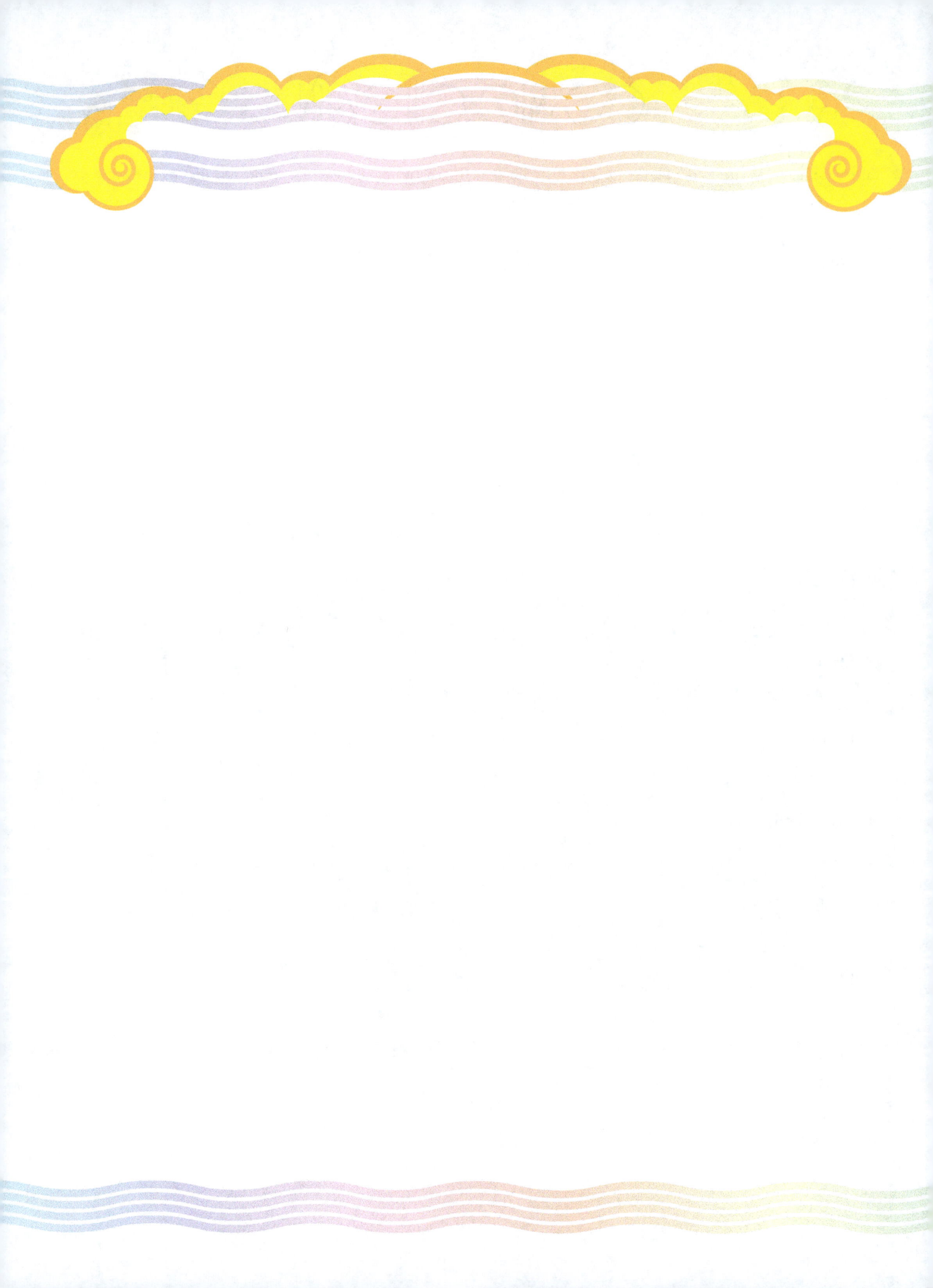

New Moon in Libra

October 16th, 12:31 PM

When the Sun is in Libra

Libra energy gives us the opportunity to bridge the gap between the higher and lower mind; abstract thinking versus concrete thinking. During Libra time, the light and dark forces are in balance and you are given a chance to experience harmony. Harmony occurs when you keep your polarities in motion and put paradox to rest, thus breaking the crystallization of polarity. Now is the time to weigh your values through the light of your Soul. Libra asks you to look at what is increasing and decreasing in your life. Start with friendship, courage, sincerity, and understanding, and keep going until your scale is in motion.

Libra Goddess

The Black Madonna is a goddess archetype associated with Isis, Mary Magdalene, Sara, Kali, and Virgin of Guadalupe. She offers compassion and understanding for the human condition. Black is all colors completely absorbed, and in her blackness she encompasses all and gives solace and miracles to any seeking comfort. She is the protectress of those who are marginalized. She is connected seamlessly to Heaven and Earth, as a fully incarnated woman and mother who has known deep sorrow, passion, joy, and love.

Grant her real life experience equal weight with the images of virginal perfection offered up as ideal, and she will help you have compassion for yourself and others experiencing the struggle of living and relating.

Build Your Altar

Colors Pink, green
Numerology 10 – Innovation is the answer today
Tarot Card Justice – The Law of Cause and Effect
Gemstones Jade, rose quartz
Plant Remedy Olive trees – Stamina
Fragrance Eucalyptus – Clarity of breath

Moon Notes

New Moon 23° Libra 53' 12:31 PM
New Moons are about opening new pathways for prosperity.

Element
Air – The breath of life that allows the mind to achieve new insights and fresh perspectives, abstract dreaming, freedom from attachments, codes of intelligence, and academic applications.

Statement I Relate
Body Kidneys
Mind Social
Spirit Peace

10th House Moon
I Produce/I Relate

Umbrella Energy
Your approach to status, career, honor, and prestige, and why you chose your father.

Choice Points
Opportunity   Curiosity
Challenge   Intrusion

Sabian Symbol
A Third Wing On The Left Side Of A Butterfly

Potential
Striving for balance when something from the past is out of order.

LIBRA VICTORIES & CHALLENGES

LIBRA NEW MOON OCTOBER 16TH

Say all of the statements in this section out loud. Then, underline the phrase that means the most to you. Use the phrase as your affirmation for manifesting throughout this moon phase.

I feel the call of the higher worlds awakening me to a new vibration. This call is to move beyond judgment and move to a place of acceptance, understanding, unconditional confidence, and love. I am at a place in my life where I can embrace the world of acceptance and wholeness, because I have birthed myself anew, beyond the imprisonment and crystallization of polarity and righteousness. My black and white worlds of right and wrong have integrated and blended into gray, the color of wisdom, where true knowledge exists. Knowledge simply is, and the need for proof does not exist where wisdom lives.

The only requirement is experience. I know that everything that comes before me is a direct reflection of my own experience and, in embracing this concept, I can now receive the gift of infinite awareness. I am in a place of awareness that came before and goes beyond where good and evil exist. I have within me, the presence of unconditional confidence to go where true love lives. I no longer need to prove myself. I am now simply being myself. I release the need to be right and accept the right to BE. I no longer need to be forgiven, because I am neither wrong nor right. I no longer need to define myself. Acceptance has no reason for defense. I no longer need to be guilty; duty motivation is no longer a reality. I know that where there is judgment, there is separation. I know understanding unifies. I accept the call of the higher worlds and express myself freely and fully without fear of judgment. I accept myself as I am, so I can learn what I can become.

Libra Homework

Libras manifest best through the legal industry, beauty industry, diplomatic service, match-making, urban development, mediation, feng shui, spa ownership, clutter-busting and space clearing, romance writing, wedding consulting, fashion design, and as librarians.

It is time to weigh and measure the values of relationship, friendship, courage, sensitivity, sincerity, and understanding. Look at what is increasing and what is decreasing in these areas.

VICTORY LIST

Acknowledge what you have overcome. Keep this list active during this moon cycle. Honoring victory allows you to accept success.

TAROT

Ask the question out loud, then draw a card. You may wish to draw it or paste a copy of it here. Then write down what you feel it might be telling you, in response to the question. Use the glossary in the appendix and record here anything about the card that captures your attention. You may wish to come back throughout the moon cycle to meditate or journal more on the card.

How is my mind supporting my manifesting?

MANIFESTING LIST

LIBRA NEW MOON OCTOBER 16TH

This or something better than this comes to me in an easy and pleasurable way, for the good of all concerned. Thank you, Universe!

Libra Manifesting Ideas

Now is the time to focus on manifesting relationships, wholeness, being loving, lovable, and loved, living life as an art form, balance and equality, integrity, accuracy, diplomacy, and peace.

New Moon in Libra

Your Personal Moon Experience

Fill in the Cosmic Check-In page. Then look up the degree of the Moon on the chart below. Take note of the "I" statement on the outside of the wheel where the Moon is located. Now, locate the same degree on your own chart and make a note of the house and corresponding "I" statement. Go back to the Cosmic Check-In page and circle the two statements from the charts and read what you wrote. This will give you an idea about what to expect from this moon phase on a personal level. For more information on personalizing your *Moon Book*, go to www.BlueMoonAcademy.com and look for *How to Use the Moon Book*.

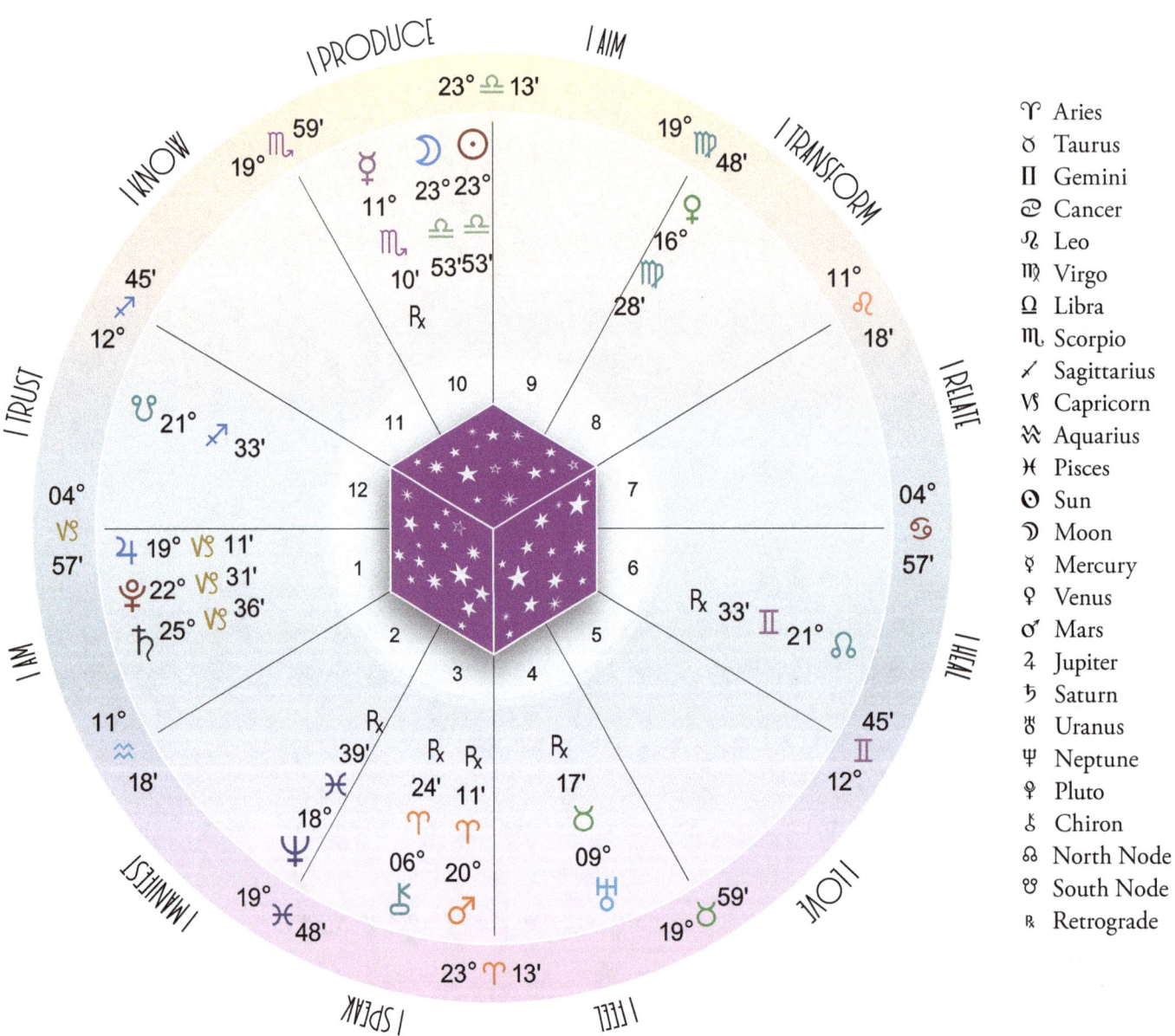

COSMIC CHECK-IN

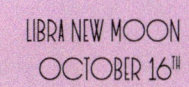

LIBRA NEW MOON
OCTOBER 16TH

Take a moment to write a brief phrase for each "I" statement. This activates all areas of your life for this creative cycle.

♎ I Relate

♏ I Transform

♐ I Aim

♑ I Produce

♒ I Know

♓ I Trust

♈ I Am

♉ I Manifest

♊ I Speak

♋ I Feel

♌ I Love

♍ I Heal

FULL MOON IN TAURUS

October 31st, 7:50 AM

When the Sun is Opposite the Moon

Full moons are always in opposition to the Sun. This creates a feeling of tension between where you want to shine and how your feelings are flowing on a sensory level about the Sun's directive. The two forces seem like they are working against each other, yet they are on the same team displaying different techniques to obtain the same mission. The Taurus/Scorpio polarity creates tension between "my" money and "our" money.

Taurus Goddess

The Roman Goddess of Abundance and Opportunity, Copia, invites you to drink deeply from her overflowing horn of plenty. As you harvest the bounties of your desires from the seeds you planted last Spring, thank Copia for the increase in your abundance factor! There is no greater prayer than the act of giving thanks.

During this Taurus moon, let receptivity and gratitude be in your attitude and actions! With open hands and heart, ask for Copia's presence at your table, and allow her to fill your cup with blessings. Encourage your gratitude to expand and generously influence all with whom you interact.

Build Your Altar

Colors Scarlet, earth tones
Numerology 8 – Sound manifests
Tarot Card Hierophant – Spiritual authority
Gemstones Red coral, red agate, garnet
Plant remedy Angelica – Connecting Heaven and Earth
Fragrance Rose – Opening the heart

Moon Notes

Full Moon 8° Taurus 38' 7:50 AM
Full Moons are about moving beyond blocks and setting yourself free.

Element
Earth – Practical, determined, structured, enduring, stubborn, traditional, stable, and stuck inside the box.

Statement I Manifest
Body Neck
Mind Collector
Spirit Accumulation

6th House Moon
I Heal/I Manifest

Umbrella Energy
The way you manage your body and its appearance.

Choice Points
Opportunity Loving Intent
Challenge Commercialism

Sabian Symbol
A Christmas Tree Is Decorated And Shines In The Darkness

Potential
There is beauty and light at the end of the tunnel.

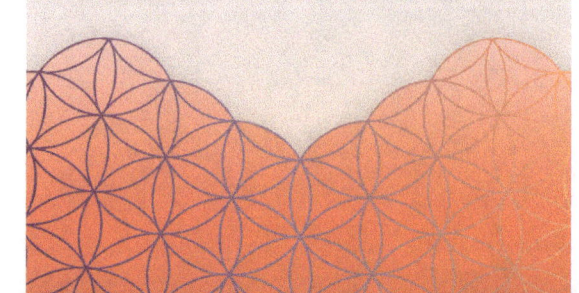

Clearing the Slate

TAURUS FULL MOON OCTOBER 31ST

Sixty hours before the full moon negative traits connected to the astro-sign might become activated to trigger what needs to be released during the full moon phase. You may notice a sudden unwillingness to share or find yourself being stubborn, wasteful, or resisting change. Make a list, look in the mirror, and for each negative trait, tell yourself *I am sorry, I forgive you, thank you for your awareness,* and *I love you.*

Taurus Victories & Challenges

Say all of the statements in this section out loud. Then, underline the phrase that means the most to you. Use the phrase as your affirmation for releasing throughout this moon phase.

Everything is possible for me today. My possibilities are endless. I have the power within me to make all of my dreams come true. I have the tools to make my talent a reality. I have the power to identify with my talent. Today, I focus my attention and intention on manifesting with my talent and, in so doing, I transform my ideas into reality. I recognize the part of me that is connected to the cosmic source of ideas and I express that source within me to manifest my creative power. I see my possibilities and act on them today. I am the creative power. I am all-knowing. I am an individual. There is no one else like me. I can manifest anything I desire. I intend it, I allow it, so be it.

Rules for Manifesting

Know what you want. Write it down. Say it out loud. Recognize that because you thought it, it can be so. Release your limiting beliefs. Override your limiting beliefs with power statements. Act as if you have already manifested your idea. Lastly, value yourself!

Taurus Homework

Taureans manifest best when buying, selling, and owning real estate, gardening and landscaping, selling and collecting art, manufacturing and selling fine furniture, singing or acting, and as a restaurateur, antique dealer, or interior designer.

The Taurus moon asks us to infuse light into form and, in so doing, the bridge between humanity and divinity is actualized and we can assume our stewardship in the physical world. When we release Spirit into matter, we become open to the idea that accumulation and actualization set us free to experience the abundance available to us here on Earth. Go shopping!

GRATITUDE LIST

Keep this list active throughout the moon cycle. This will bring you to a level of completion so that a new cycle of opportunity can occur in your life. Be prepared for miracles!

TAROT

Ask the question out loud, then draw a card. You may wish to draw it or paste a copy of it here. Then write down what you feel it might be telling you, in response to the question. Use the glossary in the appendix and record here anything about the card that captures your attention. You may wish to come back throughout the moon cycle to meditate or journal more on the card.

How is my body supporting my releasing?

RELEASING LIST

**TAURUS FULL MOON
OCTOBER 31ST**

Say this statement out loud three times before writing your list:

I am a free spiritual being and it is my desire to be free to think and to express myself fully.

From this day forward I resolve to be true – first to myself and my highest self, and then to the highest self in me which is the Source of Love That I Am.

Taurus Releasing Ideas

Now is the time to activate a game change in my life, and give up envy, financial insecurity, being stubborn, hoarding, addictive spending, not feeling valuable, and fear of change.

Full Moon in Taurus

Your Personal Moon Experience

Fill in the Cosmic Check-In page. Then look up the degree of the Moon on the chart below. Take note of the "I" statement on the outside of the wheel where the Moon is located. Now, locate the same degree on your own chart and make a note of the house and corresponding "I" statement. Go back to the Cosmic Check-In page and circle the two statements from the charts and read what you wrote. This will give you an idea about what to expect from this moon phase on a personal level. For more information on personalizing your *Moon Book*, go to www.BlueMoonAcademy.com and look for *How to Use the Moon Book*.

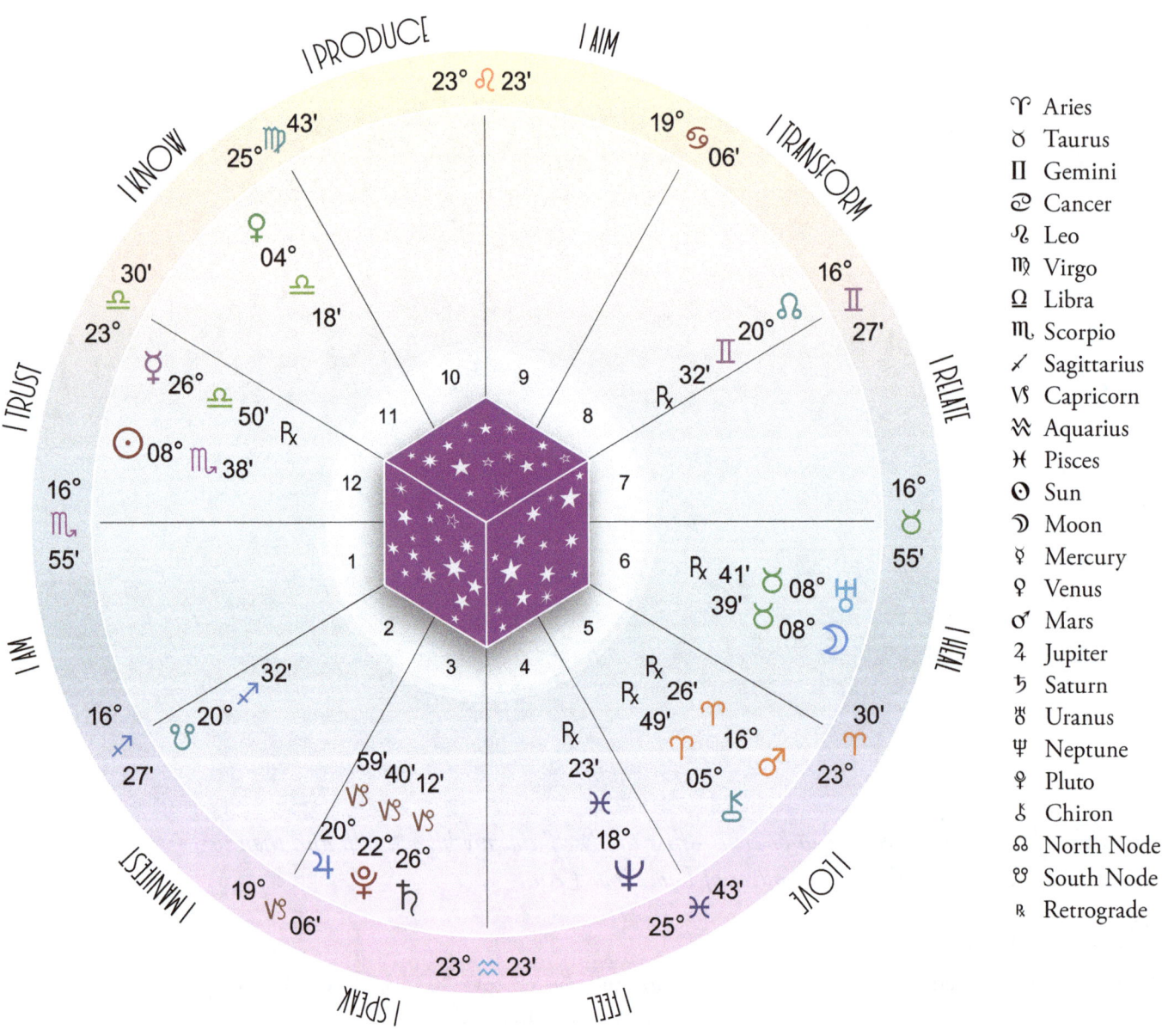

COSMIC CHECK-IN

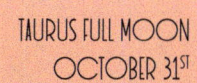

TAURUS FULL MOON
OCTOBER 31ST

Take a moment to write a brief phrase for each "I" statement. This activates all areas of your life for this creative cycle.

♉ I Manifest

♊ I Speak

♋ I Feel

♌ I Love

♍ I Heal

♎ I Relate

♏ I Transform

♐ I Aim

♑ I Produce

♒ I Know

♓ I Trust

♈ I Am

NOVEMBER

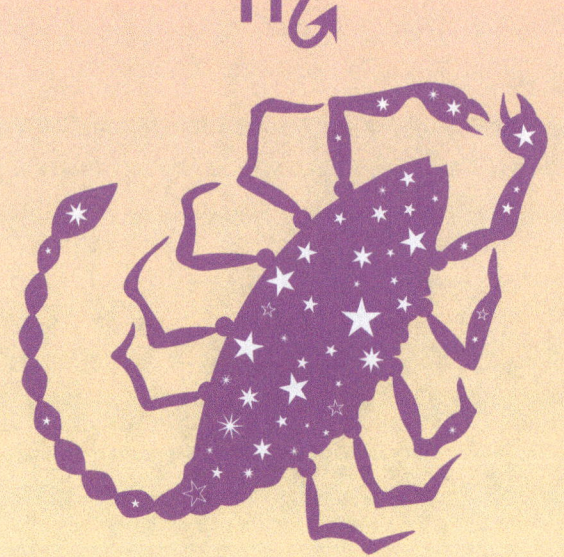

November 3rd Mercury goes out of retrograde in Libra

Time to relax the mind. Now is the time to be mindful, and not mental.

November 10th Mercury enters Scorpio

Notice how many times you think about sex every day.

November 13th Mars goes direct in Aries

The warring period is over; it's time to move forward as the champion you are.

November 14th New Moon in Scorpio

Time to open yourself to new ways of living life.

November 14th Jupiter and Pluto in Capricorn through the end of the month

Grand awakening asking us to be open to new and more beneficial financial awareness. Be willing to see what is new and different and all will be well.

November 21st Venus enters Scorpio

Expect very intense sex.

November 21st the Sun enters Sagittarius

It's party time! Optimism is in the air; let it shower you with wondrous thoughts.

November 28th Neptune goes direct in Pisces

Reality is very healing right now.

November 30th Full Moon in Gemini – Lunar Eclipse

A 19-year string gets pulled out of your consciousness today. Let it be!

November 30th Saturn, Pluto, and Jupiter are connected in Capricorn

Beware of fear tactics manipulating you into making the wrong change. Trust the eclipse to show you the way. Remember, Jupiter is involved, so it can't be too bad.

Low Vitality November 4th-5th

If you feel something is ending, let it end.

Super Sensitivity November 17th and 18th

Time to remember to buy yourself the first holiday gift. This will keep you free from holiday chaos.

SUNDAY	MONDAY	TUESDAY	WEDNESDAY	THURSDAY	FRIDAY	SATURDAY
1 ☿♂♅♆℞ PST begins 2:00 AM ☽ V/C 6:29 PM 8. Make money work for you.	2 ☿♂♅♆℞ ☽→♊ 2:00 AM 9. Meditation serves a higher purpose.	3 ♂♅♆℞ ☿SD 25°♎54' 9:50 AM 10. Be a visionary.	4 ♂♅♆℞▼ ☽ V/C 5:48 AM ☽→♋ 1:45 PM 11. Take in the vastness today.	5 ♂♅♆℞▼ 3. Go to Disneyland and dream big.	6 ♂♅♆℞ ☽ V/C 5:26 PM ☽→♌ 11:18 PM 4. Put things back in order.	7 ♂♅♆℞ 5. Time for a road trip.
8 ♂♅♆℞ 6. Invite someone out for lunch.	9 ♂♅♆℞ ☽ V/C 3:04 AM ☽→♍ 5:30 AM 7. Analytical skills serve you well.	10 ♂♅♆℞ ☿→♏ 1:55 PM 8. Lead by example.	11 ♂♅♆℞ ☽ V/C 2:58 AM ☽→♎ 8:09 AM 9. Spirit is always with you.	12 ♂♅♆℞ 10. What's new and trending?	13 ♅♆℞ ☽ V/C 3:32 AM ☽→♏ 8:18 AM ♂SD 15°♈14' 4:36 PM 11. Recognize the gift of wholeness.	14 ♅♆℞ ● 23° ♏ 18' 9:07 PM 3. Be inspired by the art you see.
15 ♅♆℞ ☽ V/C 3:12 AM ☽→♐ 7:46 AM 4. The best plans use logic today.	16 ♅♆℞ ☽ V/C 11:54 PM 5. Be dynamic and go with the flow.	17 ♅♆℞▲ ☽→♑ 8:35 AM 6. Open your heart to a new love.	18 ♅♆℞▲ 7. Through introspection find peace.	19 ♅♆℞ ☽ V/C 8:29 AM ☽→♒ 12:25 PM 8. Become friends with money.	20 ♅♆℞ ☽ V/C 4:48 PM 9. For stability use Divine resources.	21 ♅♆℞ ♀→♏ 5:21 AM ☉→♐ 12:39 PM ☽→♓ 8:06 PM 10. Expect an eye-opening day.
22 ♅♆℞ 2. Balance the facts with intuition.	23 ♅♆℞ 3. See happy possibilities everywhere.	24 ♅♆℞ ☽ V/C 2:44 AM ☽→♈ 7:05 AM 4. Dependability is a good virtue.	25 ♅♆℞ 5. Be willing to make new plans.	26 ♅♆℞ **Thanksgiving** ☽ V/C 3:45 PM ☽→♉ 7:44 PM 6. Love opens the door to more love.	27 ♅♆℞ 7. Learn by hearing other viewpoints.	28 ♅℞ ♆SD 18°♓10' 4:36 PM 8. Successful actions bring victory.
29 ♅℞ ☽ V/C 4:48 AM ☽→♊ 8:16 AM 9. Send Divine blessings to humanity.	30 ♅℞ ○ 8° ♊ 38' 1:30 AM **Lunar Eclipse** 8° ♊ 45' 1:43 AM ☽ V/C 8:21 PM 10. Take stock of completed goals.					

♈ Aries	♍ Virgo	♒ Aquarius	♀ Venus	♆ Neptune	V/C Void-of-Course	2. Balance	7. Learning
♉ Taurus	♎ Libra	♓ Pisces	♂ Mars	♇ Pluto	℞ Retrograde	3. Fun	8. Money
♊ Gemini	♏ Scorpio	☉ Sun	♃ Jupiter	⚷ Chiron	SD Stationary Direct	4. Structure	9. Spirituality
♋ Cancer	♐ Sagittarius	☽ Moon	♄ Saturn	→ Enters	▲ Super Sensitivity	5. Action	10. Visionary
♌ Leo	♑ Capricorn	☿ Mercury	♅ Uranus		▼ Low Vitality	6. Love	11. Completion

New Moon in Scorpio

November 14th, 9:07 PM

When the Sun is in Scorpio

Scorpio is the symbol of darkness which heralds the decline of the Sun in Autumn. As we watch all of nature going through a slow death, we begin to recognize the qualities of Scorpio's subtlety and depth, and the hidden forces that threaten those who live only on the surface. Scorpio rules all of the things that you try to keep hidden: ambition, pride, and fear. When you face these self-imposed limits on yourself, you take on the true power of transformation.

Scorpio Goddess

Scorpio moons ask you to delve deep into your Soul. There's no better companion in this process than Inanna, who journeyed to the Underworld and relinquished her power and possessions, one-at-a-time at each of seven gates, until she was stripped bare to her essential self, without any trappings or embellishments.

Ask your soul sister Inanna to accompany you in a candle-lit meditation to release that which you no longer need to carry in each of your seven chakras. Let go of anything encumbering your essential self, anything weighing you down. Connect with the dark, cool Earth and tune into anything that you feel like you've put behind you, but might not have completely released. Allow Inanna to empty your backpack and lighten your load, so you can rise and be reborn anew.

Build Your Altar

Colors	Deep red, black, deep purple
Numerology	3 – Let your creative juices flow!
Tarot Card	Death – Transform, transmute, and transcend
Gemstones	Topaz, smoky quartz, obsidian, jet, onyx
Plant Remedy	Manzanita – Being open to transforming cycles
Fragrance	Sandalwood – Awakens your sensuality

Moon Notes

New Moon 23° Scorpio 18' 9:07 PM
New Moons are about opening new pathways for prosperity.

Element
Water – Taking the line of least resistance, going with the flow, creativity at its best, secretive, sensual, glamorous, psychic, magnetic, escaping reality, a healer, an actor/actress.

Statement I Transform
Body Reproductive Organs
Mind Investigation
Spirit Transformation
5th House Moon
I Love/I Transform

Umbrella Energy
The way you love and how you want to be loved.

Choice Points
Opportunity   Grounded Instruction
Challenge   Condescension

Sabian Symbol
Crowds Coming Down The Mountain To Listen To One Inspired Man

Potential
New learning lessons coming your way.

SCORPIO VICTORIES & CHALLENGES

SCORPIO NEW MOON NOVEMBER 14TH

Say all of the statements in this section out loud. Then, underline the phrase that means the most to you. Use the phrase as your affirmation for manifesting throughout this moon phase.

"When the student needs to learn, the teacher appears." Today, I recognize that the Law of Reflection is in operation. I have become aware of this through my over-indulgence of judgment and criticism of other people. I am aware that when my judgment is running rampant, I am in need of a teacher who can interpret this judgment as reflection, so I can see my judgments as my teachers and use them to re-interpret myself. I seek counsel with someone who has the ability to listen to me, hear me, and give me the space I need to see myself. I have become confused by spending too much time looking outside of myself for the answers. Perhaps my authority systems, like my religion or my family traditions, no longer serve me and I need to use this confusion to become aware of a new, more self-reliant way to live my life.

The Law of Reflection

Whatever I judge is what I am, what I fear, or what I lack. I make a list of my judgments:

I rewrite each judgment in the form of a question: Am I _____? Do I fear _____? Do I lack _____?

Example 1: I judge Mary's wealth. Do I fear wealth? Do I lack wealth? Am I wealthy in my own way and forgetting to acknowledge my own ability to manifest?

Example 2: I judge John's "be perfect" attitude. Do I fear perfection? Do I lack perfection? Have I forgotten to recognize my own perfection?

In moving through this process, I reconnect to myself and find my own authority today. I send blessings to others whose reflection has so beautifully shown me myself today. I now know and cherish my judgments as my greatest teachers and set myself free today.

Scorpio Homework

Scorpios manifest best by being a private investigator, detective, probate attorney, mystery writer, mythologist, Tarot reader, symbolist, hospice worker, transition counselor, mortician, sex surrogate, or in forensic medicine.

The Scorpio moon cycle asks you to transform. In order to do this you must transmute sex drive into creativity, physical comfort into serving the greater good, money into higher value, fear into light, animosity into understanding, ambition into service to beauty, pride into humility, separation into unity, control into harmony, and power into empowerment.

VICTORY LIST

Acknowledge what you have overcome. Keep this list active during this moon cycle. Honoring victory allows you to accept success.

TAROT

Ask the question out loud, then draw a card. You may wish to draw it or paste a copy of it here. Then write down what you feel it might be telling you, in response to the question. Use the glossary in the appendix and record here anything about the card that captures your attention. You may wish to come back throughout the moon cycle to meditate or journal more on the card.

How is my heart supporting my manifesting?

MANIFESTING LIST

SCORPIO NEW MOON
NOVEMBER 14TH

This or something better than this comes to me in an easy and pleasurable way, for the good of all concerned. Thank you, Universe!

Scorpio Manifesting Ideas

Now is the time to focus on manifesting transformation on all levels, bringing light to the dark, knowing and living cycles, knowing trust as an option, accepting change, accepting my sexuality, knowing sex is natural, knowing sex as good, and knowing sex as creative.

New Moon in Scorpio

Your Personal Moon Experience

Fill in the Cosmic Check-In page. Then look up the degree of the Moon on the chart below. Take note of the "I" statement on the outside of the wheel where the Moon is located. Now, locate the same degree on your own chart and make a note of the house and corresponding "I" statement. Go back to the Cosmic Check-In page and circle the two statements from the charts and read what you wrote. This will give you an idea about what to expect from this moon phase on a personal level. For more information on personalizing your *Moon Book*, go to www.BlueMoonAcademy.com and look for *How to Use the Moon Book*.

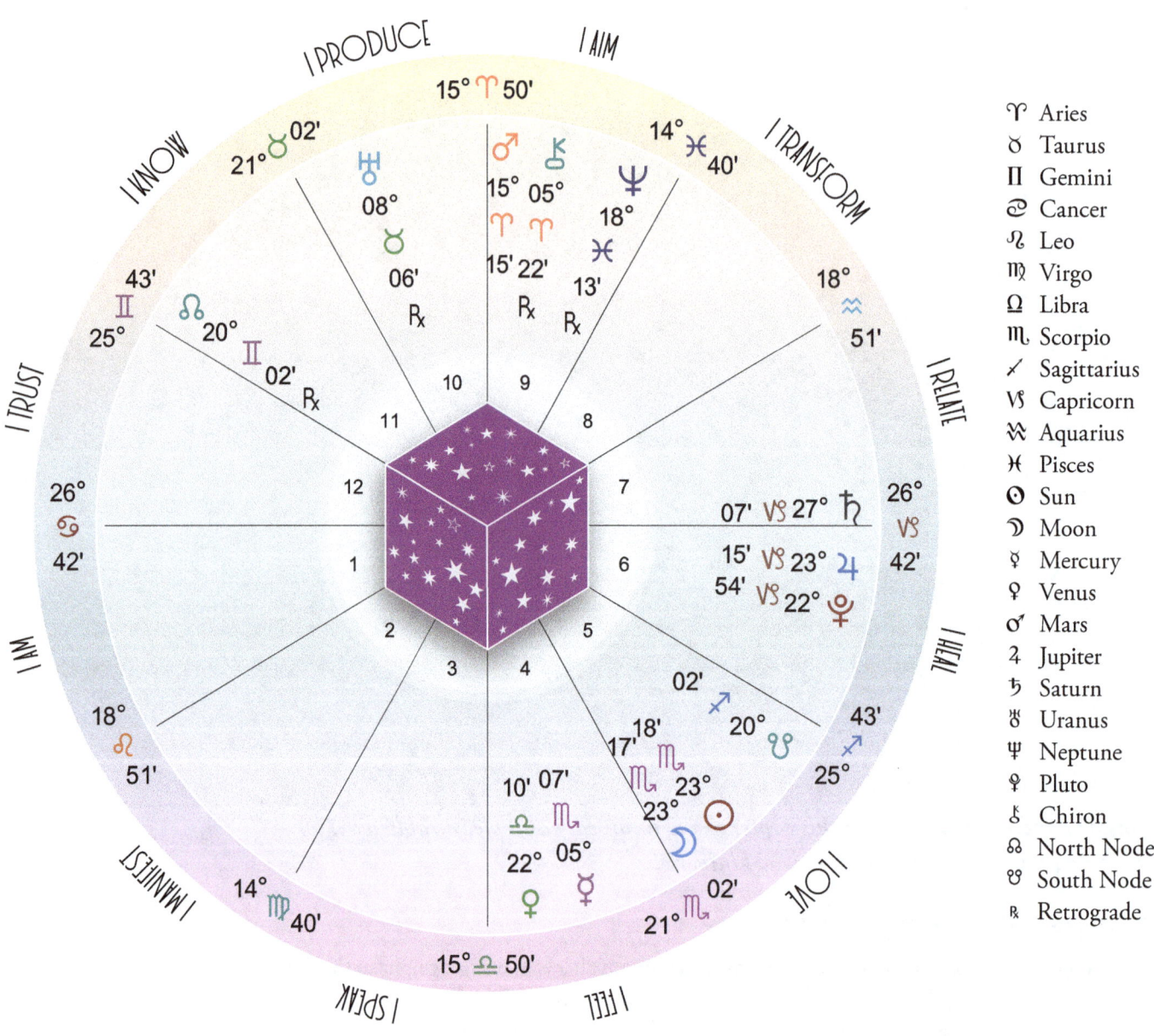

COSMIC CHECK-IN

SCORPIO NEW MOON
NOVEMBER 14TH

Take a moment to write a brief phrase for each "I" statement. This activates all areas of your life for this creative cycle.

♏ I Transform

♐ I Aim

♑ I Produce

♒ I Know

♓ I Trust

♈ I Am

♉ I Manifest

♊ I Speak

♋ I Feel

♌ I Love

♍ I Heal

♎ I Relate

Full Moon in Gemini

November 30th, 1:30 AM

When the Sun is Opposite the Moon

Full moons are always in opposition to the Sun. This creates a feeling of tension between where you want to shine and how your feelings are flowing on a sensory level about the Sun's directive. The two forces seem like they are working against each other, yet they are on the same team displaying different techniques to obtain the same mission. The Gemini/Sagittarius polarity creates tension between community ideas and global thinking.

Gemini Goddess

Saraswati beckons you to withdraw from the party scene and into the quiet, contemplative process to dream your finest creations into being. Goddess of all creative endeavors: writing, art, dance, and music, Saraswati can assist you in your waking hours and in the dreamtime.

Get out your crayons, markers, paints, and pastels, and create a massive mind map with your happiness and fulfillment at the core (your new seedpod). What sprouts from the center? What branches off? Trust the process to generate ideas to rebirth you into joyful action! Post the map where you will see it often so it can serve as an active reminder of who you are and where you're headed!

Build Your Altar

Colors	Bright yellow, orange, multi-colors
Numerology	10 – Take stock of completed goals
Tarot Card	Lovers – Connecting to wholeness
Gemstones	Yellow diamond, citrine, yellow jade, yellow topaz
Plant remedy	Morning Glory – Thinking with your heart, not your head
Fragrance	Iris – The ability to focus the mind

Moon Notes

Lunar Eclipse

Full Moon 8° Gemini 38' 1:30 AM
Full Moons are about moving beyond blocks and setting yourself free.

Element
Air – The breath of life that allows the mind to achieve new insights and fresh perspectives, abstract dreaming, freedom from attachments, codes of intelligence, and academic applications.

Statement I Speak
Body Lungs and Hands
Mind Intellect
Spirit Broadcaster, Messenger

9th House Moon
I Aim/I Speak

Umbrella Energy
The way you approach spirituality, philosophy, journeys, higher knowledge, and inspiration.

Choice Points
Opportunity Readiness
Challenge   Arrogance

Sabian Symbol
A Medieval Archer Stands With The Ease Of One Wholly Sure Of Himself, Bow In Hand, His Quiver Filled With Arrows

Potential
Setting an intention gets you everything you want!

CLEARING THE SLATE

GEMINI FULL MOON NOVEMBER 30TH

Sixty hours before the full moon negative traits connected to the astro-sign might become activated to trigger what needs to be released during the full moon phase. You may notice that you are not listening to others and overriding what others are saying by talking too much. Watch out for gossiping or omitting the truth. Make a list, look in the mirror, and for each negative trait, tell yourself *I am sorry, I forgive you, thank you for your awareness,* and *I love you.*

GEMINI VICTORIES & CHALLENGES

Say all of the statements in this section out loud. Then, underline the phrase that means the most to you. Use the phrase as your affirmation for releasing throughout this moon phase.

Today, I blend my old self with my new self, my physical reality with my spiritual awareness, my positive thoughts with my negative thoughts, my past with my present, my feminine with my masculine, my rewards with my losses, my ups with my downs, and my higher self with my lower self. It is a day for me to refine and fine tune my life by looking at my extremes. I recognize what inspires me and what keeps me stuck. I find my center today by acknowledging my extremes. I am aware that balance comes to those who are able to locate the space in the center of these opposite energy fields.

When I am in my center, my polarities are in motion. Healing cannot occur unless my polarities are moving and I know that healing is motion. I am ready for a healing today. I know that by visiting my opposites, and determining their vast opposition to each other, I can find the paradoxes that I have chosen for myself and begin to heal. I am willing to experiment with this blending of opposites and become the alchemist of my own life. When I blend all aspects of myself, rather than separating them, I can truly become whole. Today is a day to integrate, rather than separate, in order to release the spark of light that stays prisoner when my polarities are in operation. When I find balance, motion occurs and the Law of Harmony takes over, putting paradoxical energies to rest, thus breaking the crystallization of polarity. The Law of Harmony is beauty in motion and promotes the flow of color, light, sound, and movement into form. Balance is a condition that keeps my spark in motion. I become the vertical line in the center of polarity today and carry the secret of balance. Balance cannot be my goal; motion is my goal today. When I am in motion, I can take action to evolve and to express all of myself freely.

Gemini Homework

Sit still and invite silence into your space. Stay quiet and still for at least 5 minutes. During this time take an inventory and see where you have interrupted people in the middle of their sentences. Now is the time to make a conscious effort to allow others the space to express their thoughts. Keep sitting in silence and feel the frustration, while embracing the power of silence.

GRATITUDE LIST

Keep this list active throughout the moon cycle. This will bring you to a level of completion so that a new cycle of opportunity can occur in your life. Be prepared for miracles!

TAROT

Ask the question out loud, then draw a card. You may wish to draw it or paste a copy of it here. Then write down what you feel it might be telling you, in response to the question. Use the glossary in the appendix and record here anything about the card that captures your attention. You may wish to come back throughout the moon cycle to meditate or journal more on the card.

How is my mind supporting my releasing?

RELEASING LIST

GEMINI FULL MOON
NOVEMBER 30TH

Say this statement out loud three times before writing your list:

I am a free spiritual being and it is my desire to be free to think and to express myself fully.

From this day forward I resolve to be true – first to myself and my highest self, and then to the highest self in me which is the Source of Love That I Am.

Gemini Releasing Ideas

Now is the time to activate a game change in my life, and give up my attitude about unfinished business, shallow communication, old files and office clutter, broken communication devices, lies I tell myself, temptation to gossip, restlessness, over-thinking, and vacillation.

Full Moon in Gemini

Your Personal Moon Experience

Fill in the Cosmic Check-In page. Then look up the degree of the Moon on the chart below. Take note of the "I" statement on the outside of the wheel where the Moon is located. Now, locate the same degree on your own chart and make a note of the house and corresponding "I" statement. Go back to the Cosmic Check-In page and circle the two statements from the charts and read what you wrote. This will give you an idea about what to expect from this moon phase on a personal level. For more information on personalizing your *Moon Book*, go to www.BlueMoonAcademy.com and look for *How to Use the Moon Book*.

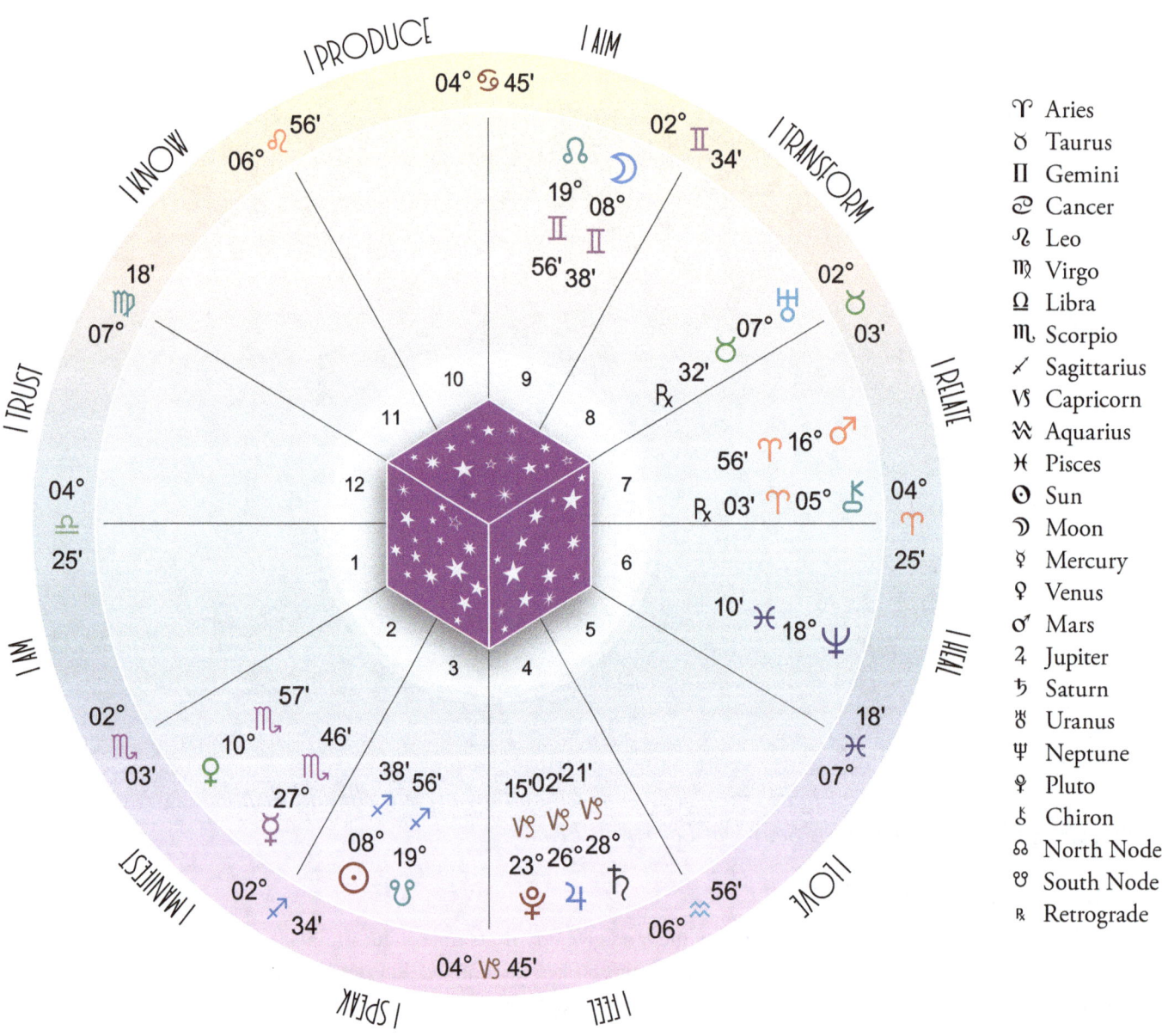

COSMIC CHECK-IN

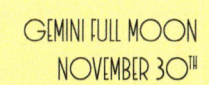
GEMINI FULL MOON
NOVEMBER 30TH

Take a moment to write a brief phrase for each "I" statement. This activates all areas of your life for this creative cycle.

♊ I Speak

♋ I Feel

♌ I Love

♍ I Heal

♎ I Relate

♏ I Transform

♐ I Aim

♑ I Produce

♒ I Know

♓ I Trust

♈ I Am

♉ I Manifest

DECEMBER

December 1st Mercury enters Sagittarius

Avoid speaking abruptly, by asking yourself: is what I'm about to say kind, truthful, and necessary?

December 14th New Moon in Sagittarius – Solar Eclipse

A 19-year pattern leftover from 2001 will release with the eclipse and bring forward an entirely new set of goals. Remember to write them down on your wish list.

December 14th the Sun, Moon, Mercury, and the South Node all connected in Sagittarius

Your inner and outer reality meet up in a conversation no longer relevant. Update yourself and speak from the present.

December 14th Pluto, Jupiter, Saturn connected in Capricorn

Power plays are in the air. Focus on the good fortune and all will be well.

December 15th Venus enters Sagittarius

Have a holiday party. It will be a blast!

December 16th Saturn moves into Aquarius

Expect to feel free at last, giving your mind a chance to get out of the box.

December 20th Mercury enters Capricorn

Speak your truth.

December 19th Jupiter enters Sagittarius

Dance on the tabletops, freedom at last! Your inventive mind will now bring you good fortune.

December 21st the Sun enters Capricorn – Winter Solstice

Honor the good you have done this year. Find the ray of light that will guide you now!

December 29th Full Moon in Cancer

Thank your ancestors for all they have given you, in talent and in service to your present family.

December 29th Jupiter and Saturn have, at long last, left Capricorn and have moved into Aquarius

The future is finally showing us a lighter and brighter view.

Low Vitality December 1st, 2nd and 29th-30th

Get rest; stay close to home!

Super Sensitivity December 19th-23rd

Be mindful, not mental, and all will be well.

SUNDAY	MONDAY	TUESDAY	WEDNESDAY	THURSDAY	FRIDAY	SATURDAY
		1 ♅℞ ▼ ☿→♐ 10:51 AM ☽→♋ 7:33 PM 11. Use your Universal connection.	2 ♅℞ ▼ 3. Have a child teach you something.	3 ♅℞ 4. Create a timetable for a project.	4 ♅℞ ☽ V/C 2:28 AM ☽→♌ 4:53 AM 5. What makes you curious?	5 ♅℞ ☽ V/C 2:27 PM 6. Make something beautiful today!
6 ♅℞ ☽→♍ 11:47 AM 7. Explore mystical teachings.	7 ♅℞ 8. Open a new path of prosperity today.	8 ♅℞ ☽ V/C 2:35 PM ☽→♎ 4:02 PM 9. Take time for inner reflection.	9 ♅℞ 10. Modernize your shopping style.	10 ♅℞ ☽ V/C 4:56 PM ☽→♏ 5:58 PM 11. The Universe has your back.	11 ♅℞ 3. Have a holiday party with friends.	12 ♅℞ ☽ V/C 5:57 PM ☽→♐ 6:40 PM 4. Grounding is important today.
13 ♅℞ 5. Being flexible is a valuable skill.	14 ♅℞ ▲ **Solar Eclipse** 23° ♐ 06' 8:13 AM ☽ V/C 8:16 AM ● 23° ♐ 08' 8:17 AM ☽→♑ 7:35 PM 6. Be love wherever you go.	15 ♅℞ ▲ ♀→♐ 8:21 AM 7. See the wisdom behind the event.	16 ♅℞ ♄→♒ 9:03 PM ☽ V/C 9:34 PM ☽→♒ 10:27 PM 8. Go shopping – circulate money.	17 ♅℞ 9. Pray for the well-being of all.	18 ♅℞ 10. A lot can get done today.	19 ♅℞ ▲ ☽ V/C 12:44 AM ☽→♓ 4:39 AM ♃→♒ 5:07 AM 11. Empower greatness in others.
20 ♅℞ ▲ ☿→♑ 3:07 PM 3. Turn on your happy music.	21 ♅℞ ▲ **Winter Solstice** ☉→♑ 2:02 AM ☽ V/C 2:24 AM ☽→♈ 2:33 PM 4. In unity there is strength.	22 ♅℞ ▲ 5. So many choices, put you first.	23 ♅℞ ▲ ☽ V/C 2:50 PM 6. Light the candles and feel the love.	24 ♅℞ ☽→♉ 2:56 AM 7. Embrace the peace of the season.	25 ♅℞ **Christmas** 8. Celebrate abundance with joy.	26 ♅℞ ☽ V/C 3:31 AM ☽→♊ 3:32 PM 9. Share your abundance with others.
27 ♅℞ 10. Notice how far you have come.	28 ♅℞ ☽ V/C 7:00 PM 11. Now, expand your horizons.	29 ♅℞ ▼ ☽→♋ 2:29 AM ○ 8° ♋ 53' 7:29 PM 3. Say yes to any social invitations.	30 ♅℞ ▼ 4. Stand tall, you are trustworthy.	31 ♅℞ **New Year's Eve** ☽ V/C 5:44 AM ☽→♌ 10:57 AM 5. Get ready for the next adventure!		

♈ Aries	♍ Virgo	♒ Aquarius	♀ Venus	♆ Neptune	V/C Void-of-Course	2. Balance	7. Learning
♉ Taurus	♎ Libra	♓ Pisces	♂ Mars	♇ Pluto	℞ Retrograde	3. Fun	8. Money
♊ Gemini	♏ Scorpio	☉ Sun	♃ Jupiter	⚷ Chiron	Ꝺ Stationary Direct	4. Structure	9. Spirituality
♋ Cancer	♐ Sagittarius	☽ Moon	♄ Saturn	→ Enters	▲ Super Sensitivity	5. Action	10. Visionary
♌ Leo	♑ Capricorn	☿ Mercury	♅ Uranus		▼ Low Vitality	6. Love	11. Completion

New Moon in Sagittarius

December 14th, 8:17 AM

When the Sun is in Sagittarius

Now is the time for greater expansion of consciousness. Sagittarius is about exterminating all of the man-eating symbols of our illusions, harmful thoughts, inertia, prejudices, and superstitions that hide behind our excuses. It is truth time, so that the Soul Goal of the Sagittarius can come into being and direct its light toward greater aspiration. Questions to ask yourself at this time are: What is my goal for myself? What is my goal for my nation? What is my goal for humanity? All goals get stimulated during this time.

Sagittarius Goddess

Let Persephone, who chose to stay in the Underworld half of the year and became the Queen of Death, be your guide as you enter the dark time of the year. Harvest is over and you now allow the land to become fallow – plowed, but unseeded. Persephone, in the version of the myth unspoiled by patriarchy, hears the cries of those stuck in purgatory, and is moved to voluntarily guide the anguished toward the completion of their spiritual journeys.

Of Persephone, also known as the maiden Kore, Plato wrote, "She is wise and touches that which is in motion." Where might you be stuck and how can Persephone get you moving in the right direction? What in your life do you seek to transform? Who do you wish to become?

Build Your Altar

Colors	Deep purple, deep blue, turquoise
Numerology	6 – Be love wherever you go
Tarot Card	Temperance – Blending physical and spiritual
Gemstones	Turquoise, lapis
Plant Remedy	Madia – Seeing the target and hitting it
Fragrance	Magnolia – Expanded beauty

Moon Notes

New Moon 23° Sagittarius 06' 8:17 AM
New Moons are about opening new pathways for prosperity.

Element
Fire – Igniting, dissolving, accelerating, cleansing, advancing awareness, impatience, leadership, passion, and vitality.

Statement I Aim
Body Thighs
Mind Philosophical
Spirit Inspiration

12th House Moon
I Trust/I Aim

Umbrella Energy
Determines how you deal with your karma, "unconscious software," and what you will experience in order to attain mastery to complete your karma. It is also about the way you connect to the Divine.

Choice Points
Opportunity   Effortless Advancement
Challenge   Forewarned

Sabian Symbol
A Bluebird, A Sign Of Good Luck And Happiness, Is Standing At The Door Of The House

Potential
Accept the power of the present moment.

SAGITTARIUS VICTORIES & CHALLENGES

SAGITTARIUS NEW MOON
DECEMBER 14TH

Say all of the statements in this section out loud. Then, underline the phrase that means the most to you. Use the phrase as your affirmation for manifesting throughout this moon phase.

Destiny is in my favor today. I know, without a doubt, that I cannot make a wrong turn today. I access my blueprint to ensure perfect timing for all opportunities to be open to me today. I promise to be open to these opportunities, knowing full well that today is my day. I am on time and in time today. My destiny is here and working in my favor. I see all that is available to me today and claim my pathway to success. I pay attention to what comes my way today and know that it is an opening for good fortune to be my reality. I am ready to accept my good fortune now. All I have to do is move in the direction of my truth. I know that my truth is my good fortune. I trust in coincidence and synchronicity to provide me with direction to my destiny. All points of action lead me to my true expression. I can see clearly into my future today with great optimism. I intend it. I allow it. So be it. All is in Divine Order.

Mantra during this Time *(repeat this 10 times out loud)*

"My truth is my good fortune. My timing is perfect. I trust that all that comes to me today is in my highest and best good. I am open to optimism. The drum of destiny beats in my favor. So be it!"

Sagittarius Homework

Sagittarians manifest best through teaching, publishing and writing, travel, spiritual adventures, and as tour group leaders, airline and cruise ship personnel, evangelical ministers, philosophers, anthropologists, linguists, and translators.

The Sagittarius moon cycle creates a magnetic matrix that stimulates us to take direction towards becoming one with a goal and then sheds light on the path. In the ancient mystery schools, Sagittarius moons were used to set the stage for candidates to reach higher levels of awareness by inspiring their desire to reach a goal and then to step toward the goal. It is time now to become one with your goal.

VICTORY LIST

Acknowledge what you have overcome. Keep this list active during this moon cycle. Honoring victory allows you to accept success.

TAROT

Ask the question out loud, then draw a card. You may wish to draw it or paste a copy of it here. Then write down what you feel it might be telling you, in response to the question. Use the glossary in the appendix and record here anything about the card that captures your attention. You may wish to come back throughout the moon cycle to meditate or journal more on the card.

How is my spirit supporting my manifesting?

MANIFESTING LIST

SAGITTARIUS NEW MOON
DECEMBER 14ᵀᴴ

This or something better than this comes to me in an easy and pleasurable way, for the good of all concerned. Thank you, Universe!

Sagittarius Manifesting Ideas

Now is the time to focus on manifesting truth, teaching and study, understanding advanced ideas, optimism and inspiration, bliss, goals, travel and adventure, and philosophy and culture.

New Moon in Sagittarius

Your Personal Moon Experience

Fill in the Cosmic Check-In page. Then look up the degree of the Moon on the chart below. Take note of the "I" statement on the outside of the wheel where the Moon is located. Now, locate the same degree on your own chart and make a note of the house and corresponding "I" statement. Go back to the Cosmic Check-In page and circle the two statements from the charts and read what you wrote. This will give you an idea about what to expect from this moon phase on a personal level. For more information on personalizing your *Moon Book*, go to www.BlueMoonAcademy.com and look for *How to Use the Moon Book*.

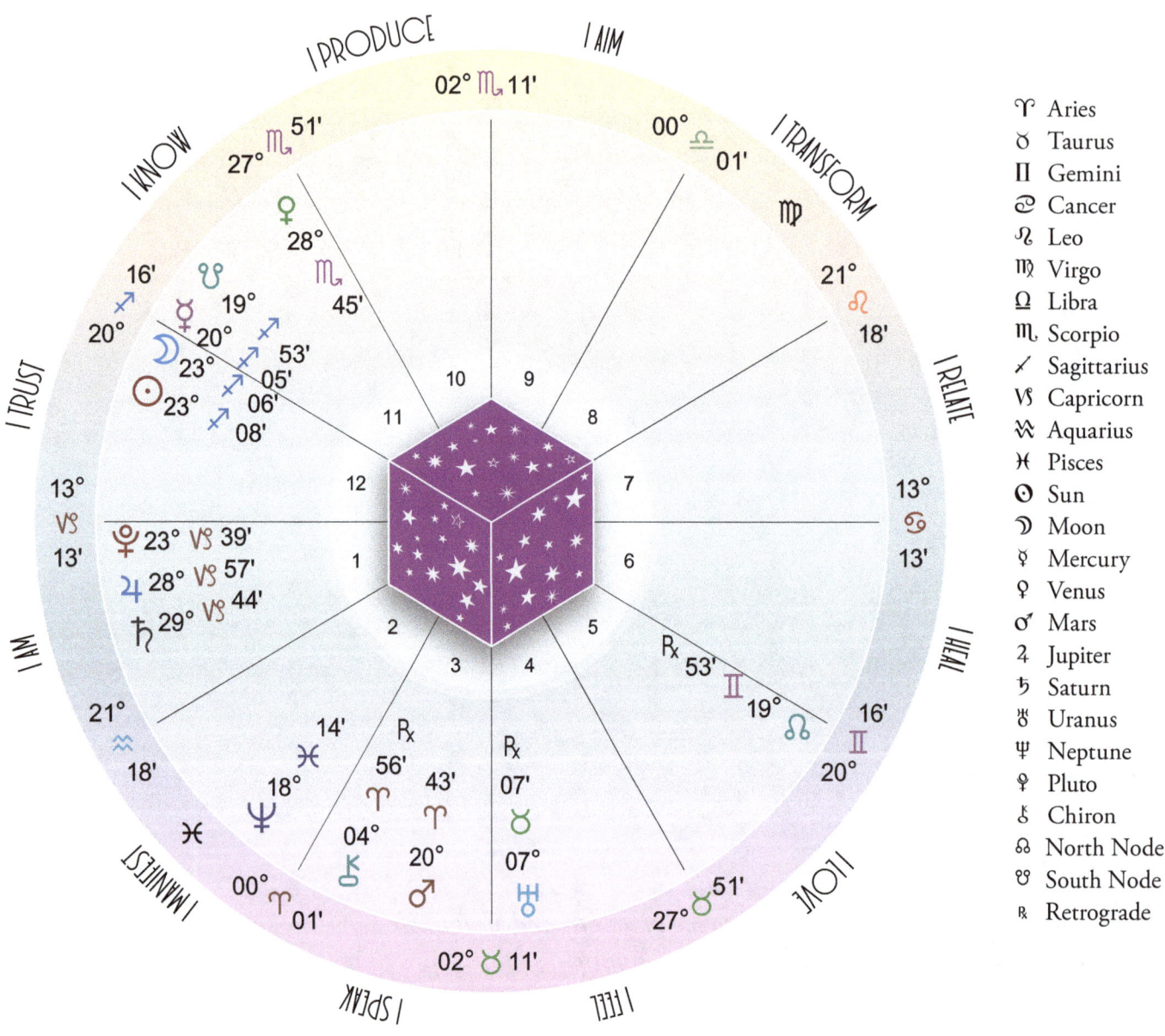

COSMIC CHECK-IN

**SAGITTARIUS NEW MOON
DECEMBER 14TH**

Take a moment to write a brief phrase for each "I" statement. This activates all areas of your life for this creative cycle.

♐ I Aim

♑ I Produce

♒ I Know

♓ I Trust

♈ I Am

♉ I Manifest

♊ I Speak

♋ I Feel

♌ I Love

♍ I Heal

♎ I Relate

♏ I Transform

Full Moon in Cancer

December 29th, 7:29 PM

When the Sun is Opposite the Moon

Full moons are always in opposition to the Sun. This creates a feeling of tension between where you want to shine and how your feelings are flowing on a sensory level about the Sun's directive. The two forces seem like they are working against each other, yet they are on the same team displaying different techniques to obtain the same mission. The Cancer/Capricorn polarity creates tension between being at home with your family or being at work positioning yourself for success.

Cancer Goddess

Birds are the symbol of expanded consciousness because they are born twice; once into the egg and once out of the egg. They are associated with rebirth and self-realization. Bird Woman is the Cancer goddess. She teaches us that, although we live in the illusion that security comes from our identity in the outer world, our true cosmic significance must be found within. Bird Woman directs us toward discovering our way home to our Soul, the place of lotus light. She has the ability to fly between Heaven and Earth, bringing communications from the angels and the spirit guides. She inspires souls to infuse matter with light—the true essence of co-creating.

Build Your Altar

Colors	Shades of gray and milky, creamy colors
Numerology	3 – Go dancing, celebrate with friends
Tarot Card	The Chariot – The ability to move forward
Gemstones	Pearl, moonstone, ruby
Plant Remedy	Shooting Star – The ability to move straight ahead
Fragrance	Peppermint – The essence of the Great Mother

Moon Notes

Lunar Eclipse

Full Moon 8° Cancer 53' 7:29 PM
Full Moons are about moving beyond blocks and setting yourself free.

Element
Water – Taking the line of least resistance, going with the flow, creativity at its best, secretive, sensual, glamorous, psychic, magnetic, escaping reality, a healer, an actor/actress.

Statement I Feel
Body Stomach
Mind Worry
Spirit Nurturing

11th House Moon
I Know/I Feel

Umbrella Energy
Your approach to friends, social consciousness, teamwork, community service, and the future.

Choice Points
Opportunity   Innocence
Challenge   Out of Reach

Sabian Symbol
A Small Naked Girl Bends Over A Sparkling Pond Trying To Catch A Fish

Potential
Focus on your ability to manifest.

CLEARING THE SLATE

**CANCER FULL MOON
DECEMBER 29TH**

Sixty hours before the full moon, negative traits connected to the astro-sign might become activated to trigger what needs to be released during the full moon phase. You may notice an unusual amount of worry, moodiness, addiction to the past, or challenges related to the energy of mothering. Make a list, look in the mirror, and for each negative trait, tell yourself *I am sorry, I forgive you, thank you for your awareness,* and *I love you.*

CANCER VICTORIES & CHALLENGES

Say all of the statements in this section out loud. Then, underline the phrase that means the most to you. Use the phrase as your affirmation for releasing throughout this moon phase.

Today, I take advantage of my ability to take action and position myself for success. I clearly know that the road to success is before me, and all I need to do is move forward. I am aware that when I take action and move forward, the Universe fills in the dots. Whether I move left, right, or straight ahead doesn't matter—what matters is that I am in movement. Today, I release indecisiveness that keeps me stuck. Today, I let go of vacillation that exhausts my mind. Today, I take my foot off of the brakes and find the gas pedal. I allow movement to occur, even if I don't know where I am going. When I take action, I trust the guideposts will appear. I am aware that action leads me to my new direction. Today, I know and GO! I remember that karma comes to the space of non-action, while success comes through action. Action brings me to my victory. Standing still leads to regret, resentment, and chaos. I am aware that action can be as simple as taking a walk on the beach, buying fresh flowers to add a new dimension to my home, or simply going to a new restaurant for lunch. I take action today to break up a crystallized pattern and, in so doing, my life begins to show me newfound awareness and light to guide me.

Cancer Homework

It's now time to conquer pride and ambition, overcome fear of loneliness, release the need for money, security, and possessions, discover the value of emotions, and connect to beauty. Submerge yourself in a tub of water, relax, and let the clean water flow through your cells to wash away all of your hurts, resentments, and history that keep you trapped in the past. Pull the plug and let the spiral of water carry away your pain. Be prepared to boldly claim your presence in the present. Look around your kitchen and throw away the pots and pans that continue to feed your past, rather than vitalizing your life now.

GRATITUDE LIST

Keep this list active throughout the moon cycle. This will bring you to a level of completion so that a new cycle of opportunity can occur in your life. Be prepared for miracles!

TAROT

Ask the question out loud, then draw a card. You may wish to draw it or paste a copy of it here. Then write down what you feel it might be telling you, in response to the question. Use the glossary in the appendix and record here anything about the card that captures your attention. You may wish to come back throughout the moon cycle to meditate or journal more on the card.

How is my heart supporting my releasing?

RELEASING LIST

CANCER FULL MOON
DECEMBER 29ᵀᴴ

Say this statement out loud three times before writing your list:

I am a free spiritual being and it is my desire to be free to think and to express myself fully — to move about my life toward Truth and Wisdom — to accept and enjoy all good which is mine in living my truth.

I am now free and ready to make choices beyond survival!

Cancer Freedom Ideas

Now is the time to set myself free from self-pity, defensive behavior, nurturing everyone else but me, living in the past, being a mother, and having a mother.

Full Moon in Cancer

Your Personal Moon Experience

Fill in the Cosmic Check-In page. Then look up the degree of the Moon on the chart below. Take note of the "I" statement on the outside of the wheel where the Moon is located. Now, locate the same degree on your own chart and make a note of the house and corresponding "I" statement. Go back to the Cosmic Check-In page and circle the two statements from the charts and read what you wrote. This will give you an idea about what to expect from this moon phase on a personal level. For more information on personalizing your *Moon Book*, go to www.BlueMoonAcademy.com and look for *How to Use the Moon Book*.

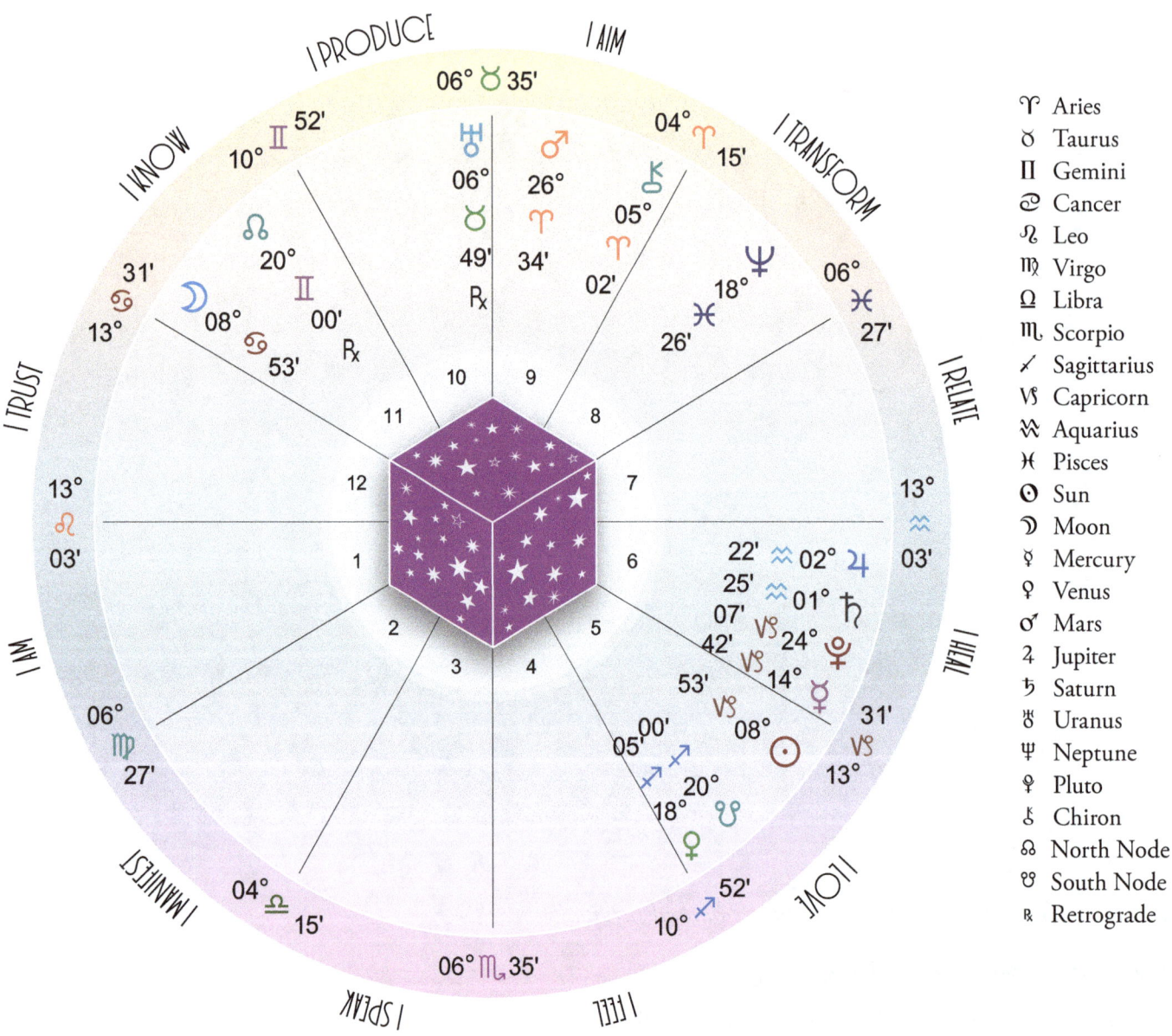

COSMIC CHECK-IN

CANCER FULL MOON
DECEMBER 29TH

Take a moment to write a brief phrase for each "I" statement. This activates all areas of your life for this creative cycle.

♋ I Feel

♌ I Love

♍ I Heal

♎ I Relate

♏ I Transform

♐ I Aim

♑ I Produce

♒ I Know

♓ I Trust

♈ I Am

♉ I Manifest

♊ I Speak

APPENDICES

Eclipses

Lunar	January 10th	♋	Cancer
Lunar	June 5th	♐	Sagittarius
Solar	June 20th	♋	Cancer
Lunar	July 4th	♑	Capricorn
Lunar	November 30th	♊	Gemini
Solar	December 14th	♐	Sagittarius

Retrogrades

	Begins			Stations Direct		
Uranus	August 11th, 2019	♉	Taurus	January 10th		
Mercury	February 16th	♓	Pisces	March 9th	♒	Aquarius
Pluto	April 25th	♑	Capricorn	October 4th		
Saturn	May 10th	♒	Aquarius	September 28th	♑	Capricorn
Venus	May 12th	♊	Gemini	June 24th		
Jupiter	May 14th	♑	Capricorn	September 9th		
Mercury	June 17th	♋	Cancer	July 12th		
Neptune	June 22nd	♓	Pisces	November 28th		
Uranus	August 15th	♉	Taurus	January 14th, 2021		
Mars	September 9th	♈	Aries	November 13th		
Mercury	October 13th	♏	Scorpio	November 3rd	♎	Libra

Tibetan Numerology of the Day

2	**Balance**	Be decisive and move past vacillation.
3	**Fun**	Have a party. Take on a creative project. Express the "Disneyland" side of yourself.
4	**Structure**	Take the day to organize. Get the job done. Work and you will sail through the day.
5	**Action, exercise, travel**	Exercise—join a gym, take a dance class, play tennis, go for a walk. Travel—go for a drive, travel the world, visit your travel agent. Make a change.
6	**Love**	Go out for a night of romance. Work on beauty in your home. Nurture yourself and take care of your health.
7	**Research**	Read a book. Learn something new and get smart. Take a class.
8	**Money**	Have a business meeting. Meet with your accountant. Make a sales call. Start a new business.
9	**Connecting with the Divine**	Meditate. Take part in a humanitarian project. Do community service.
10	**Seeing the "big picture"**	Take an innovative idea and run with it today!
11	**Completion**	Do what it takes to be complete.

The Astro Wheel

	Statement	Ruling Sign		Key Notes
1st House	I Am	♈	Aries	Your outer appearance, the way you present yourself, the way you dress, the way you enter a room, and what you leave behind when you leave the room.
2nd House	I Manifest	♉	Taurus	The way you make your money and the way you spend your money.
3rd House	I Speak	♊	Gemini	How you get the word out and the message behind the words.
4th House	I Feel	♋	Cancer	The way your early environmental training was and how that set your foundation for living, and why you chose your mother.
5th House	I Love	♌	Leo	The way you love and how you want to be loved.
6th House	I Heal	♍	Virgo	The way you manage your body and its appearance.
7th House	I Relate	♎	Libra	One-on-one relationships, defines your people attraction, and how you work in relationships with the people you attract.
8th House	I Transform	♏	Scorpio	How you share money and other resources, what you keep hidden regarding sex, death, real estate, and regeneration.
9th House	I Aim	♐	Sagittarius	The way you approach spirituality, philosophy, journeys, higher knowledge, and aspiration.
10th House	I Produce	♑	Capricorn	Your approach to status, career, honor, and prestige, and why you chose your Father.
11th House	I Know	♒	Aquarius	Your approach to friends, social consciousness, teamwork, community service, and the future.
12th House	I Trust	♓	Pisces	Determines how you deal with your karma, "unconscious software," and what you will experience in order to attain mastery to complete your karma. It is also about the way you connect to the Divine.

Heavenly Bodies

☉	**Sun**	Outer personality, potential, director, the most obvious traits of the consciousness projection
☽	**Moon**	Emotion, feelings, memory, unconsciousness, mother's influence, ancestors, home life
☿	**Mercury**	The way you think, the intention beneath your thoughts, communication, academia (lower mind)
♀	**Venus**	Beauty, value, romantic love, sensuality, creativity, being social, fun, femininity
♂	**Mars**	Action, change, variety, sex drive, ambition, warrior, ego, athletics, masculinity
♃	**Jupiter**	Benevolent, jovial, excessive, expansive, optimistic, abundant, extravagant, accepting good fortune
♄	**Saturn**	Teacher, karma, disciplined, restrictive, father's influence
♅	**Uranus**	Liberated, revolutionary, explosive, spontaneous, breakthrough, innovation, technology
♆	**Neptune**	Mystical, charming, sensitive, addictive, glamorous, deceptive, illusions
♇	**Pluto**	Money, wealth, transformation, secrets, hidden information, sexuality, psychic power
⚷	**Chiron**	Wounded healer, healing, holistic therapies
☊	**North Node**	This represents where you are headed in this lifetime. In other words, it represents the direction your life will take you, your future focus. In Eastern astrology, this is sometimes called the "head of the dragon."
☋	**South Node**	This represents what you brought with you this lifetime and what you are moving away from. It is sometimes called the "tail of the dragon" in Eastern astrology.

Astrological Signs

Each sign of astrology has a particular quality or tone that is described in more detail with the moons.

Sign	"I" Statement		Element	Key Words
♈ Aries	I Am	Sign of the Ram Ruled by Mars ♂ Begins the zodiac year with the Spring Equinox	Fire	Ego, identity, championship, leadership, action-oriented, warrior, and self-first.
♉ Taurus	I Manifest	Sign of the Bull Ruled by Venus ♀	Earth	Self-value, abundant, aesthetic, business, sensuous, art, beauty, flowers, gardens, collector, and shopper.
♊ Gemini	I Speak	Sign of the Twins Ruled by Mercury ☿	Air	Versatile, expressive, restless, travel-minded, short trips, flirt, gossip, "nose for news," and the messenger.
♋ Cancer	I Feel	Sign of the Crab Ruled by the Moon ☽ Begins with the Summer Solstice	Water	Emotional, nurturing, family-oriented, home, mother, cooking, security-minded, ancestors, builder of form and foundation.
♌ Leo	I Love	Sign of the Lion Ruled by the Sun ☉	Fire	Willful, dramatic, loyal, children, child-ego state, love affairs, decadent, royal, show-stopper, theatre, adored and adoring.
♍ Virgo	I Heal	Sign of the Virgin Ruled by Mercury ☿	Earth	Gives birth to Divinity, perfectionist, discernment, scientific, analytical, habitual, work-oriented, body maintenance, earth connection, attention to detail, service-oriented, earth healer, herbs, and judgmental.
♎ Libra	I Relate	Sign of the Scales Ruled by Venus ♀ Begins with the Autumnal Equinox	Air	Relationship, social, harmony, industry, the law, diplomacy, morality, beauty, strategist, logical, and over-active mind.
♏ Scorpio	I Transform	Sign of the Scorpion Ruled by Pluto ♀ and Mars ♂	Water	Intense, passionate, sexual, powerful, focused, controlling, deep, driven, and secretive.
♐ Sagittarius	I Aim	Sign of the Archer Ruled by Jupiter ♃	Fire	Optimistic, generous, preacher-teacher, world traveler, higher knowledge, goal-oriented, philosophy, culture, publishing, extravagance, excessive, exaggerator, and good fortune.
♑ Capricorn	I Produce	Sign of the Goat Ruled by Saturn ♄ Begins at the Winter Solstice	Earth	Ambitious, concretive, responsible, achievement, business, corporate structure, world systems, and useful.
♒ Aquarius	I Know	Sign of the Water Bearer Ruled by Uranus ♅	Air	Inventive, idealistic, utopian, rebellion, innovative, technology, community, friends, synergy, group consciousness, science, magic, trendy, and future-orientation.
♓ Pisces	I Trust	Sign of the Fishes Ruled by Neptune ♆	Water	Sensitive, creative, empathetic, theatre, addiction, escape artist, glamor, secretive, Divinely guided, healer, medicine.

Colors

- **Red** — Passion, bloodline, circulation, ancestry
- **Pink** — Shy passion, learning to stand up for yourself, unconditional love, timid, colors in between the vertebrae of the spinal cord teaching you to stand up yourself
- **Orange** — Money, sex, power, creativity, Christ healer, integration of the physical at a deeper level
- **Yellow** — Enlightenment, a bright mind (perhaps too logical), happiness, joy, playful, higher mind, purist form of logic, the Sun
- **Green** — Natural, nature, envy, abundance, heart, go
- **Turquoise** — Sky power, spontaneous, futuristic, innovative
- **Blue** — Third-eye perception, moody, water, the flow of emotion, depth, psychic, fantasy, throat, communication, emotional body
- **Indigo** — Absence of guilt, opening to aspects of the future, creating new pathways
- **Violet** — Magical thinking, abstract thinking, abstract mind, guilt-ridden
- **Purple** — Ego, royalty, controlling version of power
- **Rainbow** — Indicates a good future, open to all possibilities
- **Gold** — Personal value, self worth, valuable
- **Silver** — Intuition, reflective, ability to see yourself, the Moon
- **White** — Major change, includes all colors
- **Clear** — Clarity, cleaning, getting it clear, no color
- **Black** — Intuitive, receptive, emptiness, absence of color, inner self, the void

TAROT GLOSSARY

A Universal Support System: The Major Arcana Cards

The first 22 cards in the deck, numbered with Roman numerals 0-21, are the most potent cards in the deck and are a model of wholeness. Each Major Arcana card singles out a stage of development on the spectrum of wholeness. Each has a law (shown in capital letters) and a lesson reflecting the values of our times and promoting the evolution of experience on the internal and external planes of awareness. The law is what you have to learn while traveling here. The lesson is the experience which allows the law to be learned.

Reversals

After drawing a card, turn it over side-to-side, like a page in a book. Reversals are cards that are upside-down to you as you read the cards. This is true whether you are reading for yourself or for someone else since the cards are always laid out for the reader, the person interpreting the cards. The qualities listed under the Reversed heading are merely showing you the inner place and inner work that is needed in your development.

THE FOOL – 0

POTENTIAL. The promise of things to come. The energy you are bringing into yourself in the moment. A leap of faith. A new beginning. A go-for-it attitude. Accessing your potential (not caring if you look foolish). Remember, the guy with the lamp shade on his head may be having more fun than you. Willing to play full out. Going through life lightheartedly.

REVERSED: Unwilling to take risks. No faith in yourself. Worry. Holding yourself back. Being afraid of looking foolish. Afraid to let go and "let God." No faith to take the leap. Taking life too seriously.

THE MAGICIAN – I

TALENT. Ability to convert from the ethereal to the physical. Masculine polarity in its purest form. All things are possible for you. Having all the tools for success. Time to focus your intention and attention. A man who symbolizes every woman's fantasy.

REVERSED: Misuse of power. A master of illusion. Seeing everything as impossible. Lacking self-confidence. Doubting your ability to manifest or create. Not accessing your tools (talent).

THE HIGH PRIESTESS – II

INTUITION. The Feminine polarity in its purest form. Purity, the Virgin Goddess within. A woman who symbolized every man's fantasy. Dispenser of wisdom and knowledge.

REVERSED: Not trusting your intuition. Overriding intuition with logic. Diluting your femininity. Prostituting yourself. Selling yourself short. Time to ask, "What intuitive hit am I not listening to?"

THE EMPRESS – III

LOVE. The epitome of the Natural Woman. Fertility. Nurturance. The ability to get your needs met. Flowing with what feels natural. Knowing how to take care of yourself and others. Being touchable, lovable and nurturing. The perfect wife/mother. Creativity at its best.

REVERSED: Not nurturing self or others. A poor self-image manifests in feeling unloved. Ask, what it is you want in order to get your needs met. Do for yourself rather than expect others to do for you. Remember, you can only be loved to the extent you love yourself.

THE EMPEROR – IV

SUCCESS. Ability to respond to success and manifest in the outside world. The perfect husband/father. Successful in business. Structured, logical and grounded. Having a foundation for success. Chairman of the Board type.

REVERSED: Not assuming responsibility – in the world, in a relationship, in business. Disorganized. A social dropout. Unable to work the system for success in the world. Disconnected. Rebellious against the system. A man who has turned his back on a woman.

THE HIEROPHANT – V

TRADITION. The authority figure. The bridge between humanity and divinity. The teacher's teacher. The interpreter of life (teacher, lawyer, therapist, preacher, rabbi, doctor) through listening and reflection. Seeking interpretation through traditions, social awareness, church, dogma, society's rules. Needing advise and interpretation through the eyes of an authority.

REVERSED: Learning to interpret life for yourself. Breaking away from tradition, dogma, ritual, church, society's rules. Learning to live by using your own intuition and becoming your own authority. Knowing there is more to life than what meets the eye. Seeing beyond the physical.

THE LOVERS – VI

RELATIONSHIP. Integration of the masculine and feminine life energy. Perfect inner balance of the masculine and feminine principles. Union of opposites. Healthy relationship. Commitment. Marriage. Good health.

REVERSED: Broken partnerships. Selfishness. Love for all the wrong reasons. Divorce. Separation. Bad health. Lack of commitment. Disharmony.

THE CHARIOT – VII

ACTION. Taking action for victory in life. Broad, sweeping changes. Positioning yourself for success. Take action now to move forward in life.

REVERSED: Upheaval in your life from not taking action. Putting your foot on the brakes when it needs to be on the gas pedal. Chaos.

STRENGTH – VIII

PASSION. Understanding the dynamics of the beauty and the beast within. Learning to express your higher and lower selves without judgment. Integrating consciousness with the physical, thereby creating a passion for life.

REVERSED: Denial of natural expression. Giving power away to your lower forces. Out of control. Stubborn. Lacking courage. Health issues. Exhaustion.

THE HERMIT – IX

INDIVIDUALITY. Knowing ourselves as an individuals. Recognize your inner qualities. Your God-self uniqueness manifests your inner light. Time to take your spirituality off the mountaintop and shine your light out into the world.

REVERSED: Contemplating and observing. Hiding out and retreating from life. Denying your own individuality. Not sharing your knowledge; keeping it to yourself. Caution: Do not stay on the mountaintop too long.

THE WHEEL OF FORTUNE – X

LIFE LESSON. In time and on time with your life's blueprint. The drum of destiny beats in your favor. Applying the knowledge of your life lessons and experiencing good fortune. Being in the right time at the right place to experience what appears to be a miracle.

REVERSED: Denying your destiny. Taken off your path. Everything out of sync. Denial of life lessons. Getting stuck in feeling sorry for yourself. Misfortune.

JUSTICE – XI

KARMA. Activating the laws of Cause and Effect. (Every action has a reaction; what you put out you get back.) Expect compensation for actions taken. Actions now get equalized and balanced. Winning a lawsuit. Reaping benefits.

REVERSED: Not accepting responsibility for your actions. Being forced to face what you do not want to see. Blaming others rather than seeing the balance of action. Feeling as if an injustice has been done.

THE HANGED MAN – XII

DETACHMENT. Learning to accept rather than control. Taking time out to reflect. Being willing to "hang out" and do nothing. Being calm in the midst of the storm.

REVERSED: Clinging to the past. Living life through a rear view mirror. Not willing to change. Afraid to just hang out and observe. Trying to control. Being a martyr.

DEATH – XIII

TRANSFORMATION. There is no compromise – change is imminent. Make a clean break. Time to let go of the past. Rejuvenation. Regeneration. New beginnings.

REVERSED: The Universe has you on hold. Delays are appropriate. Do not personalize the feeling of "stuckness." Take time to play rather than pushing. Let go of what you think the action "should" be. Be willing to stay in the void.

TEMPERANCE – XIV

BALANCE. Experimentation and modification. This is a time of learning to manage life by blending extremes, knowing boundaries and setting limits. Inner and outer congruity is very important now. Know what it takes to keep yourself centered.

REVERSED: Life is unmanageable. Moderation is needed. Obsessive and compulsive behaviors are causing imbalance. Could indicate poor health, exhaustion, stress. Out of alignment with spiritual and physical realities. Time to set limits and boundaries.

THE DEVIL – XV

CONFINEMENT. Feeling confined, constricted, limited. 360-degree test with 180-degree vision. Options required. Ask yourself, how many different ways can I look at this situation.

REVERSED: The light at the end of the tunnel appears. The testing period is over. The road to freedom has been found. You have seen your options. The solution to your problem has been found.

THE TOWER – XVI

SPONTANEITY. Learning to live in the moment. An unexpected event leads you into freedom. Do not put anything off until tomorrow. Do whatever is appropriate in the moment. Clear the way so new consciousness can appear.

REVERSED: Resisting change. Staying stuck by trying to control the outcome. Refusing to go with the flow. A blessing in disguise.

THE STAR – XVII

NEW DIRECTIONS. Breakthrough to a new level of consciousness. On track. Golden opportunities on the horizon. Support coming from higher sources to provide guidance and direction.

REVERSED: Search for inner direction rather than outer guideposts. A missed opportunity. Time to ask, "Where am I being thrown off course and not willing to accept a new level of consciousness?"

THE MOON – XVIII

FEARS AND PHOBIAS. A time to face up to and look at what you keep hidden from yourself. A warning to stay on the path and avoid outside influences of negativity. Being deceived or deceiving yourself. Absorbing toxic or poisonous energy; i.e., drugs or alcohol. Drug or alcohol abuse. Time to face your darker side and bring it into the light.

REVERSED: A warning of personal safety. Danger in the dark. Doing anything to avoid facing the truth. Secrets, lies, deception, depression and repression. Denial, cheating, illegal activities.

THE SUN – XIX

ENLIGHTENMENT. The source of energy, happiness, abundance, success, prosperity, fulfillment, playfulness. The child-ego state revealed.

REVERSED: Not seeing that all is available to you. Where you are denying yourself happiness? Your dimmer switch is turning down the sunlight!

JUDGEMENT – XX

FREEDOM. Freedom from judgement. A clean slate is now available, a new life on a new level of consciousness. Congratulations! You have let go and integrated beyond black/white, right/wrong, good/bad and have moved into a more integrated version of yourself.

REVERSED: Being your own worst enemy, judging yourself constantly, beating yourself up, making yourself wrong, afraid of what people think, feeling guilty. Low self-esteem. Stop punishing yourself for past deeds and let go.

THE WORLD – XXI

ATTAINMENT. Unlimited opportunity for success. Attainment. Having it all. Your full potential realized. Victory in life. Mastery of the inner and outer planes of awareness. Acknowledge your accomplishments.

REVERSED: Fear of failure. Not willing to take responsibility for success. A loser attitude. Never bringing anything to completion. Feeling defeated. Walking to the door of success and saying, "Oh well, it wouldn't have worked, anyway."

The Cards

Use these to cut and paste the card you have pulled into the Tarot section of each cycle as you work through the year. You will likely want to make copies in case you pull the same card more than once.

Continued...

THE EMPEROR.   THE HIEROPHANT.   THE LOVERS.

THE CHARIOT.   STRENGTH.   THE HERMIT.   WHEEL of FORTUNE.   JUSTICE.

THE HANGED MAN.   DEATH.   TEMPERANCE.   THE DEVIL.   THE TOWER.

THE STAR.   THE MOON.   THE SUN.   JUDGEMENT.   THE WORLD.

SKY POWER YOGA

By Astrology Sign

After manifesting, setting yourself free, and recalibrating by facing your trigger points, and after becoming open to being victorious, yoga allows the body to hold the position for manifesting or for releasing.

Please consult your doctor if you need to determine whether yoga exercises are suitable for you. If a pose is contraindicated for you, energetic benefit can still be obtained by envisioning the steps rather than doing them physically. Otherwise, proceed from a modified stance that has been medically-approved for you.

Before following any advice or practice suggested by this book, it is recommended that you consult your doctor as to its suitability, especially if you suffer from any health problems or special conditions. The publishers, the author, and associates cannot accept responsibility for any injuries or damage incurred as a result of following the exercises in this book, or using any of the therapeutic methods described or mentioned.

Aries

Aries New Moon: Mountain Pose

No props are needed. Stand with your feet hip-width apart. Lift your toes, spread them wide, and place them back on the floor.

To massage the bottoms of your feet, rock back and forth and side to side for 30 seconds. Gradually make your movements more subtle until you find the sweet spot where your weight is balanced evenly across your feet.

Squeeze your thighs to lift your kneecaps. Slightly tuck your tailbone down and feel your hips align over your ankles.

Inhale, lengthening your spine. Exhale, rolling your shoulders back and down, reaching your fingertips towards the floor. Gently lift your chest from the sternum and turn your palms out slightly. Imagine a strong line of vertical energy running from the bottom of your feet to the top of your head.

Relax into the pose. Close your eyes. Breathe in and out slowly and deeply several times through your nose with your awareness on your head.

Inhale deeply. Envision the energy of your breath coming up from the earth into your feet, up your legs, up your spine, and out the top of your head.

Say or think to yourself the mantra *I Am*. Exhale slowly. Envision the breath returning back into your head, down your spine, down your legs, out your feet and back into the earth. Repeat as desired.

Aries Full Moon: Resting Pose

You need one pillow and one blanket for the prop. Lie on your back with your legs spread shoulder-width apart. Place your arms by your side at a 45-degree angle with your palms facing down. You may place a pillow under your neck for support or cover yourself with a blanket to stay warm.

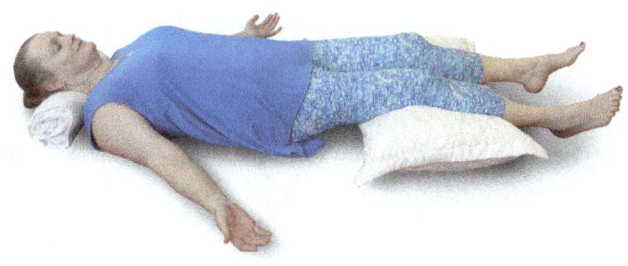

Relax. Close your eyes. Breathe in and out slowly and deeply several times through your nose with your awareness on your head. Allow your body to soften and relax until it feels like you are melting into the floor.

Feel the gentle rhythmic massage of the body as your belly subtly rises and falls with each breath. Allow this awareness to increase your sense of being grounded and supported.

Inhale and envision the energy of your breath coming up from the earth into your feet and then up your legs, your spine, and out the top of your head. Say or think to yourself the mantra *I Am*.

Exhale softly and slowly as you envision your breath flowing back into your head and down your spine, your legs, and out your feet back into the earth. Repeat as desired.

Taurus

Taurus New Moon: Seated Neck Rolls

You need one chair for the prop. Sit one hand-width forward from the back of the chair. Back is straight and feet are placed hip-width apart on the floor. If your feet require more solid contact with the floor, place pillows or folded towels under your feet.

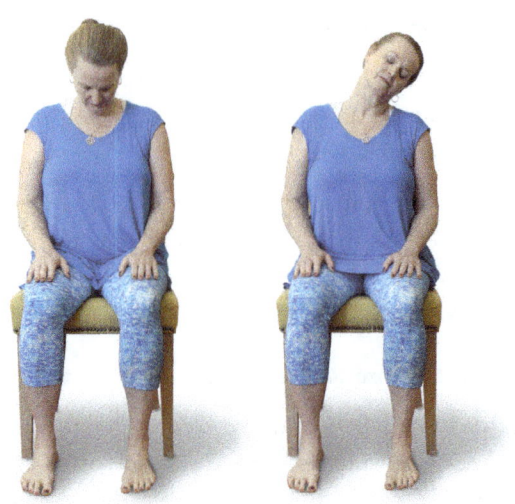

Relax and close your eyes. Breathe in and out slowly and deeply several times through your nose, with your awareness on your throat.

As you exhale, drop your head forward rolling the right ear toward the right shoulder.

Inhale and tip your chin up slightly while you envision the energy of your breath coming into your neck. Say or think to yourself the mantra *I Manifest*.

Exhale softly and slowly as you roll your head forward and to the opposite direction with the left ear towards the left shoulder.

Inhale, tipping your chin slightly up and repeating the mantra, then exhale rolling back toward the right shoulder. Repeat as desired.

Taurus Full Moon: Seated Fish

You need one chair for the prop. With your back straight sit one hand-width from the back of the chair with your feet on the floor hip-width apart. If your feet require more solid contact with the floor, place pillows or folded towels under your feet.

Place hands on the sides of the chair with elbows pulled in slightly and pointing towards the chair back.

Gently lift your chest from the sternum with your head and neck remaining neutral.

Relax. Close your eyes. Breathe in and out slowly and deeply several times through your nose with your awareness on your neck.

Inhale softly as you say or think to yourself the mantra *I Manifest*. Tilt the chin upward slightly as you envision the energy of mantra in your throat. Remain for three breaths.

On the next exhale, softly and slowly release the chin and the elbows. Ground your breath and the mantra into the earth as you release the pose. Repeat as desired.

Gemini

Gemini New Moon: Seated Camel

You need one chair for the prop. Sit one hand-width forward from the back of the chair. Your back is straight and your feet are placed hip-width apart on the floor.

Lengthen the spine and slightly tuck your chin. Then interlace your fingers behind your back with your knuckles facing down.

Relax. Close your eyes. Breathe in and out slowly and deeply several times through your nose with your awareness on your lungs and hands.

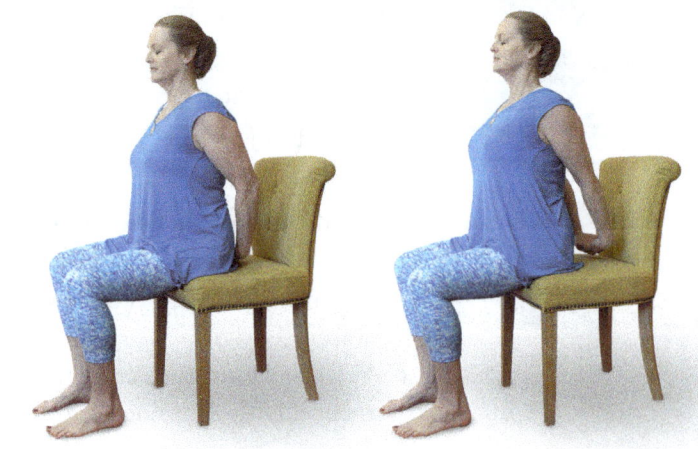

Inhale deeply. Lift your chest and press your hands down and backwards. Say or think to yourself the mantra, *I Speak*.

Exhale slowly. Release the pose by bending your elbows and dropping your chest back to normal. Repeat as desired.

Gemini Full Moon: Reclined Heart Opener

You need two bath towels and one to two pillows for the prop. Fold two towels in half lengthwise, roll them into a log, and place them on the floor. Put both pillows on top of the rolled towels to support your back, neck, and head in the pose. Sit on the floor with the support prop behind you.

Lean back onto your elbows and then lower your back onto your support prop. This creates a gentle opening across your chest. If you find your head dangling over the top edge, shift your prop towards your head to support your head and neck fully.

Place your arms out at a 45-degree angle with palms facing upward at your sides.

Relax. Close your eyes. Breathe in and out slowly and deeply several times through your nose keeping your awareness on your lungs and hands.

Inhale and keep your awareness on the expansion of your lungs. Exhale softly and slowly as you say or think to yourself the mantra *I Speak*.

Relax fully into the support prop and the pose. Enjoy breathing with the mantra for a few minutes.

Cancer

Cancer New Moon: Child's Pose

You need two bath towels and one to two pillows for the prop. Fold the two towels in half lengthwise, roll them into a log, and place them on the floor. Put both pillows on top of the rolled towels to support you in the pose.

Begin kneeling, placing your support prop in front of your knees then come onto hands and knees. Align your knees under your hips and your hands under your shoulders.

Close your eyes. Breathe in and out slowly and deeply several times through your nose with your awareness on your stomach.

Exhale and drop your hips back towards your heels so your front torso lowers onto the support prop. Slide your hands forward slightly and rest your head on the support prop. Turn your head to whichever side is most comfortable.

Inhale deeply. Exhale slowly as you say or think to yourself the mantra *I Feel*.

Relax fully into the support prop and the pose. Remain with the mantra and breath as long as desired.

Cancer Full Moon: Seated Cat/Cow

You need one chair for the prop. With your back straight sit one hand-width from the back of the chair with your feet on the floor hip-width apart. If your feet require more solid contact with the floor, place pillows or folded towels under your feet.

Sit comfortably with a straight back and gently cup knees. Breathe in and out slowly and deeply several times through your nose with your awareness on your breasts.

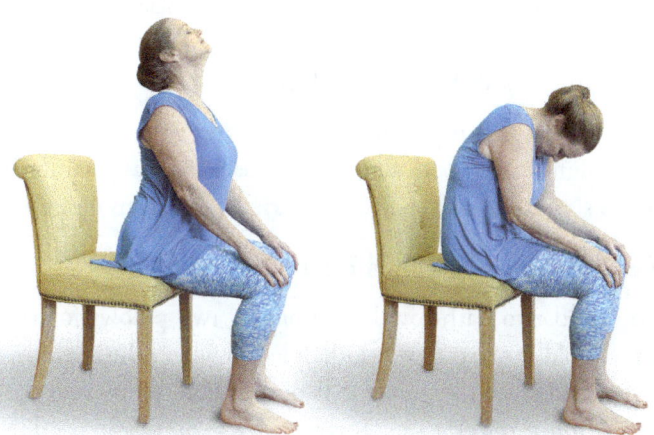

Inhale and allow your belly to drop down as your pelvis tilts back into a subtle back bend.

As you inhale, say or think to yourself the mantra *I Feel*.

Exhale slowly as you tilt your pelvis forward and round your back slightly into a gentle forward bend while gazing down. Repeat with a smooth, continuous movement as many times as desired.

Leo

Leo New Moon: Seated Cactus Arms

You need one chair for the prop. Sit one hand-width forward from the chair back with your feet on the floor hip-width apart. Feet should have solid contact with the floor. Use pillows or folded towels to support your feet, if necessary.

Lengthen your spine to straighten your back. To make the cactus arms, lift and bend arms so that your hands are at a 90 degree angle from your elbow.

Relax and close your eyes. Breathe in and out slowly and deeply several times through your nose maintaining your awareness on your heart center.

Inhale deeply and squeeze your shoulder blades together, then press elbows back, and lift your sternum slightly. Say or think to yourself the mantra *I Love*.

Exhale slowly. Bring your elbows together and round your back slightly. Your body does a subtle back bend as you inhale and a subtle forward bend as you exhale. Repeat as desired.

Leo Full Moon: Reclined Heart Opener

You need two bath towels and one or two pillows for the prop. Fold the two towels in half lengthwise, roll them into a log, and place them on the floor. Put both pillows on top of the rolled towels to support your back, neck, and head in the pose. Sit on the floor with the support prop behind you.

Lean back onto your elbows and then lower back onto your support prop. This pose creates a gentle opening across your chest. If you find your head dangling over the top edge, shift your prop towards your head to support your head and neck fully.

Place your arms out at a 45-degree angle with palms facing upwards at your sides.

Relax. Close your eyes. Breathe in and out slowly and deeply several times through your nose keeping your awareness on your heart center. Allow your body to soften and relax.

Inhale deeply as you say or think to yourself the mantra, *I Love*. Exhale slowly and relax fully into the support prop and into the pose. Enjoy breathing with your mantra for a few minutes.

Virgo

Virgo New Moon: Seated Spinal Twist

You need one chair for the prop. With your back straight sit one hand-width from the back of the chair with your feet on the floor hip-width apart. If your feet require more solid contact with the floor, place pillows or folded towels under your feet.

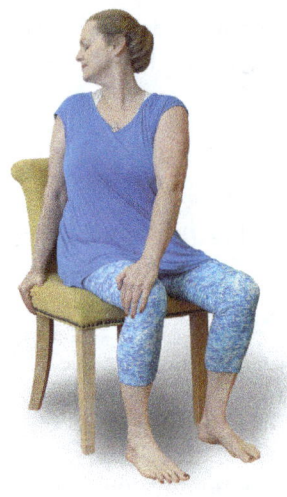

Reach your right hand back to hold the chair just behind your sitting bones. Reach your left hand diagonally to cup the right knee.

While gazing forward, anchor your sitting bones into the chair. Then inhale and lengthen your spine.

Relax. Close your eyes. Breathe in and out slowly and deeply several times through your nose with your awareness on your intestines. Inhale deeply as you say or think to yourself the mantra *I Heal*.

As you exhale softly, twist to turn your head towards your right shoulder using a subtle, gentle rotation. Feel your breath expanding your rib cage on the left side as well as massaging the spine and internal organs.

After several breaths, gently release the pose, return to facing forward, and repeat on the opposite side.

Virgo Full Moon: Prone Spinal Twist

You need two bath towels and one pillow for the prop. Nest the two towels, fold in half lengthwise, and roll them into a log. Place the towel log on the floor with the pillow on top for your support prop. Sit on your side with your right hip on the floor. Place your support prop at a 90-degree angle to your thigh.

Inhale anchoring your sitting bones to the floor and lengthening your spine. Exhale and gently lower your upper torso down onto the prop. Your gaze is the same direction as your knees. This creates a subtle restorative twist. Walk your hands forward in order to release your shoulders.

Relax. Close your eyes. Breathe in and out slowly and deeply several times through your nose with your awareness on your intestines. Inhale deeply as you say or think to yourself the mantra *I Heal*.

Exhale slowly and relax more deeply into the pose.

Breathe with your mantra for a few minutes before repeating on the opposite side.

Libra

Libra New Moon: Seated Forward Fold

You need one chair for the prop. With your back straight sit one hand-width from the back of the chair with your feet on the floor hip-width apart. If your feet require more solid contact with the floor, place pillows or folded towels under your feet.

Place hands on thighs just above knees. While gazing forward, anchor your sitting bones into the chair. Then inhale and lengthen your spine and neck towards the ceiling.

Relax. Close your eyes. Breathe in and out slowly and deeply several times through your nose with your awareness on your kidneys.

Inhale softly as you say or think to yourself the mantra *I Relate*. Exhale slowly, hinging at the hips with a straight back (hands slide forward over knees and down shins towards the floor). Stop once you feel any tightness in the back of your legs.

Release the neck and drop your head slightly. Inhale and exhale in this position for a few breaths.

Bring your head back to neutral in line with the spine, engage your abdominals, straighten your spine and return to sitting upright facing forward. Repeat as desired.

Libra Full Moon: Elevated Legs

You need two bath towels and one to two pillows for the prop. Nest two towels together. Fold them lengthwise and roll into a log. Place the towel log on the floor and place your pillow on top for your support prop.

Sit on the floor with your legs straight in front of you and your feet hip-width apart.

Place your prop between your feet and then place each foot on the prop.

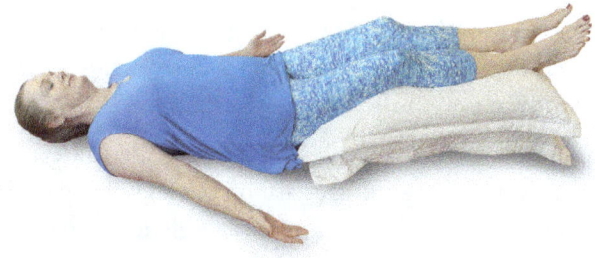

Sit up straight. Lower yourself onto your elbows and then onto your back. Relax. Close your eyes. Breathe in and out slowly and deeply several times through your nose with your awareness on your kidneys.

Inhale deeply. Say the mantra *I Relate* either out loud or in your head. Exhale slowly. Enjoy breathing with your mantra for a few minutes in this relaxing and rejuvenating pose.

Scorpio

Scorpio New Moon: Seated Cat/Cow

You need one chair for the prop. With your back straight sit one hand-width from the back of the chair with your feet on the floor hip-width apart. If your feet require more solid contact with the floor, place pillows or folded towels under your feet.

Sit comfortably with a straight back and gently cup knees. Breathe in and out slowly and deeply several times through your nose with your awareness on your reproductive organs.

Inhale and allow your belly to drop down as your pelvis tilts back into a subtle back bend. As you inhale, say or think to yourself the mantra *I Transform*.

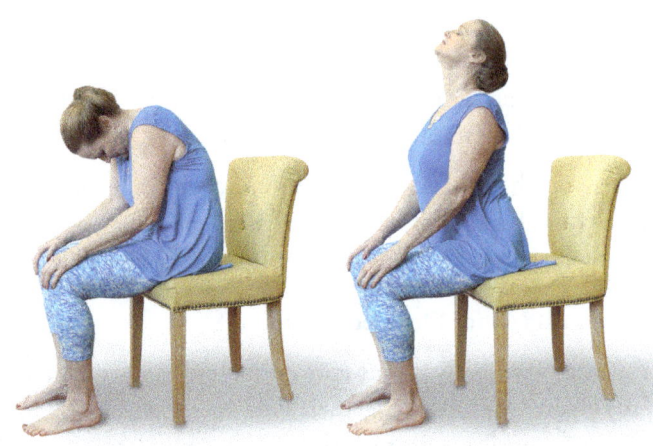

Exhale slowly as you tilt your pelvis forward and round your back slightly into a gentle forward bend while gazing down. Repeat with a smooth, continuous movement as many times as desired.

Scorpio Full Moon: Reclined Goddess on a Chair

You need one chair for the prop. Sit on the floor close to your chair with the right side of your upper torso facing the chair seat and your lower torso close to the chair legs.

Lean back onto your left elbow and lift your right leg onto the chair seat. With your back flat on the floor, lift your left leg to rest on the chair seat next to the right leg.

Place the bottoms of your feet together in the center of the chair seat. Allow your knees to fall towards the edges of the chair seat. Adjust your knees to allow your thighs to open comfortably.

Relax. Close your eyes. Breathe in and out slowly and deeply several times through your nose with your awareness on your reproductive organs. Inhale deeply as you say or think to yourself the mantra *I Transform*.

Exhale slowly and relax into the pose more deeply with each out breath. Repeat as desired.

Sagittarius

Sagittarius New Moon: Reclined Windshield Wipers

No prop is needed. Lay on the floor face up with your legs bent and feet on the floor hip-width apart. Place arms out at your sides with palms facing down.

Relax. Close your eyes. Breathe in and out slowly and deeply several times through your nose with your awareness on your thighs. To create the windshield wipers movement, rock both your knees to the left and then to the right.

Connect the movement with your breath—inhale and move knees to the left and exhale moving knees to the right.

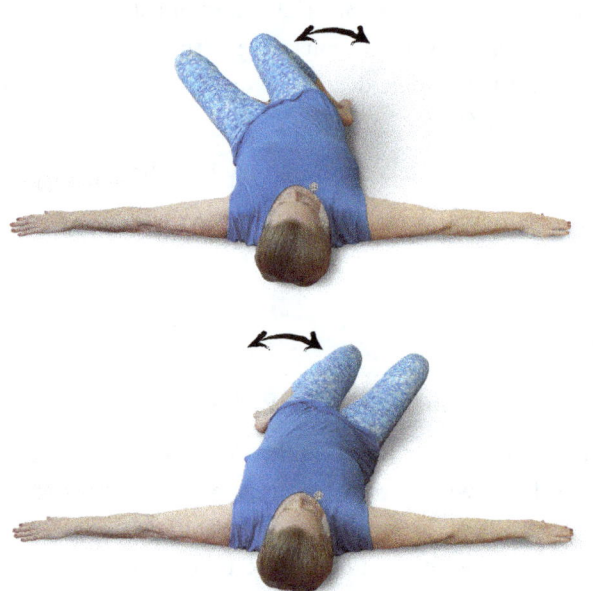

Inhale softly as you say or think to yourself the mantra *I Aim* and move your legs to the left.

Exhale softly and move legs right. Repeat as desired.

Sagittarius Full Moon: Seated Pure Hip

You need one chair for the prop. Sit one hand-width forward from the back of the chair. Back is straight and feet are placed hip-width apart on the floor. If your feet require more solid contact with the floor, place pillows or folded towels under your feet.

Bring your right foot up over your left knee. Rest your right ankle on your lower-left thigh.

Relax. Close your eyes. Breathe in and out slowly and deeply several times through your nose with your awareness on your

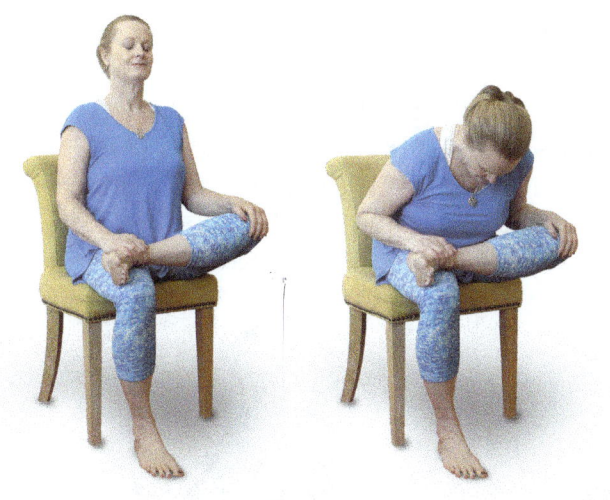

thigh. Inhale deeply and lengthen your back. Say or think to yourself the mantra *I Aim*.

Exhale slowly as you hinge at the hips and shift your weight gently forward.

Remain for several breaths. Inhale, engage your abdominals, and return your upper torso to an upright position. Repeat as desired.

Capricorn

Capricorn New Moon: Standing Knee Circles

No props are needed. Stand with your feet placed 4-6 inches apart with your legs straight and knees soft (not locked back). Place your hands on your hips and your gaze forward.

Close your eyes, and take several slow deep breaths in and out, through your nose. Inhale and exhale slowly, with presence. Breathe and settle into the pose before adding the mantra with the breath.

Inhale, standing tall with a long spine. Pause and say or think to yourself the mantra, *I Produce*.

Bend at the knees and circle both knees in a clockwise direction while exhaling slowly.

Inhale while coming back to the upright and straight-legged starting position for a pause. Repeat as many times as is comfortable.

Capricorn Full Moon: Seated Egg Beaters

You need two bath towels and one or more pillows for the prop. Nest two towels, fold in quarters, and place on the chair. Place the pillow on top of the towels. Sit on the chair to see if your feet hang freely without touching the floor. Add additional pillows or folded towels to elevate you so that your feet don't touch the floor.

Sit one hand-width forward from the back of the chair. Back is straight and head is neutral. Reach behind with both hands to hold the side edges of the chair.

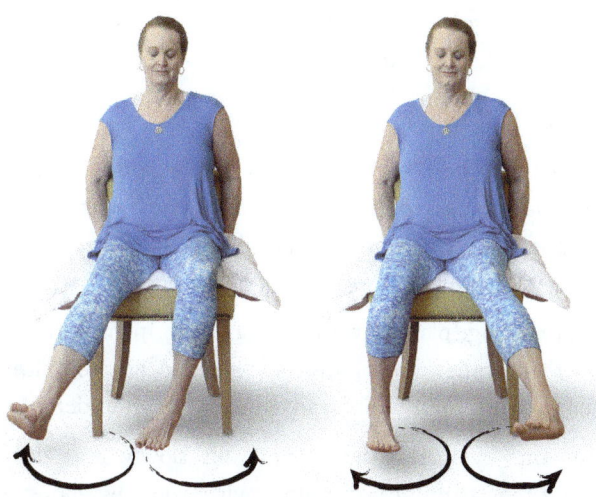

Relax. Close your eyes. Breathe in and out slowly several times through your nose with your awareness on your knees.

Swing your feet forward, out, and around with each foot circling in the opposite direction like an egg beater. The right foot circles clockwise, the left counterclockwise. Allow the movement of the right foot to propel the left. This movement gives a relaxing massage to the knee joint and surrounding muscles.

Inhale deeply and say or think the mantra *I Produce*.

Exhale as you slowly circle your feet. Once your breath is fully exhaled, pause, and repeat as desired.

Aquarius

Aquarius New Moon: Elevated Legs

You need two bath towels and one to two pillows for the prop. Nest two towels together. Fold them lengthwise and roll into a log. Place the towel log on the floor and place your pillow on top for your support prop.

Sit on the floor with your legs straight in front of you and your feet hip-width apart. Place your prop between your feet and then place each foot on the prop.

Sit up straight. Lower yourself onto your elbows and then onto your back. Relax. Close your eyes. Breathe in and out slowly and deeply several times through your nose with your awareness on your ankles.

Inhale. Say the mantra *I Know* either out loud or in your head. Exhale softly and slowly. Enjoy breathing with your mantra for a few minutes.

Aquarius Full Moon: Child's Pose

You need two bath towels and one to two pillows for the prop. Fold the two towels in half lengthwise, roll them into a log, and place them on the floor. Put both pillows on top of the rolled towels to support you in the pose.

Begin kneeling, placing your support prop in front of your knees then come onto hands and knees. Align your knees under your hips and your hands under your shoulders.

Close your eyes. Breathe in and out slowly and deeply several times through your nose with your awareness on your stomach.

Exhale and drop your hips back towards your heels so your front torso lowers onto the support prop. Slide your hands forward slightly and rest your head on the support prop. Turn your head to whichever side is most comfortable.

Inhale deeply. Exhale slowly as you say or think to yourself the mantra *I Know*.

Relax fully into the support prop and the pose. Remain with the mantra and breath as long as desired.

Pisces

Pisces New Moon: Seated Foot Flex

You need one chair for the prop. With a straight back sit in a chair with your feet on the floor hip-width apart. Feet should have solid contact with the floor. Use pillows or folded towels to support your feet, if necessary.

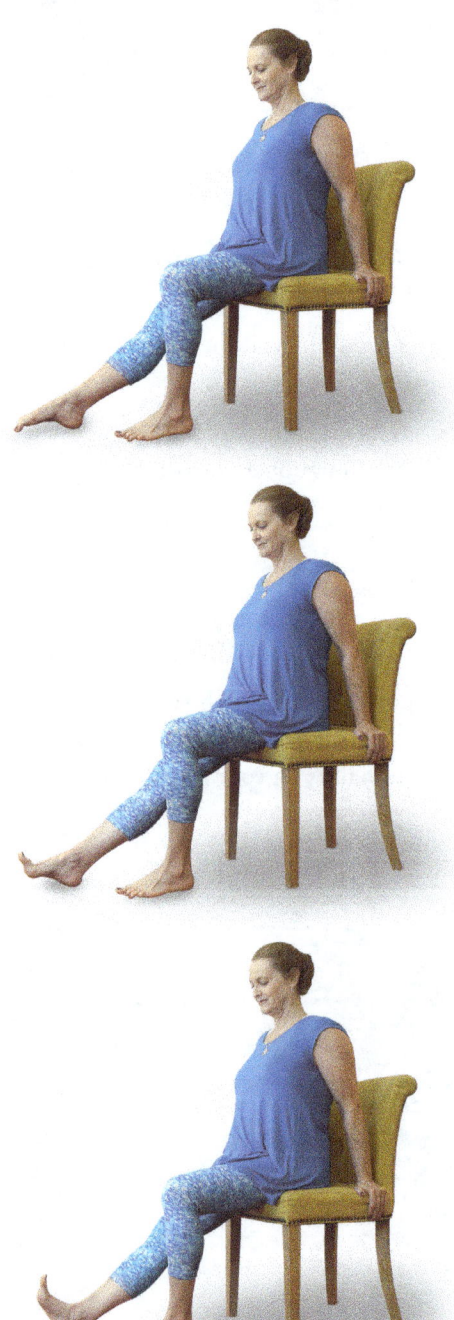

Bring your right foot forward. Relax. Close your eyes. Breathe in and out slowly and deeply several times through your nose with your awareness on your feet.

Point your right toe. Inhale deeply.

Say the mantra *I Trust* either out loud or in your head. Then pause and lift only your toes.

Exhale and flex your whole foot. Relax and breathe. Repeat three times and change legs.

Pisces Full Moon: Rocky Mountain Pose

No props are needed. Stand with your feet hip-width apart. Lift your toes and wiggle them for 30 seconds. Spreading your toes wide, place them back on the floor.

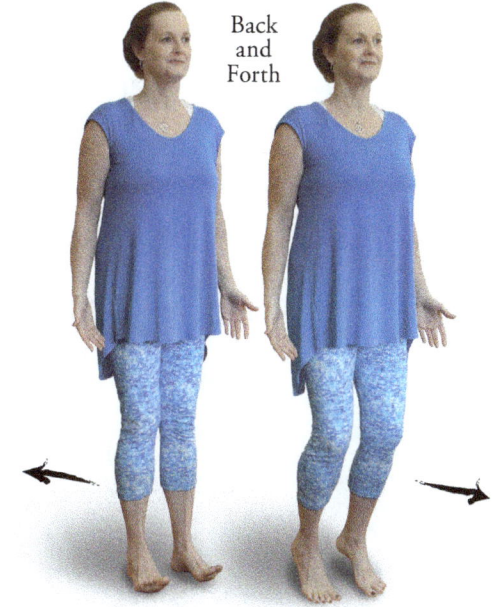

Back and Forth

As you exhale, rock back and forth and side to side—massaging the bottoms of your feet. Feel yourself grounded, stable, and strong amidst movement.

Settle into mountain pose. Squeeze your thighs to lift your kneecaps. Slightly tuck your tailbone down and feel your hips align over your ankles.

Lengthen your spine. Roll your shoulders back and down reaching your fingertips towards the floor. With your chest gently lifted from the sternum, turn your palms out slightly. To add support: imagine a strong line of vertical energy running from the bottom of your feet to the top of your head like a tree with strong roots running deep into the earth.

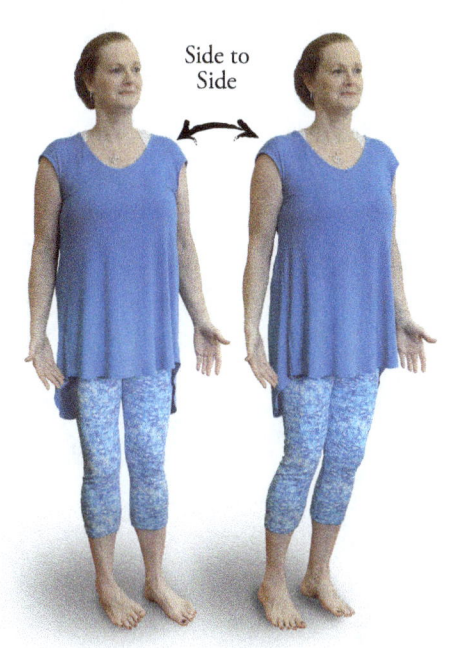

Side to Side

Relax. Close your eyes. Breathe in and out slowly and deeply several times through your nose with your awareness on your feet.

Inhale deeply as you say or think to yourself the mantra *I Trust*. As you exhale slowly, your exhalation roots you more deeply into the earth. Repeat as desired.

ABOUT THE AUTHOR

Beatrex Quntanna

Tarot expert, published author, symbolist, poet, lecturer—Beatrex is one of the luminaries of our time. Synthesizing 44 years of spiritual teachings, intuitive skills, and conventional counseling, she translates this wealth of wisdom into practical language making it accessible to all and applicable in today's world. Known for being "the teacher's teacher," her experience and advice has served as an invaluable support for many of today's spiritual teachers and professional psychics. She guides with profound insight, compassion for the human experience, and humor; inspiring personal growth and activating an inner-knowing in her students that sparks a self-confidence to walk tall in this world as a spiritual being.

Her life's work is showing how to Live Love Every Day by *living* astrology, not just intellectualizing it—teaching others how to ebb and flow with the natural cycles of the Moon and the cosmos, rather than working against them. She teaches this through Moon Classes held regularly throughout the year, and is the creator of *Living by the Light of the Moon*, a popular annual workbook that takes you step-by-step through her process.

The ultimate book on the Tarot and its symbols, *Tarot: A Universal Language* by Beatrex Quntanna, has been reviewed by magazines in Europe as well as in the United States. Her expertise in symbolism and Numerology, as well as her extraordinary psychic insight, make this book unique among Tarot books.

Beatrex also creates jewelry that heals and enlivens, *Spirituality on a String*. More than just necklaces and accessories, these are power pieces you will want to wear every day. She strings every bead by hand, with love, drawing from her vast collection of unique and hard-to-find pendants and beads from Tibet, Nepal, India, and the Far East.

Beatrex's many print credits, as well as numerous radio, TV, and video appearances include:

- Guest blogger for Satiama.com and True Nature Healing Arts
- Contributing author to two anthologies by Maria Yracébûrû – *Prophetic Voices* and *Ah-Kine Remembrance*
- *How to Use the Moon Book* online video course produced by Blue Moon Academy
- *Tarot: A Universal Language* online course produced by Blue Moon Academy
- *Tibetan Numerology* online course produced by Blue Moon Academy

Beatrex teaches ongoing Astrology classes and continues to be available for private group workshops in Encinitas, California.

Interested in Ongoing Moon Classes and workshops with Beatrex?

Contact her at beatrex@cox.net
or visit **www.Beatrex.com**

OTHER PUBLICATIONS BY BEATREX

2020 The Year of Unity – Wall Calendar

Created by Beatrex Quntanna

Numerology by Michelenne Crab
Art and Design by Jennifer Masters

Live by cycles instead of by time

This is the calendar from Beatrex's *Living by the Light of the Moon* workbook as a stand-alone work of art—for your home, your office, or a gift for someone special—putting all of Beatrex's information at your fingertips as a quick and easy reference to guide you day by day!

To order, go to www.Beatrex.com
or call 1-760-944-6020

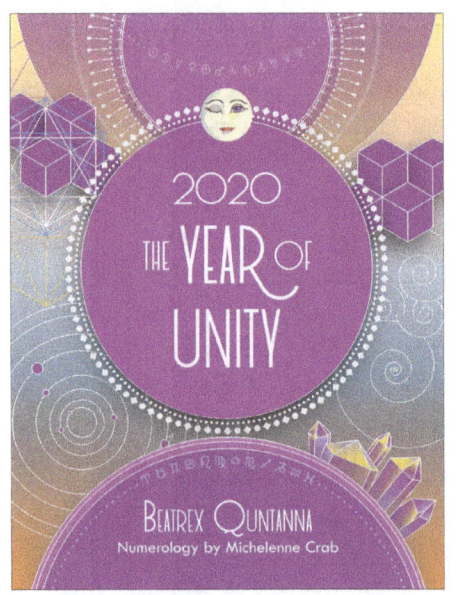

Tarot: A Universal Language

By Beatrex Quntanna

Experiencing the Road of Life Through Symbols

Embark on this fascinating journey through the unfolding Story of Life as told by the Universal Language of the Tarot. This book contains innovative avenues to understand the tarot through the author's in-depth knowledge of symbology.

Learn how to quickly read and interpret the Tarot by following this simple, informative, and illustrated guide. Use the expanded symbology section to understand each symbol depicted on the Minor and Major Arcana cards.

This book includes an interpretation of all 78 Tarot cards, plus readings created by this nationally-known Tarot teacher, reader, and symbolist.

To order, go to www.Beatrex.com
or call 1-760-944-6020

ONLINE CLASSES WITH BEATREX

How to Use the Moon Book

Everything you need to know about using the *Living by the Light of the Moon* workbook to create magic and abundance in your life!

How to navigate your life by the light of the Moon and its cycles, this annual workbook—also known to Beatrex's students as "The Moon Book"—will show you step-by-step when and what to do to release whatever holds you back, and when and what to do to manifest what you truly want in your life.

Following along with this video class series helps you understand how to use the workbook easily and effortlessly.

The course includes:
- High-quality instructional videos on each aspect of the book
- A handout that makes it easy to follow along
- And the warmth and wisdom of Beatrex to carry you on your journey

For more information or to enroll now go to www.BlueMoonAcademy.com

---

Tarot: A Universal Language

Experience the amazing interpretation and wisdom behind each and every Tarot card from Beatrex. This course is now available online for the first time ever. Beatrex has over forty-three years of experience giving Tarot readings and teaching the Tarot to her students.

Now this wealth of knowledge is available to you to study at your leisure.

In this online course you will...
- Get to know the meanings and symbols of the Tarot cards
- Understand how to increase your intuition by using the cards
- Receive special reading spreads appropriate for different issues
- Meditate with the cards—let the symbols speak to you
- Learn how to set up a vortex in your office for doing readings
- Understand how to care for and treat your Tarot deck

The course includes high-quality instructional videos, study aids, fun quizzes, and insightful activities. Whether you are on a journey to learn the Tarot for your own enlightenment or whether you want to do Tarot card readings for others, this is the course for you. Beatrex fills the course with her insightful wisdom, funny stories, and deep, anchored knowledge of the Tarot. Don't miss this course.

For more information or to enroll now go to www.BlueMoonAcademy.com

ONLINE CLASSES WITH BEATREX

Tibetan Numerology

How to Build a Powerful Personal Force

Names are important. Understand the power that exists in your name and how it informs your personal attraction force. Knowing the numerological value of your name gives you the ability to advance your personality power, understand your karma, and enliven your attraction force. Take the course at your own pace, any time, any place.

The course includes:

- High-quality instructional videos on how to calculate the numerology of names, words or numbers
- What your name says about you now and how to turn it into a powerful attraction force to help you easily manifest what you desire
- The importance of and how to calculate your personal timing cycle, as well as your business name, house number, area code, and more
- A handout that makes it easy to follow along
- And the warmth and wisdom of Beatrex to carry you on your learning journey

For more information or to enroll now, go to www.BlueMoonAcademy.com